The Keneman Chronicles

The
Keneman
Chronicles

AOC Harry L. Keneman, U. S. Navy (Retired)

Order this book online at www.trafford.com
or email orders@trafford.com

Most Trafford titles are also available at major online book retailers.

Printed in the United States of America.

ISBN: 978-1-4269-9598-9 (sc)

Trafford rev. 11/10/2011

 www.trafford.com

North America & international
toll-free: 1 888 232 4444 (USA & Canada)
phone: 250 383 6864 ◆ fax: 812 355 4082

Short excerpts of interest
During a 22 year period

October 1937 thru
January 1959

Unusual Events, People and Places
Experienced
During One Sailor's Naval Career

By AOC Harry L Keneman
Chief Petty Officer, U. S. Navy (Retired)

In memory of those Bluejackets
That sailed the blue green waters
Of the "Old Navy"

And

The loved ones they left behind.

Table of Contents

INTRODUCTION
to
THE KENEMAN CHRONCLES

Ninety nine percent of the historical books written about the U.S. Navy are large heavy documents praising our mighty big-gunned vessels and the gold encrusted Naval Officers that commanded them at sea during battle action. Now that might sound offensive and a little bitter but it's not meant to be. You see, your writer is extremely proud to have spent a major portion of his life serving on these vessels while working for those Gold Braded officers. In fact, at one time earlier in life I was definitely interested in becoming a member of their commissioned group.

However, coming close in a competition never won a cigar! I fell short in the necessary qualifications. Therefore, in October 1937 I enlisted because I was still interested in a naval career. By 1943 during World War II I had been promoted through the ranks to Chief Petty Officer, the senior ranking enlisted man. I can assure you it is an outstanding senior enlisted position as well. After all it's more then obvious the Chiefs actually run the Navy because they are closer to the problems and the necessary action to resolve them. If you doubt this statement, you just ask any Chief. They would be very willing to clarify this claim for you.

This introduction, as well as the enclosed stories, had been prepared for the specific purpose of defining the average life style of our Navy Bluejackets. In some cases, it directly introduces you to Navy personnel, both enlisted and officers, with whom the writer served with, knows about, or was influenced by, during the early years of the twentieth century. Plus, it includes a description of contacts and events during the twenty-two years of my uniform service.

From the very beginning of this new nation, the early life style of our American sailors was originally shaped from the British seaman mould dictated by the Royal Navy. As our service expanded and grew, changes emerged which allowed the crew to react more like a professional sports team

The average military book is normally prepared as a continuous detailed story covering a selected period or series of connected events. This volume has been assembled in the same basis format. However the material will be presented in individual small short stories covering a single subject that will be complete in themselves and will eliminate the fluff material that normally ties our military books flow of events together. The short story approach has provided the writer the opportunity to exert full concentration on the subject material of the basic story. I hope the reader enjoys my simple attempt to entertain.

The Author's Biography

Assembling this volume has been the author's first attempts at preparing true stories of personal military experiences or observations for publication as a series of individual short stories. Here each presentation will attempt to cover a single subject. However, occasionally there might be a small subject crossover to insure proper continuity of subject material.

Most of Mr. Keneman's previous writing efforts were formal military documents prepared as an employee of the U. S. Navy Department. His attempts at true personal efforts reported herein began after his almost 42 years of combined military uniform service and as a civilian employee of the Department of the U.S. Navy. His career began when he enlisted in the Navy in 1937 at age 18. The Navy trained him for Ordnance duty in shipboard and aviation ordnance. In that particular time frame aviation appeared to be an area with the most potential. However, his first sea duty began in the 2nd Deck Division of the Light Cruiser USS Memphis, CL-13. It took over a year to obtain his desired change into aviation. However, he never regretted the early days as a deckhand because it provided him the basic Navy philosophy, of when you learn you earn. His first Aviation tour began with Patrol Squadron 11 flying Consolidated Catalina PBY-2's, where his ordnance background knowledge earned this young sailor a 3rd Class Petty Officer rating as an Aviation Ordnanceman.

Shortly thereafter, he returned to the USS Memphis to aid in forming a new Aviation Unit. He began flying South Atlantic neutrality patrols as a rear seat crewman in the Curtiss SOC-2 Seagull. During this duty, he was promoted to Petty Officer 2nd Class while sharing with others the thrill of catapult flight until the end of his enlistment. He was then shipped back to the

Naval Receiving Ship, New York for discharge. His arrival at the Receiving Ship was just a few days after the Pearl Harbor bombing. It was obvious it would be a long war. On reenlisting he began what became a lifetime career. This period began at the Naval Air Station, Argentia, Newfoundland; here he was responsible for the establishment of an ordnance supply depot. For said duty the Department of the Navy, Bureau of Navigation automatically promoted him to Petty Officer 1st Class.

He then received orders to the Naval Air Station, Pensacola, FL. Those individuals, who were proficient Combat Aircrewman, were assigned to instructing in aerial gunnery. During this tour he was selected for promotion to Chief Petty Officer. Having been selected at age 25, he had to be one of the youngest, if not the youngest E-7 in the Navy!

This tour was followed by a transfer to Shore Duty at the Aircraft Overhaul and Repair Department, NAS Norfolk. His favorite job at said facility was Chief in Charge, Aircraft Multi-Engine Flight Test. Next he spent over 2 excellent duty years serving in the USS Coral Sea CVA-43. Immediately followed by Patrol Squadron 44. When selected for duty on the staff of the Commander, Naval Air Forces U.S. Atlantic Fleet, the tour on the Vice Admiral's staff, in reality guaranteed a lifetime career. After Navy retirement he spent 20 years as a civilian employee of the Department of the Navy, retiring from the Naval Air Systems Command, on 7 December 1978 as Head of the Naval Air Documentation Policy and Programs Office.

PREFACE
It's Purpose

For several years following my forty-one year, eleven months and seven day retirement from my combined Navy uniformed service and with the Department of the Navy, very little thought had been given to writing about my personal past experiences, events or accomplishments. In those days I was more interested in what the future had to offer as I took enjoyment in a blank retirement schedule.

As I grew older a Congressional Representative friend advised me on the subject of preserving Veteran's Oral History's being collected by the Library of Congress. It seemed that many veterans, myself included, began to wonder whether future generations might actually be interested in reading about sea-going experiences that these old sailors might have had while serving their country during the twentieth-century.

I was very surprised to discover that many individual's, especially family's, might be very interested in some sort of history of what old granddad have contributed in the past' that might live into the future long after this old man becomes a distant memory. It's very possible that many individual, face to face, happenings might be a heck of a lot more interesting than the bland generalized writings produced by a future Historian. A perfect example, were the personal letters hand written sent home by Civil War soldiers, which became more interesting reading than the standard history book descriptions of action during that war.

Thinking hard I felt my brain had stored many, both good and bad memory's that had to be classified from both to a possible good to a not so good Naval experience. How hard could this memory chasing possibly be? It actually turned out to be slightly more difficult than anticipated. Written accounts concerning personal affairs and events requires an entirely different flow of subject material than the 1, 2, 3, lay out of a Navy aircraft technical document. Based there on, my first attempt to prepare a description of 1937 Navy recruit training experiences had to be rewritten a couple of times before this writer was satisfied with the layout of the written subject material prior to beginning the follow up information that would lead me on to the next item.

This so-called document, which would eventually turn into a book project a couple of years later. It's hard to believe it finally reached about 200,000 words and well over several hundreds of pages before it could be considered a near finished project.

Just about the same time, our son's talked us into selling our Florida home and moving to Nevada. As a result this volume lay dormant for several months while we were getting settled into what now represents our final home. A few months later it was in work again to get it ready for publication. As the review began, I found myself beginning to make changes or corrections! Well, what the heck let's refer to calling it a final edit.

Now I would like you to know I was born into an old-fashioned manual typewriter era and didn't find my fingers on a computer keyboard until my late 70's or early 80's. Actually this darn machine can at time make me very angry. For 20 years I worked for the Navy Department traveling around the country making speeches and I was successful at it. Now, I can sit down at the computer and begin writing and quite often this machine will draw a big red line under something telling me I was doing it wrong! However, I did read the entire volume and made several corrections of my own as well as those suggested by the computer. I do enjoy inserting Navy jargon which drives the computer nuts trying to figure it out!

On conducting the editorial review one thing began to worry me. A detailed book covering several years tends to speak in generalities rather than specifics. Therefore, it became obvious the reader interest factor would tend to rise and fall based on their depth of Naval history knowledge. It seemed to feel like the reader would have to have served time in the military, in order to understand, or hold interest in some of the material.

At that moment it was determined that the book should remain as is, but it also gave birth to a new idea. In an effort to improve and hold the readers interest, it was determined a short story format should be used to allow the written information to focus on a single subject or detailed action analysis to clarify the subject matter. Further, it was determined that additional interest might be enhanced by the inclusion of humorous satire and wherever possible, something extremely serious or comical. In addition, wherever possible my personal opinion of the success or failure of either side had to be included.

Also, comparing something that happened 60 or more years ago with something similar today might in some way spice up the story making it more interesting. Thus the contents of much of this volume were born.

Several short descriptive stories have been published in monthly veterans publication or newsletters. Comments submitted proved the format change really worked. However, this approach in some cases might result in some slight repetition and occasional cause certain overlaps between stories.

I seriously hope you will enjoy reading about some of my experiences and the people I met or served with, or was rather close to, as well as the events described herein. On my part this has been a serious attempt to keep a small part of our military past alive long after being transferred to where old military personnel report to serve their final tour.

Respectfully,

CPO Harry L. Keneman, U. S. Navy (Ret.)

CAPTURING MILITARY & WAR EXPERIENCES

Many veterans, myself included, who were lucky enough to have lived through the devastation of World War II, saw small reason to express a desire to relive many of the experiences they lived through during the tough war years. As they grew older it finally began to register, that it might be important to some individuals, especially family members, to understand what Dad or Grandpa really experienced during the big war.

In particular our immediate off springs, should have a true understanding of certain events that transpired between the 1930's and 1970's. Such knowledge might be of special value as it might relate to their having to be mentally and physically prepared for the possibility of coping with the reality of all out war at some point in their lifetime.

Listening to news and much of the public reaction to the current Middle Eastern situation, it becomes a positive indicator that most of our current politicians and our politically correct educational system has done little to prepare young citizens with the ability to understand, analyze, or be able to react in support of the troops currently deployed in harms way.

Many of our older veterans viewing the situation are stating they are now sorry for not having kept a journal of the things they had witnessed or experienced during their own period of service. For one thing they actually didn't have the time to spare. Fellow veterans stop worrying and think, you automatically kept a complete record of your experiences. All the information you might like to pass on had been stored for years in the best computer God or man ever devised, your brain! You can be assured if you would take the time to write it down, or store it on the family computer, you will be utterly amazed at the mass of information that will flow out of your brains deep storage and appear on your paper or monitor screen.

In earlier times, many of you, like myself in 1937, enlisted in the military. There we learned a lot about life and a system of survival that was never taught in any college. At age 18 little did I realize that many of my experiences would be of value 60 or more years later. Not so long ago it was brought to my attention that what had been experienced suddenly was of instant value to those developing oral history programs like the Library of Congress Veterans History Project. Believe it or not, this is our government saying they need your verbal history information.

Once you start storing your memory on paper or in the computer, your memory begins to rush backwards. I was amazed to discover how clearly the so-called trials and tribulations of years long past flashed through the mind. Naturally what was written required editing and even some rewrite. The words that begin to appear on your paper or computer screen will begin to return a fairly accurate accounting of what transpired years ago. What will be documented are the average individual G.I.'s description and the opinion of his fellow veterans of what transpired around them. What you are preserving are the thoughts of what you had experienced over 60 years ago! It not only gives you something to keep yourself busy, it begins to be interesting and enjoyable as well. Things that transpired so many years ago can now be approached from a totally new point of view. What might have been very serious many years ago may be viewed with a completely different viewpoint as serious, funny, in extreme, kind of silly or even stupid. At the same time some of your experiences might literally scare the Hell out of you and still you would be able to do it again! But you're still alive and able to remember! Therefore, the people of this nation need to know you had that experience and in a way you may have helped preserve their freedoms and life styles.

In closing, it is recommended that every veteran give this memory chasing a try. Lots of individuals especially the youngsters might be happy to know about some of the things old Grandpa had to put up with in the past. Plus it opens up a whole new avenue for keeping us old guys mentally and physically active. It's definitely better than physical exercise as well as a good job of keeping us out of the wife's way!

Freedom of Speech

The freedom of speech is defined in the first amendment quoted in the Bill of Rights. I'm certain our forefathers intended it should apply specifically to the spoken or written word. Over the years it developed as the centerpiece of our nations declared freedoms. For example, what is printed herein is an example of ones right of free expression. However, during the same period it has been subject to many controversial interpretations. In fact, it's beginning to appear that anyone can voice a thought, or an opinion, in any fashion or manner they may desire. That really is not the case.

When our forefathers first put their words down on paper, I believe they felt that the people, or at least most people, would read and interpret the language with a certain amount of common sense. True, it extends everyone the right to express an opinion, state a disagreement, as well as render a protest. However, it didn't mean expressing it haphazardly without serious thought or a review of the facts. It was intended that the subject matter of the statement being made had not been snatched out of mid-air. It was expected that the speaker would be a semi-authority familiar with his subject having a logical reason, or suggestion, for agreeing, objecting or protesting,

Again, this may not be true with sensitive subjects such as politics, religion, marriage, finances, crime etc. In the heat of discussion, impolite terminology like liar, inappropriate foul language, stupidity, and derogatory family references may be blurted out. These applications don't really qualify under the right of Freedom of Speech! One must be careful to state their opinion, or comments as clearly as possible to ensure that those listening, enjoy, understand, or disagree with the material being discussed. Points may be emphasized by change of wording or expression. However, this should not include boisterous, slanderous, or sarcastic expressions supported with inappropriate body language.

Despite recent claims, speech means just that, speech. It does not apply to inappropriate acts of violence, burning a national flag, threatening another person or causes possible injury, or damage to property. No matter what some radical judge or public official might rule, it is in error if they claim some malicious act is an expression of freedom of speech. Said freedom applies appropriately to the spoken or written word.

AN ODE TO THE MEN OF THE SEA

What manner of man is he?
This man drawn to the lore of the sea,
and the wonder of exotic shores.
While sharing a deep-set love of home and country.

A man willing to forgo the luxury of life ashore.
To live a regimented military existence,
working, eating, and sleeping. Steadfastly responding,
to the tone of a shrill pipe, bugle command or,
the demanding call of GQ, man your battle station!

For over 200 years, since the time of sail.
He has been lulled to sleep,
By the creaking of wet shifting timbers,
and the brisk snap of canvas in a freshening wind.
Today our sailor listens to the slap of green water on steel,
as the whispering and rumbling of blowers and machines,
invade his land of dreams.

He serves diligently in times of peace,
or bravely through the rumblings of war.
Pray tell, what does all this gain him?
Maybe a small shiny heart with a purple ribbon
or, eternal sleep in a canvas sheath.
Slipped quietly into the deep beneath a brightly colored ensign.
Never again to enjoy a happy reunion at voyage's end.

This strange, wandering sea going man,
Who willingly forgoes a normal family life.
To bravely serve with distinction
while sailing into possible harms way.
This is a special breed of man,
With a true love of country and the sea.
He deserves to be honored with special recognition
by both family and a grateful nation.

Harry L. Keneman 2002

A VETERAN, ANALYSIS

Military Personnel that served this nation in times of international conflict are known as **VETERAN'S.** Once that service was completed, whether it was just during the term of the conflict, or professional retirement that person was reborn. They departed the military a very different individual than the one that marched off to war. A series of possible qualities may have contributed to their survival. Some of which may be reflected herein.

V:—Our "**V**" might describe the **VIGOR and VITALITY** displayed by our veteran's mental and physical strength exercised in order to endure and survive during times of conflict.

E:—Our first "**E**" may represent the **ENERGY** that gave them the inherent power to respond to the force of arms and overcome resistance while performing under adverse hostile conditions.

T:—The "**T**" might stand for the mental **TEMPERMENT** required to adjust to the lack of privacy experienced during the military life style and the close personal relationships fostered by combat survival.

E:—Our second "**E**" may have stood for **ENDURANCE** which provided with the tolerance and intestinal fortitude or guts to carry on and keep going despite the fatigue, pain and suffering experienced during the conflicts duration.

R:—The "**R**" might have referred to the **RESOLVE,** which gave them the ability to analyze complex situations, determine necessary action and carry it to a conclusion.

A:—The "**A**" could possibly refer to our natural inherent **ABILITY.** The power of inventive talent during our schooling years and expanded upon through our work and military experiences.

N:—The **"N"** may identify the veterans **NATIONAL** Pride; The love of Country, our Constitutional freedoms, and our independent capability to set and achieve personal goals.

S:—Last but not the least, the **"S"** might stand for their **STAMINA,** which allowed them to endure and overcome unbelievable conditions, resistance to hardship, fatigue, illness and Mental stress.

The term **VETERAN'S** may include all, or part of the qualities or abilities covered above. However, on second thought, we might look back and face the fact that our survival may have been due to damned outstanding **GOOD LUCK!**

A VETERANS VIEW OF WAR!!

The dictionary defines WAR as the final solution between two or more disputing nations or, factions within a given nation, (Civil War), to declare that a state of hostilities exists to resolve territorial or political differences. Political problems that fail to be resolved by diplomatic negation, usually results in a declaration of war being initiated by the controlling factions of the most powerful activity, with the victor forcing his will and desires upon the loser

For the average native or citizen, and the man in uniform, who in all probability wasn't mad at anybody, is instantly caught up in an armed conflict that really hadn't been his choice. His short definition of war can be expressed in one small phrase, KILL OR BE KILLED. The situation now becomes a simple matter of self-preservation or, a process of elimination. No matter what his feelings, he must destroy the enemy before that enemy has a chance to destroy him.

Therefore, serving as a warrior, despite his personal preference for diplomatic negations, his destroying the enemy serves two major purposes. It eliminates the enemy, while extending his ability to serve his country as well as his own life span. As the troops deploy, the military personnel who in all proximity also might not be angry with anybody either, yet being patriotic, their reaction may also vary from one extreme to another. Lots of cheering, flag waving, music and, believe it or not fireworks! Just what the nervous recruit needs as he marches off to God only knows where. Those that really deserve pity are the grieving mothers, who have the weight of a bowling ball in the pit of their stomach; as she watch's her only son disappear from view.

As to the disappearing young man in uniform, no matter what the depth of his training, is probably worrying about his first reaction to combat. No need to concentrate on fear because there is probably plenty of that to go around within his fellow troops, marching along with him. There also exist the odd feeling of being "all alone" even though completely surrounded by troopers you know.

However, once approaching a combat condition the last thing you could possibly want was to be alone. Once that adrenaline begins to flow, take full advantage of what happens to your body. You will be stronger, quicker, and your senses will be sharper but now is the time to proceed with caution, it seems you tend to live longer that way. Many Medal of Honor recipients, who acted impulsively, throw caution to the wind while performing miraculous feats of bravery. As a result they often received the Medal posthumously. Some that did survive admitted later that they didn't have a clear picture of what they had done. Others, when physically possible, kept a short journal. What they committed to paper can be extremely valuable later in life when they eventually began to discuss it.

The young recruit and his buddy's mentioned above, on their return were no longer the same happy young soldiers in their spiffy new uniforms. Those young men no longer existed. They had become entirely different individuals. They had been to see the elephant and returned as a serious thinker with a definite new outlook on life.

War's either won or lost, is always a losing proposition. To the uninformed population, the tragedies of war seemed to normalize and fade into the past when peacetime conditions set in. However, the tragedies of war really never totally fade away for the veteran. The crosses of honor for those that made the supreme sacrifice still rest quietly row on row, on row. Also there are a good percentage of our living veterans who continue to survive and succeed despite being broken in body or mind. However, eventually they will again find total peace as two sharply dressed men in uniform tightly fold that beloved tricolor ensign into a cocked hat triangle for presentation to the grieving next of kin.

THE NAVY BLUEJACKET

For more than two century's The United States of America has maintained two or more naval fleets to roam the seas of this world for the specific purpose of protecting the integrity of our vast shorelines. These fleets are also dedicated to the protection of our Constitutional freedoms, democratic interests and American life styles second to none. Our overall ability to perform this feat nationwide is mainly due to a group of sharp individuals entitled, The Navy Bluejackets.

A Bluejacket is actually a young enlisted person who has raised his right hand and swore before God that he would donate a few years of his life to the service of his country. He and many others like him swore an oath to become the heart and soul that breathes life into the U.S. Navy's massive cold steel, fighting machines. Their knowledge, voices and manual labors provides the power that forces these giant metal machines to move, maneuver, keep it clean, man its guns and even dies if necessary to keep it afloat.

These young men, and now, women, come from the nations towns, villages and all walks of life of this country and swear to willingly serve their nation in this capacity. They all look pretty much alike in their blue or white uniforms but in reality like all humans they fall in various categories. First we have the patriots, those that willingly serve in times of national conflicts, who volunteer till peace returns, then return to civilian life, join the American Legion or Fleet Reserve Association and faithfully vote for the continued support of veterans rights.

Then there is the middle group with a wide-open lifestyle that considers their naval vessel a home away from home. They are happy go lucky free spirits, who willing serve because of the luxury of not having to worry about where their food, clothing and place to sleep were coming from.

Then there is a group known as the "lifers." The serious career Bluejacket's who recognize the advantages available to each willing individual. While serving in the military you automatically become the manager of your own destiny. The military will provide the facilities and materials to achieve but the effort is 100% personal. If properly applied, it will advance you into the upper echelon ranking personnel toward the Chief Petty Officer's position where if you succeed you will become a senior enlisted individual with a certain amount of command and upper management authority. Advancement above this level, may also be attained by special selection to the Warrant or Commissioned Officer ranks.

All three of these groups meld fairly well together and become ships company, or the "crew" that controls the operation of the vessel. They become Shipmates that, work, fight their ship and develop pride in their vessel and what they do. In the natural interest in advanced positions, our Bluejacket can take interest in specialty training. They have the rights to choose and study for a specific trade qualification. Once they become proficient therein, the insignia for that specialty will appear under the white eagle, better known as the "Crow" on their left sleeve.

The number of stripes below the specialty insignia indicates their level of proficiency. The strips on the lower left sleeve indicate years of service. Four years for each single stripe. After thirty years of service they become eligible for full retirement, or at twenty years they are eligible for transfer into the Fleet Reserve with a financial retainer. The latter is the most popular approach.

Interested? Please report to the nearest Navel Recruiting Office!

U.S. NAVY RECRUIT TRAINING, MID 1930'S THE FIRST DAY

During your scribes extensive life cycle, that October 1937 date of my entry into "boot" training is a very clear memory. It began the military history of a cocky 18 year old that enlisted at the U.S. Navy Recruiting Office, Brooklyn Navy Yard. He had just signed his life over to serve a term of four years as a U.S. Navy enlisted man.

He had broken family ties and was actually happy to be headed toward a brand new life of his own far away from home. This fresh new 21 buck a month Apprentice Seaman was immediately shipped via the old over-night Fall River Steamship lines departing from New York City to Providence, R.I. for further transfer, by Navy bus to the Naval Training Station, Newport, R.I.

As the bus passed through the USN Newport training gates, that cold dreary morning, our new recruit's mental impression was, those ominous gray field stone buildings appeared to look more like the entry to a penal institute than a Naval Training Station. It didn't take more than a few days for those recruits to realize how close a call that really appeared!

Once on board, (how nautical can you get in less than 24 hours?), we were lead directly to the mess hall. There we picked up a metal tray and a large clay mug without a handle. They were amazed to receive a double scoop of bake beans generously splashed with a large scoop of red lead, a large square of yellow corn bread, and a mug of black brew, ironically it was called coffee. Damned if it tasted like coffee. Besides, it had been whispered about that it was laced with saltpeter!

In less than an hour, the shine of this new life was rapidly starting to tarnish! We wondered who could have possibly qualified bake beans as breakfast food? What was going to happen next? Get use to it boot, your going to learn to enjoy a heck of a lot of those beans in the next few years!

After eating we were verbally assaulted by a five hash mark Chief Boatswain's Mate. He loudly stated he was our new Company Commander and that for the next 16 weeks he would be first cousin to God almighty. When you desire to address him you will do so by his suggested title, "Chief Sir". He also stated we must wait for authorization to speak. For the first three weeks, we were advised that individual responses were not permitted aloud unless you were authorized to do so!

Our next stop for our 70 or more of us was a haphazard march to the clothing stores building. We were immediately ordered to remove all our civilian clothing, and were provided a shipping container to mail our clothing home. Now it's embarrassing to be lined up stark naked trying not to look self conscious or em-bare-assed! (Just a little spot of humor.) Slowly the line of naked recruits passed in alphabetical order through a team of pharmacist mates and doctors. With a couple of shots in the right arm and a couple in the left, with a "bend over and spread your cheeks" and a "turn your head and cough", plus whatever else you might imagine, we finally passed through the line. Thank God, at that point we were issued a undershirt and a pair of regulation shorts to cover our bare ass's! The rest of the morning was consumed with the issue of a hammock, a sea bag, and the clothing allowance. We were instructed on how to roll and store cloths in the sea bag. The instruction also included how to dress in a suit of undress blues. At least we were now beginning to look more like recruit sailors

The next adventure took us to a barracks and centered on learning to swing a hammock. Contrary to the normal home practice of swinging a hammock, the navy's hammock had to be stretched out about five feet off the ground taut as a bowstring. How the hell are you supposed to get in it? Tightly stretched out like that it closely resembled an unpeeled banana. Now the mattress, its cover and blankets had already been made up inside the hammock. The trick was to swing yourself up like a trapeze star, slip your feet in to open it up, then center your butt in the middle of your mattress. Sounds simple, right? Like hell it was! It took a lot of practice, because, if you landed a couple of inches off center, the damn thing would flip you out as fast as standing up in a canoe! However, in time, what was really surprising was how quickly we learned how to do it. Plus it was also a lot more comfortable to sleep in it than you would think

Chief, Sir then marched us to the barbershop. By now it had become obvious the military's only assurance you could get a large group of guys from one place to another without losing anybody was to march them there. Those barber's had to have a pool going to see who could sheer the most sheep in the shortest period of time. Following five, four and aft sweeps and a quick flick over each ear they yelled, Next! In less than 20 minutes all 70 plus of us looked like Kojak with a day old beard! From that day forward I was sure I would be bald before the end of the year, because my nice reddish hair slowly began to do a real disappearing act!

Eventually, we lined up for evening chow. What was the hurry? We were getting a lesson in military philosophy that seniority hath its privileges. At this very moment we had been aboard about 8 or 9 hours. Guess who ate last.

It was then early to bed early to rise. During the first night on board there were quite a few who suffered the hammock barrel roll blues. This left them hanging upside down by their safety lines. Thank the Lord, it wasn't me. I slept warm and soundly until sleep was destroyed by flashing lights and the brassy blare of the reveille bugle. What going on, it still dark? Holy cow, Chief Sir's voice was harsher than the bugle. He was accenting his order to roll out by whacking the bottoms of occupied hammocks with the heavy end of a sawed off pool cue! He was yelling, "Alright men strip down to your shoes and socks, grab you soap and towels and fall in."

What was the Navy's obsession with mass nakedness? For the first three weeks we took mandatory showers each morning at 5:00am. In single file the company ran into and out of the shower room through two banks of about 16 showers. Every other one hot the next one cold. We soaped down on the way in and rinsed off on the way out. It was obvious the Navy was trying to tell us they didn't approve of dirty sailors.

We then dried off and dressed for breakfast. As we marched to morning chow the following thought crossed my mind, "Wow, I've been in the Navy for about 24 hours. There was about 15 weeks and 6 more days till the end of boot camp and 3 years and 36 weeks after that. If this 1st day is a sample, what other incredible things could possibly happen between now and then?" Today, over 70+ years later, the events of this first day of my naval career is as vivid today as if it were yesterday!

U. S. RIFLE, CALIBER .30, MODEL 1903

The American 1903 Springfield rifle was the first military bolt action repeating rifle manufactured for use with a new cartridge with a non-corrosive primer and smokeless powder. It probably remained in our inventory as a first line rifle longer than any other approved firearm. As indicated by the model number 1903, when it was approved for adoption, it served in one modification or another until well after the Vietnam War.

Because of its accuracy and the desirability of its various users it remained in service in spite the fact it had been displaced by the semiautomatic Model M-1 Garand in the late 1930's. The well liked '03 was a modified smooth operating bolt action, five round clip loader, partially copied from the basic German Mauser design. The rifles mounting, the "Star Gauged" target barrel version was one of the most accurate military rifles ever manufactured.

My first contact with this said firearm was during Navy recruit training. Well used, battle scared, beat up versions of this rifle had passed through the hands of many military recruits during their initial training phase. When they were issued to our recruit company they sure didn't look like much. However, our Chief Petty Officer Company Commander was a stickler about things being neat, clean and shinny bright. He reminded us we would be married to that rifle by the serial number impressed on the top of that forward receiver ring and it better look fairly good no matter what its age or condition. In order to accomplish this he first taught us how to disassemble and clean it.

Because of my personal interest in firearms, this was the first weapon other than a .22 that I held in my hands. So I determined I would do my best to improve its condition, as the receiver and barrel assembly was removed from the stock. My thoughts raced back wondering if some heroic soldier or Marine had carried it into battle or, had it always been a prop for training other recruits? The bore was worn and slightly pitted, indicating it had been fired extensively with early government corrosive primed ammunition.

So it had seen action even if only on the firing range. Most of the blue finish had long since disappeared at the hands of its previous users. The bore was cleaned and oiled and the outside metal cleaned up with soft steel wool. The wooden stock required a lot of work because it was very dark from prior handling and oil accumulation. It took several periods of scraping to get down to where the wood grain began to become visible. Except for the metal bright spots, that rifle began to take on the appearance of a fairly worn but well cared for piece.

We recruits spent hours mastering the manual at arms and physical drill with arms. However, there was also a down side connected to the rifle. Company punishment could turn that eight-pound rifle into an instrument of physical torture. When being disciplined under arms, there were two positions favored by most Company Commanders. They consisted of standing erect, the rifle held horizontally across the chest with the arms fully extended or, quick stepping back and fourth the length of the drill area, rifle in hand, with the arms extended over the head

It didn't take long for your arms to begin to twitch, while shoulder muscles begin to ache and knot up. In no time at all, that fine old rifle took on a new personality. About every thirty seconds it began to double, triple and quadruple in weight. When you start to sag, that old Chief was already there to suggest you return it to its extended position. Once or twice being subjected to this feat of strength and endurance quickly taught you that making mistakes was a condition to avoid.

Recruit training did nothing to faze my love for this old rifle. In less than a year I qualified Marksman in 1938 with that 1903 and shortly thereafter earned the Navy Expert Rifleman Medal. Now over 60 plus years later I still own two of these old rifles that I purchased years ago from Uncle Sam. You know what? They may have been designed over a hundred years ago but I can assure you they still shoot as good as the day they came off the assembly line!

FIRST NAVY SHORE LEAVE
Newport, Rhode Island

Three weeks of detention at the Naval Training Station had us all feeling like we had been sentenced to hard labor on a chain gang. But now the recruits of Company 17 were finally getting a break. We had been released from detention and were at this moment eligible for shore liberty in the old town of Newport. It was about the second week in November. The damp Rhode Island fall weather had already began warning us of the arrival of winter.

The company personnel had just experienced their first Navy pay line and had received between seven and eight dollars. Curiously, it was paid mostly in two-dollar bills. When we quizzed the Company Commander, the Chief responded, "That's a dumb question men. By now you should know that in an old Navy town, the ladies of the evening don't make change."

Saturday we received our first authorized liberty pass. With a seven-buck limit, a trip to the gyp-joint, (ship Service) would be a frugal one if I expected to have sufficient funds for liberty. So, my purchase consisted of a small box of Hershey' bars and two bags of Bull Durham. With six bucks in my kick and almost 2 weeks to pay day I had already determined this liberty definitely would not be one big ball of fire.

Another problem, recruit liberty came with limiting restrictions. Instead of decking out in our dress blues and that good looking blue flat hat, our boot uniform of the day for new recruits was undress blues, white hat and boot leggings. This rig was to make everyone in town aware we were lowly boots not allowed in dance places or bar rooms. It was not bad enough to have only six bucks in pocket; we had to advertise our low position in life as well.

Now Newport was, and still is, a historical town whose credentials ranged from the America's champion sailing cup, plus 10 mile Drives millionaire's row, then it was down the down the hill to the lowly $21.00 a month recruit, Apprentice Seamen from the Naval Training Station. The crossroads of town at Broadway, Thames St. and Long Wharf there was a combination of narrow streets, some still paved in lumpy, bumpy cobblestones. The proud older building with their small brass plaques attached to the well-kept building's front, bragging about their ancestry and time of construction. Quite a few of them had been built long before George Washington got the idea to chop down the cherry tree.

From Broadway to cobble stoned Thames St., which was a narrow one way passage through way past Government Landing. Here off shore anchored Navy vessels discharged their liberty parties at fleet landing. There was also a small ferryboat that carried the Naval Torpedo Station working personnel back and forth to Goat Island. This was the heart of the city. Here there were wall-to-wall restaurants, bar rooms, an occasional nightclub and many other commercial activities.

For Boots, bar rooms, nightclubs and alcohol were off limits. This sort of limited recruit activities to the Navy YMCA on Broadway across from the court house, which by the way was fairly new. It was built some time after 1700 and something. The two movie theaters on the other side of the court house and the small sandwich and ice cream shops, (fast food joints like McDonald's hadn't been invented yet), and, last but not the least, the Seaman's Institute where you could get involve in a high stake game of 8 Ball!

I had been wandering around town for almost two hours and had only been able to spend a little over a dollar. As to the possibility of meeting and conversing with a nice young lady was out of the question. Not only was she the possible pride and joy offspring of some big old Chief Petty Officer, plus, with her living in this city she probably knew more about the navy than you did, and could tell by your outfit you probably couldn't afford to buy her a double deck ice cream cone! Now, I wouldn't want you to believe I was hard to please, but boot liberty in Newport was definitely a sandwich short of a picnic!

Well, it was back to the base for me. At least there was someone there to talk to and besides I'd be able to catch up on my letter writing. It would be easy to explain to everyone back home what a wonderful time was had on my very first liberty. After all, letters cost only a couple of cents each!

"HOW FAR CAN YOU ROW A SWIMMING POOL?"

Having lived most of my life in close proximity to salt water, boating and swimming was my normal summer leisure recreation. Everyone I knew had learned to row a boat, but very few had ever been involved in any team rowing efforts. The Navy's mid 30's recruit training schedule involved training to man a long boat under oars. But, with winter moving in, all the boats had been beached for the winter.

Now if anyone could teach recruits how to row a boat on land, it had to be some crusty ole Chief Petty Officer. Just leave it to my old Chief Petty Officer; he would surely have a way! He just marched those young boots into a large indoor swimming pool. Would you believe? A bunch of sharp Carpenter's Mates had equipped both sides of that pool with rowing thwarts, gunwales, row-locks, and oars! What type comment did we make? Our young recruits just laughed and made smart cracks like, "How far do you think we can row this swimming pool?"

However, when that sharp old Chief got the first two squads positioned on their thwarts, darned if it didn't look like the galley slave scene in the first Ben-Hur movie! Our Chief was damn serious about these recruits learning the proper rowing commands and responding in perfect team like fashion. At the command "Stand by your oars", you were supposed to shove the oar over the gunwale just far enough to position the oar leather in the row-lock. This had to be done without getting your oar tangled with the ones fore and aft of you. This action took a little getting use to.

Just imagine an approach along side a dock situation, the command, "Up Oars" required to bring all oars to a straight

24

upward position and holding it. At first this seemed rather dangerous because we had oars falling in every direction including in the water! Just the same, it was repeated until this feat was accomplished without the danger of decapitating a single recruit.

On, the command "Out Oars" the rowers tossed the oar blades outboard while allowing the oar leather to fall into the rowlock. Then on the command, "Standby, Give way together", everyone was to follow the stroke oarsman and pull and feather together. Now how do you do that in a pool that wasn't about to move? Somebody had conveniently drilled several holes in the oar blades! These neophytes started with a great amount of splashing and clashing. But eventually, after several trying sessions, they began to stroke and feather together giving the general appearance of a rowing team. They were not exceptional, but good enough to qualify.

For a final comment, I was never able to figure out why such a big deal was made about those rowing lessons. In my many years at sea, during my naval career, Not once did I see a boat propelled by sailors under oars! All the sea fairing men I ever knew, personally thanked God for the internal combustion engine!!

SAILORS WERE FIGHTING MEN, OH YEA!

My memory of naval boot training in the late 1930's was a harsh, trying experience designed to convert a youngster into an experienced bluejacket. Now 70 plus years later my thoughts of this former experience leaves a warm humorous memory through my mind. It took a tough bunch of old Chiefs to convert a bunch of happy go lucky youngsters into serious fighting men. I hope this story will amuse you about one of these efforts.

Along with the marching, they did have periods of entertainment and recreation, mandatory of course. Now this particular recruit, being too short for basketball, too slow for track, too lazy for weightlifting, real lousy at pool shooting, as left-overs we actually got signed up for boxing training. Actually, it seemed like fun. First we got us out of marching a few hours a week. Also from some of the tall tails I had heard, the ability to handle yourself ashore could be an advantage. A little knowledge of boxing might be beneficial later in life. Was it possible that learning a little about self-defense might be a good idea in the event of a future altercation?

From what we heard from some old salts, a few boxing moves might be important knowledge to have, especially after consuming a few beers with tough guys from a different ship or service. For a few weeks we spent a couple of hours a day working on light and heavy bags, jumping rope, and shadow boxing. Boy, did we kick the crap out of a lot of guys in that shadow boxing practice! However, we had no experience whatsoever inside the ring ropes competing against another individual.

One day the coach lined us all up, weighed and took our measurements. He stated that in a couple of days they would be holding a smoker. Several of us commented, "Wait a minute, we haven't boxed in the ring before." The Chief replied, "Don't worry about it. You guys have done well in the preliminary training. The ring experience will teach you a lot." Well, its just for fun, what harm could it be?

When the big night arrived. The ring had been set up in the indoor drill hall surrounded by chairs. Those of us in the locker room had been issued cups and trunks. Once dressed, or undressed, if you prefer, I sat on a stool looking down at those big red gloves waiting for event #4. A funny feeling began to grow in the pit of my stomach as I sat on that stool listened to the shouting, screaming and cheering. Hey, this has got to be more than just a sparring match! Somebody out there sounds like they really mean business! How the devil did I ever get my fanny involved in this?

The word was finally passed, "OK #4 time to go." Reluctantly, they led me out and helped me into the ring. The coach rattled off a bunch of instructions that I didn't even hear. My eyes concentrated on that nice looking guy sitting on the stool opposed me. I began wondering what might be possible. I'm sure we may be in the same boat!

At the bell we met in the center of the ring for instructions. As we touched gloves he smiled. While returning to the corner, my mind registered, "Hey, that's a good sign." At the bell we, bouncing off the stools, I noted that he was right handed and I was a lefty. Maybe he wasn't used to southpaws! Oh, Oh, there's an opening, quick jab with the right! POW! What the devil was I doing crawling around on my belly on the canvas. Three, four, five, wait a second I'm trying to get up! Back on my feet, as I backed away, this guy advanced, still smiling, he had both hands cocked for action. Again he led with a left, which I was able to block but I failed to see him cross with that right. BAM! Down I went. I could hear the crowd booing as I crawled around on my belly listening to three, four, five. Screw the crowd, the number I was looking for was 10!

Thus ended a short boxing career. Later my nice looking opponent visited me wanting to know if I was OK. It seems I had been pitted against a New York Golden Gloves Champ with over 60 amateur fights! He could not believe they had placed me in the ring with him. My response, "I guess I was just the right weight!

This great shipmate, who's name I hate to admit I have long ago forgotten, became my best friend for the remainder of our recruit training tour. I had to assume that he thought I needed the protection!

A 1930's STYLE NAVY WATCH STANDING EXPERIENCE

Watch standing has always been one of the major functions within the navy's operational system. The common expression was, and still is, "The Navy never Sleep's". To accomplish this feat the 24-hour day is divided into four watch sections and each day into a series of six watches. Every individual, (this term is used because we now have mixed company aboard), on the ship or station has the duty every 4th day. The section leader is responsible for the preparation of the watch list and all assignments of those individual watch standers for his watch stations.

There are various types of watch standing depending on the rating and skill structure. For this particular watch we will define an actual road Sentry under Arms, Rifle. For an individual assignment the loneliest watch of the day, or I should say night, is the 12:00 to 04:00 in the morning. The watch standers major concerns at this time of night may consist of trying to stay awake or keep from freezing to death.

In the mid 30's, a winter watch, your equipment would consist of a wool watch cap, wool long handles, undress blues, a peacoat, leggings and a 1903 Springfield rifle, Caliber .30-06, unloaded!

Now tonight's young sailor in question was a Seaman 2nd Class. He was fairly new to the Navy, which was the real reason for being assigned this particular watch. The Chief of the Watch had stationed him at his post at the entrance to officer's country. He had been thoroughly checked out as to his duties and was mentally running the procedure through his mind in order to have something to do.

At approximately 01:15 flashing headlights penetrated the moonless darkness indicating a vehicle was approaching down the road to Officers Country. As instructed, the sentry smartly faced the approaching car and brought his rifle to port arms. The auto continued to proceed on unabated. The sentry then yelled, "Advance and be recognized!" As the car continued to approach, the young man now began to panic! He yelled, "Stop! Stop!!" at the top of his lungs.

The vehicle failed to slow down. By now the young sailor lost it completely! He stepped back, grabbed the rifle by the muzzle and let fly at the advancing car! Luckily, the rifle passed butt first through the windshield of the car on the passenger's side. Instantly, all four of the cars brakes locked bringing the vehicle to a screeching halt!

The station executive officer staggered out of his car, also yelling at the top of his lungs. "What the Hell is going on out here!" The young sailor, still in a panic whimpered, "I'm the guard. Who are you Sir? Are you hurt, Sir? May I have my rifle back Sir?" Naturally, this amazing incident was quietly hushed up. However, the ever-smiling storytellers quietly passed this story completely around the station. Seriously, as I remember it, the young sailor departed the station with a written duty citation in his record signed by the same officer he assaulted. There have been a lot of various watch standing stories passed down through the years, but in my opinion this was one of the better ones.

TRAINING COMPLETION & FOLLOW UP

Our Recruit Company 17 had completing twelve weeks of Naval-Training, which finally advanced seventy some recruits to the rating of Seaman 2nd Class. Plus we were extremely happy to have graduated from under our former Chief Boatswain Mate's strict Command. Only one day had passed and now our tough old Chief treats us like old time shipmates as we were transferred to the Sea Unit for assignment.

The part that pleased us most was at last we now looked like real sailors. Those damn leggings were now at the bottom of all our Sea Bags. Another pleasing factor our promotion to Seaman 2nd Class was accompanied by a pay raise to a rip roaring 36 bucks a month. It made us all feel like we hit the big time.

It was easy to wonder why our dress uniform was called "blues". That blue color was so dark it looked just like black! Without leggings, our lower trousers flapped lightly in the breeze, the pea coats were neatly buttoned and the blue flat hats, slightly cocked, looked kinda salty. Especially with a small match pack stuck inside the lining to make it stand up in the front. We actually looked like real sailors despite the fact we hadn't been hit in the face with any salt spray as yet!

Now the Petty Officer in Charge of the Sea Unit didn't want us to get lazy waiting for our first set of orders. Each morning he lined us up and assigned duties. For some fool reason he seemed to think that yours truly was the type to enjoy working with a heavy canvas bag over one shoulder and a long pointed stick in the other hand. Now this training station always looked neat. Until now, we hadn't noticed it was guys like us with a pointed stick that made it look that way! We had to admit that this job in no way strained our mental capability much, but it sure was boring.

One morning the Petty Officer in Charge asked if there were any of us that would like to work on a real ship to please step forward. With the exception of about a half dozen of us new comers, everyone took one step backwards! It was a put up job. Next time we would know to step backward too! Just a few minutes later we were going up the brow of an old three mast frigate, the USS Constellation.

My memory might be a little hazy; this vessel was built, or rebuilt, some time back in the 1850's. Again, I believe she mounted about 24 muzzle loading cannon. Like the famous USS Constitution, she was still in commission as a floating museum. In the 1930's it had been preserved at the Training Station as a monument to our former naval history. It was on this old sailing vessel we first learned how to holy stone teak wood weather decks.

The tools of the trade involve one half of a fire-brick with a small hole in the center large enough to accept a sawed off swab or broom handle. Once inserted in the brick, with the aid of a Seaman 2nd it can be worked back and forth on the watered down deck plates. It's a tough job but I'll assure you the deck will appear almost pure white once it was sun dried.

For working aboard this grand old vessel we all received a small certificate proclaiming us a crew member of the USS Constellation. I really hate to admit it, but this valuable document disappeared some time during the World War II era.

During the training period I had noted that my interest was to attend the Navy's Aircraft Photography School. At first, I was slightly disappointed when the Navy actually selected me for the Class A Ordnance School at the Naval Training Station, San Diego. However, as I followed my career advancement, it seemed the Navy actually knew what was best for me, Therefore, I mentally thank them monthly every time the Federal Retirement electronic deposit reaches my bank account!

On the arrival of our travel orders to San Diego we were happy to be trading Newport's cold weather for the warm sunshine of San Diego, California! However, there was a slight catch involved. Naturally I had to get stuck with a job. Apparently I was four weeks senior to a busload of graduating Apprentice Seaman. I had been assigned the responsibility of escorting these characters to San Diego. They provided me a briefcase of instructions, personnel orders, and a bundle of meal tickets. Well, the Navy never moves without somebody in charge. So I guess this was my entry into telling other people what to do! Now try and guess how much attention they were going to pay to me!

Back in the 30's fancy airline travel was none existent. Especially for a bunch of low paid sailors. We were scheduled the old fashion way, by bus and train. A bus to Providence, RI, then a short train ride to New York. Here we did receive Pullman Car for the zigzagging trip across the country. Upon arrival in Chicago a Naval Recruiting Officer met us at the train were he conducted an inspection during the Layover. In Chicago I lost one of the kids. He must of thought that joining the Navy was a grave mistake. I really felt sorry for him. The police were going to hunt him down, turn him back over to the Navy, then charge him and lock him up. As the trip continued it began to get boring as the days passed by.

The only problem we had was with the meal tickets and the dining car personnel. They seemed to feel that Navy meal tickets permitted them to feed us anything they had left over in the galley. With the information I had been provided prior to departure we convinced them that would be a grave mistake. From that point on we had no trouble ordering from the menu. By the seventh day we finally reached San Diego. This Naval base was palace compared to the penitentiary appearance of the Newport station. As we split up and went our separate ways there were short so longs and good bys all around.

I then reported officially to the administrative office of the Class A Ordnance School. I was assigned to a barracks, a bunk and a locker. I also received a bundle of station and school requirements and regulations. Class would begin instantly on Monday.

There would be no liberty for the first three weeks on board. I never understood the rationality for a 21 day lock down on reporting to a new station. Did they think we would get lost in town and be unable to find our way back to the Naval Station?

The Spanish style tan stucco buildings with bright red roofs surrounded by green lawns and tropical shrubbery looked great compared to what we had to put up with in Newport. The barracks double deck bunks were lined up wall to wall on red linoleum flooring. For a while there would be no hammocks. I was assigned a lower bunk with an attached locker positioned next to. Except for sleeping in the same room with sixty or more guys, it looked like a hotel compared to boot camp.

Our schedule called for eight hours classes for four days with field day and barracks inspection on Friday. Personnel inspection would be conducted each Saturday morning with liberty beginning at 13:00 on the fourth week. This next may sound unusual, but true. Because of family complaints, letters to family had to be turned in each week prior to receiving your liberty card! Can you believe the U. S. Navy had complied with this childish request?

Come Saturday morning everyone began preparing for personnel inspection. Shoes had to be spit shined. I started unrolling my brand new undress whites that had rested in the bottom of my sea bag for almost five months when I noticed they had taken on a yellowish tan that failed to match anybody else's pure white uniforms. The barracks Petty Officer suggested I spend the morning in the gear locker with a bucket of hot soapy water, so I could bleach my two sets of whites until they finally matched every body else's.

On Monday my education on the various weapons mounted in the Navy's combat vessels began. We were issued special school materials which included a hard backed lose-leaf note book which we were to keep hand written record's of study material. Believe it or not, the cost of said materials was actually deducted from our pay the following payday.

We kind of joked about the fact we were doing the studying so we could help the Navy maintain their weapons. Concurrently, we were actually paying for the privilege. We would be covering the ordnance rating of Gunners Mate, Turret Captain, Torpedoman, and Aviation Ordnanceman. On weapons that discharge projectiles we began with the Colt .45 ACP, the Springfield 1903, with which we were already familiar, 30 and 50 caliber machine guns, all the way up to the battleship 16 inch rifles. That rifle fired projectiles in the thousand pound category. The study subjects would also include mines, torpedoes, depth charges and their various launching devices.

The days passed by quickly as we began learning about the various items previously identified. The final weeks our efforts concentrated on Naval aviation and the ordnance elements related there to. I was personally convinced that the Navy's combat future was going to depend heavily on the use of aviation in warfare future which appeared to be moving faster with the development of aviation ordnance weapons development. Based thereon, my mind kept advising me to concentrate within this area of endeavor. It also appeared to be the most interesting. My study book expanded rapidly with my concentrated efforts to store as much information as possible. Even I was over-whelmed by the amount of weapons data I was submitting to hand written paper.

The 16 weeks at the trade school seem to rush by to graduation and it now became my time for my formal introduction to the fleet. The paper work being filled out requested we indicate three possible choices of sea duty. Quickly I inserted my three choices, a Fighter Squadron, a Patrol Squadron, and a carrier, especially the USS Saratoga CV-3. I would have been satisfied with any of the three.

Graduation Day and the results were posted. I had finished in the top ten per cent of the class with the rating of 3.841. Not bad, not bad at all. On the assignment sheet it read KENEMAN, Harry L. Jr., S2c, 223-41-87, USS Memphis CL-13. What the devil happened! Three strikes and your out! Better luck next time. Looks like I'll be sleeping in a hammock again for awhile.

A SEAMAN'S FIRST SEA TOUR

It was early 1938 when this Seaman 2nd graduated from the San Diego's Class A Ordnance School. After receiving my assignment orders to the USS Memphis, CL13 I found myself climbing the port gangway of said vessel. I faced aft and saluted the colors. I then turned to the Officer of the deck, saluted and requested permission to come aboard. The Officer of the Deck granted me permission; I then advised that I was reporting for duty. The Quarter Deck messenger was then directed to escort me down to the Main deck and the Executive Officers Office.

It was obvious they didn't care a tinkers damn about how proud he was of his excellent 3.8 average gained in that school. He was a Seaman 2nd and Seaman 2nd's did not pass go, they went directly into a deck division no matter how damn smart you thought you might be. Prior to my arrival I had already been assigned to the 2nd Deck Division aft. The division's four hash mark Boatswain's Mate 1st Class arrived; welcomed him aboard and gave him the 2nd division area of responsibility tour of the vessel. Old Boats then located and assigned me an empty locker, identified a berthing space to swing my hammock and familiarized him with the Watch, Quarter, and Station Bill and explained his duty assignments.

It was actually easy to become friendly with the division personnel, they were always glad to gain a new face. I was surprised how easy it was to cope with the general routine of on board maintenance in the assigned work areas. The day always began on the morning watch with black coffee in the lower after citadel between the Port and Starboard six-inch guns. These were the early times before the installation of electronic sound systems. It was the responsibility of the Boatswain Mates to pass all major, and routine on board communications and directions with his nice silver Boatswain's pipe. The first announcement each day was usually, "Clean sweep down fore and aft. Sweep down all decks and Ladders." This particular command was passed at least five times a day! Said order was normally followed by direction to clamp down with damp swabs and general polishing of all bright work. A new young sailor just assumed that these efforts were repeated daily to brush away the hammock cobwebs and work up everybody's breakfast appetites.

On Monday mornings, the ship would drop its mooring get underway and put out to sea. We would steam slowly past Point Loma for the purpose of making headway for conducting a series of drills. The Navy has always been famous for practicing drills. There were all kinds, fire drills, plus All kinds and types of emergency drills. Naturally General Quarters, which directed man immediately to their battle stations and gun loading drills. Every GQ was timed to determine how long it took the crew to batten down all hatches and report that all hands had manned their battle stations. Conducting drills did not mean that general cleanup and ships maintenance was ever neglected! Whether spotlessly clean or just slightly dusty, the sweeping and swab downs were never missed.

During GQ drills we often had a sea going tug and a floating towed target available to give the gun Pointers teams aiming practice. The 6"53 single gun mounts had telescope sights secured to the sight yoke, a "Y" shaped steel unit mounted which cranks in the deflection information from the mechanical Fire Control director. Looking through their telescopes, the Pointer in the left seat was responsible for maintaining the scopes horizontal wire on the target by raising and lowering the gun muzzle in elevation to compensate for the ships role. The Trainer, in the right hand seat, had the responsibility to keep his vertical crosshair on target by moving the gun horizontally in azimuth.

The sight yoke is kept in proper alignment by the Sight Setter. He received his deflection directions by sound power head set from the Fire Control Director. The recommended deflection was cranked into the sight yoke immediately. The term "Set" was shouted loudly so both the Pointer and Gun Captain knew the gun was properly aligned ready to fire. Once everything was pre-set correctly and the gun sight was on target, the Pointer could fire the gun with his electric firing key.

Every Friday we conducted Field Day and compartment inspection while steaming back to our San Diego mooring. Those off-duty married men would hit the washroom to prepare for weekend liberty. That was unless the Captain had scheduled Captain's Inspection for Saturday morning. It was rumored that Captain's Inspections depended strictly on how early a tee-time the skipper could get at the North Island Naval Air Station Country Club.

My arrival aboard was timely due to the fact all gun crews were in training for up and coming short-range battle practice. This annual program was important to everyone. There was the extra gunnery "E" money, as well as other awards for excellence in gunnery. A 6" gun practice-loading machine was mounted on top of the after deckhouse. At least twice a day, our gun crews practiced on that machine.

Our practice went something like this. With the order "Load", the Gun Captain would instantly open the interrupted screw breech block. The Rammer instantly identified the bore's condition, clear or foul. In the event of a foul bore he must block the gun loading with his ram for the safety of the gun crew. On "bore clear" the tray man would insert the loading tray in the open breach to protect the interrupted screws. Then, with a mighty heave the 1st shell man tosses the 100 pound plus projectile through the tray into the breech, then the Rammer with his ram shoves the projectile all the way home to engage the shell's copper rotating band with the bores rifling. As the ram is quickly removed so the Powder man can rapidly shove the powder bag all the way into the chamber with the red ignition end visible the tray is withdrawn. The Gun Captain completes the load by inserting a primer in the firing lock. As he closes and locks the breech; he yells "Ready One" to advise the pointer the gun is ready to fire. This loading cycle takes only seconds to accomplish. On the "Fire" the reloading procedure instantly begins again.

Eventually, the day arrived when the ship swung into line for short-range live firing battle practice. As we prepared for the firing run, my mind wrestled with the fact that I had never heard a gun larger than a .22 Long Rifle fired before. In nervous anticipation, we heard the word "Load" passed. The breech of the 6"53 gun mount opened and he could see the blue sky at the muzzle as he screamed, "bore clear". The shell went through the tray into the bore as he slammed it home with the ram. The powder bag was inserted and the breech closed as the Gun Captain announced, "ready one". On the command "fire" there was one hell of a loud boom as the large breech leaped back at me in recoil.

As the breechblock swung open, I saw flame and smoke swirl out the muzzle under air pressure. "Bore Clear," I yelled as he rammed home shell number two. In went the powder bag and the breech closed. "Ready two" mouthed the Gun Captain. Again the monstrous breech recoiled back at him. From that moment until the "Cease fire" command everything seemed automated.

At the completion of the exercise, I discovered I was shaking with excitement, and covered with sweat. I realized that firing a naval six-inch battery was a hell of a lot more exhilarating than a .22 rifle. Aboard this vessel in my late teens, my thoughts all revolved around the fact that the events of this day had been the most exciting happening in my short life.

Once the scoring results of the exercise were posted, it was announced that our gun crew had qualified for the gunnery efficiency "E". Old Boats, my Gun Captain, congratulated me personally with a "You did good Kid." He handed me a small ¾" inch white E on a blue background. "Sew this on your dress blues son." He was positive that this young Seamen 2nd Class would hit the beach with a much saltier feeling now that I had a gunnery "E" prominently displayed on my jumpers left sleeve. After that day I no longer felt like a boot recruit. I had finally arrived as a seasoned sailor!

USS MEMPHIS CL 13 AT SEA
IT WAS GREAT TO GET UP
IN THE MORNING!

As the vessel penetrated the moonless night darkness, the bow of the old USS Memphis CL 13 was cutting deeply through the green waters of the rolling Pacific Ocean. Our vessel had been under way for several days and the Third Section of the Port watch was manning the 4 to 8.

As the eastern sky began to gray it was obvious we were still steering a direct northerly course. The ships bow slowly rose and fell in the swell. The breeze from the northeast was cool and wet but had little effect on trimming the ship to remain on the Captains selected course. As the morning sun slowly began to peak over the eastern horizon the Starboard first section was making preparations to relieve the Port third section.

It was still a little early with the Main deck lined with sleeping hammocks swaying gently with the slight motion of the vessel. Below the hammocks were the folding cots of the personnel who had been aboard slightly longer than the Hammock dwellers. Looking aft along the main deck at the line of sleepers, it was hard to believe that each individual knew his exact sleeping location and would return to it religiously each evening.

Along the decks came the piping Boatswains ordering the removal and storage of all sleeping materials. At first, with everyone turning out it looked like the start of a mass disaster. However, in just a matter of minutes the hammocks, cots and bedding were stored in the Hammock Nettings and all hands were shower bound to prepare for the new Day. There were a few bunks down but they were the sleep in's from the 12 to 04 watch.

Again the Boats were piping, "Clean Sweep down fore and aft, Sweep down all decks and ladders!" As stated previously, cleanliness was a major element so this would happen usual four more times before the day would end. By now, all the divisions would be settled in their special place for their hot mug of black tar like coffee before going to work on the morning watch. "Its bright work time." The tart salty air just loved brass. The morning watch, and brass polish, was God's gift to the sailors to make sure that, when the sun rose in the morning, the brass turn buckles on the life lines, and all other visible brass shone like the day it was first made.

The next event was more appealing. Now that everyone had worked up a massive hunger it was time for chow down. The bugler blew mess call and the Boats with their little tin whistles, made out of pure silver, blew Chow down at the top of every ladder. The mess cooks (the lowest rated persons on the ship) had lowered the mess tables and benches from the overhead in preparation for breakfast. The one thing I never figured out was, if the boats, blowing mess call at the top of the ladder, how come they got to be the first ones to sit down at the mess tables?

Usually the food was excellent. The only time you had to be careful was when they served hard boiled eggs. You had to be careful to make sure you didn't get a bloot. You don't know what a bloot is? That's an over aged egg with a little bitty unborn chick in it. Them little bitty feathers are damn hard to get out from between your teeth!

Well, can't tell you more about our wonderful day. Time to go to work!

1930's SEAMANSHIP & IT'S ASSOCIATED TOOLS

During the mid 30's we suffered a deep depression, purchased gasoline six gallons for a dollar. And enjoyed what we could during the good old pre-war days. This was the time when I enlisted as a pink cheeked teenage sailor sent to Newport recruit training to be taught "old Navy" Seamanship. My instructions was conducted by a chubby, middle aged 2nd Class Boatswains Mate, approaching age 35 to 40. These older Boats always wore severely squared white hats, displayed their Brest pocket badge of authority, a shiny silver whistle, called a Boatswain's Pipe, that rested majestically upon their chests.

The tools of their trade were nautically unique, not normally known to the landsman. However, if recognizable, it had to be known by an entirely different name. For example, men of war vessels in the heavy cruiser or battle-wagon classes had uniquely beautiful white teak wood decks. Under no circumstances were these beautiful white decks ever allowed to remain slightly dusty or dirty, whatever matter was dragged over, spilled on, or even dumped there strictly by mistake! I think even the seagulls knew better than to deliberately deposit anything there on.

I'm sure you may be wondering how they keep those decks so clean and white? It was easy, good SEAMANSHIP. There was a special tool called a holy stone. Now this item has never seen the inside of a church. It was an ordinary white fire brick broken in half with a small hole chopped in the top, which accommodated a pole made from a broom or swab-handle. Once the deck was wet, the machine that operated this holy stone was normally a Seaman 2nd Class who was also invented to give these old Boats somebody to order around. When so directed, that seaman would stick a pole in the hole of that brick and briskly work it back and fourth over a wet deck until that deck got clean again! Once rinsed the bright sun will take over and dry it back to a lovely creamy white!

The smaller vessels, light cruisers, destroyers, gun boats were constructed with steel decks which required daily maintenance because they were subjected to all kinds of continuous wear, tear, and five times a day clean sweep and clamp down with a swab. This was another seamanship tool known to the general public as a mop. Excessive passage and other forms of basic work traffic, tend to thin the protective coating. All good sailor's know steel and salt water hate each other. When they get together, they form rust, rust forms pits, which makes it more difficult to keep things neat and clean.

Rust cannot be tolerated and must be dealt with immediately. For this special purpose we had age old tools, chipping hammers, manual and compressed air, wire brushes, two types, hard and soft, foxtails, (dust brush's) for cleaning up paint chips. For the finishing touch the Navy has never run out of Red Lead, anti-corrosive paint to prevent more rust, and the Peace de resistance topping, the Navy's good old choice of color, Battleship Gray. All of which would be applied with the item of choice, the famous Navy four-inch brush. Sorry, Shipmate, the soon to become famous paint roller hadn't been invented yet!

Now all such good SEAMANSHIP always must begin on the morning watch around 06:00 hours. Many years ago an old 1st class Boatswain's Mate claimed that long ago, God himself called all the Admirals together and told them to invent the Morning Watch, and good old bright work polish. That was so all brass work on board could brightly greet the morning sun. He also told them to invent the lowly Seaman 2nd's to do the polishing, and perform the first clean-sweep and clampdown of the day. Last but not the least, they invented the Chief Petty Officer who would be charged with the responsibility to see that everything worked perfectly and that these old sea fairing men properly trained the young Canoe College Boys to make sure they would be promoted to LT (jg) in four or five years.

Many often wondered who in the Navy was responsible for buying all those damn four inch brushes. He must have owned stock in the company!! When he retired he could tell everybody, "I made my fortune on purchasing four inch brushes for the Navy."

There has got to be a couple of old guys somewhere in this world with vivid memory of how ten crazy goof-offs who, in 1938 painted the old Light Cruiser, USS Memphis CL 13 from stem to stern and vice versa, from weather deck to water line beautifying the hull of said vessel's 1,110 feet in less than 10 days. The work was completed in its entirety with those damn magical Navy four-inch brushes.

Oh, how those Seaman 2nd's hated those 4 inch brushes. You had to be one to fully understand!

THE CONNING OF A VESSEL
USS MEMPHIS CL 13, 1938

A combat vessel no matter what its size or description, receives all underway commands and management controls from a single station, The Captains Bridge. The Bridge is strategically positioned in the forward section of the vessel in order to provide maximum visibility for the navigation and steering control of the ship. It is centrally located at a high point forward of the ships foremast. At least that's what my 1917 copy of the Bluejacket's Manual says.

Due to the major electronic advancements of the past 60 or more years, today's vessels are controlled primarily by preset microminiaturized electronics. Simplified it's like pushing a button marked "Take us to Pearl Harbor," and it's away we go. Now that description is a little far fetched. Despite all the famous new electronics The Commanding Officer is still entirely in Command of the vessel. Not a piece of fancy electronics command.

As I understand it, his orders are directed to the Navigator, who with the aid of the bridge watch set up the electronics to perform in accordance with the Skippers desires. Some times I wonder what would happen if the modern electronics disagreed with the Captain. Many timers I often thought if it wasn't more interesting to respond to the Skippers orders being performed manually by the Bridge watch.

As words appeared on this line my mind slowly drifted back to 1938 and the old USS Memphis CL 13. There I again visualized the Bridge lay-out on one of the newest of the 10 speedy slick light cruisers of the 1924 vintage Omaha Class.

Centrally located on the Bridge was, wait a second, what happened to the helm? Where was as the large steering wheel with all the spokes? Oh Yea, We were high class. Our helm was now a state of the art 1925 electric drive system for rudder control. The Helmsman steered this baby with a device that made him look like a Trolley Car Driver! However, he had to stand up rather than have a nice soft pillow to sit on like the Trolley Car Captain. Normally, the Helmsman stood the watch for two hours then was relieved by his back-up Lee Helmsman.

Directly forward his steering mast was a large brass Binnacle stand complete with its old fashion magnetic compass as well as the more modern gyrocompass. This trained enlisted man was the most important sailor on the Bridge. It was his job to keep the ship on an assigned course despite the power of the wind and water. With the aid of the gyrocompass and the manipulation of the rudders with our electric steering mechanism, he could in most cases offset the power of the wind and water.

On the Starboard side forward was the Captains Chair positioned to best observe the sea ahead. While underway, the skipper spent a good part of his day in that chair. When the Captain was on deck the Bridge became the central point for all shipboard commands. Directly behind the Captains chair was the Navigators table. Here all the charting was performed to insure we remain on a predetermined course to our selected destination. Each and every change in course or direction was instantly plotted and timed. As an after thought, I would also like to mention the entrance to the Skipper's underway Sea Cabin was also aft on the Starboard side.

Forward on the Port side, due to the fact at that particular time we lacked sound powered phones for passing information throughout the vessel. Therefore, we had a human messenger's station. His standby position was the left forward corner of the bridge. This spot usually belongs to one of the deck division bright boys in training for future positions in the Bridge watch. Their job was the human communication link between the Skipper or the OOD and other elements of Ships Company.

Another mission was to be observant of the workings on the Bridge from the skipper on down. This was especially true during the night watches. Having stood these watches personally, it was actually a good time to get to know the new young officers who were familiarizing themselves with the real world duties of the Officer of the Deck. One thing was certain; there really wasn't much need for message delivery in the middle of the night! So it gave this young sailor time to learn the standard Bridge watch procedures

Just to the left, approximately two or more feet from the steering control mast was the Annunciator. This was a signaling device for transmitting orders to the engine room. It permitted the Bridge to direct the increase or decrease in screw turns to adjust our speed through the water or to reverse the direction of the screw's rotation for backing down. In the event of an emergency and failure or loss of the Annunciator, there was a voice tube attached to the forward bulkhead so that an emergency order to the engine room could be passed verbally. The Lee Helmsman usually performed control of engine room signals based on the Skippers or Officer of the Deck's orders.

The sole remaining member of the Bridge team was the Officer of the Deck. In the Captains absence below, or sleeping in his sea cabin the OOD had direct control of the Conn as the Skippers representative. It was his responsibility to see that all changes, or events, and the timing thereof are in accordance with the Captains standing orders.

Young Officers might have the Captain return to the Bridge to just observe. If the Captain takes his seat without stating "I have the Conn," it definitely means the young OOD was still in charge. Now it's pretty obvious the young OOD might be under observation. So he had to keep his cool. Control the nerves when the Captain is on Deck! After all you're a Commissioned Officer standing a watch in temporary command of an operational combat vessel. Quit worrying youngster, straighten up and fly right, as a ring knocker your bound to make Lt. (jg) in 4, maybe 5, more years!

"SAILOR CAN YOU SPARE A DIME?"

While on liberty way back in the 30's sailors can end up having some rather weird experiences. The average Navy sailor's made little money. When ashore he was always in the position of seeing how far his funds might be stretched. Actually the simplest solution was not to go ashore. Almost everything on board was free except for smokes, candy at the Gyp-Joint (Ship Service) and an ice cream sundae at the Gee-Dunk Stand. In those days as a Seaman 2nd Class I drew $36.00 a month. With a $2000.00 G.I., insurance policy withdrawal his bi-monthly pay day averaged about $16.00. Two cartons of Sea Store smokes consumed a buck. Incidentals like toilet articles and candy, etc. consumed another five bucks total. Using my excellent high school math this left about $11.00 for a couple of liberties and maybe a G-dunk or two at the ice cream stand.

In order to relax, everyone has to get off the ship occasionally or go bananas. In the mid 30's simple items purchased ashore were rather inexpensive. A hot roast beef sandwich sold for about 35 cents, a coffee, with refills, went for a nickel. If you wished to splurge, a T-bone steak with fries and dessert went for a buck fifty. Movies, usually a double feature, cost about 35 to 50 cents.

If you were the type that yearned for female companionship there were the dance palaces. There you could meet young lady's and dance your fool head off for fifty to seventy-five cents an evening! In those days many a lonely sailor or soldier met their future spouses in that fashion. Less we forget, a tall slim draft beer could be had for a nickel, a bottle about 15 cents and a mixed drink like a rum and coke went for a quarter.

Following a shave and shower on this particular day I shifted to my dress blues, stuck 6 dollars in the watch pocket of my pants, (a Seaman 2nd's financial status does not allow a watch for that pocket.) I drew liberty card, proceeded to the port gangway to catch the motor launch that came along side. The liberty party requested permission to depart the ship. Facing aft, saluting the colors, I then proceeded down the gangway into the launch.

On arrival at Fleet Landing everyone leaped ashore and headed for town. Walking ashore was not only good exercise it failed to dent the pocket change. On deciding to get something to eat, I entered the first diner and ordered a sandwich and a glass of water. After all water was not only good for you, it was free. My next course of action took me to the theater district where a couple of hours were killed watching a double feature. Departing the movie it now was dark and old San Diego was a mass of colored lights. Walking back toward the landing I came to a small tavern that I had patronized previously. Well, why not, at least have one drink then head back to the ship.

On entering said tavern, who did I bump into but shipmates sitting at a table with a couple of fairly nice looking ladies. I was invited to sit down with them and have a drink. Could this be a lucky break where I would meet a local girl? Things were progressing nicely and the young lady next to me was easy to talk to. So I called for another round of drinks while my shipmate began to really cozy up to the other girl.

Suddenly, my friend swore, leaped to his feet, dragged his lady out of the chair and began to punch her out! The other girl quickly grabbed up her friend and they raced out the door. What happened?" I yelled, "You jerk, what's wrong with you? Why did you hit her?" My friend yelled back, "What her? She's a he!"

What a tragedy. I was out two bucks and a quarter I hadn't expected to spend. Plus the waitress advised us the shore patrol was on the way. Rapidly we departed the facility and headed back to Fleet Landing. There we were able to catch a nickel snatcher back to the ship. Thus ended a perfect example where shore liberty scored a complete zero!

FEMALES AND THE
YOUNG SAILOR MAN

During the early years of the 20th century prior to World War II our Navy Chief Petty Officers, (CPO's), trained their young sailors to be strong, mean fighting men. He wanted them tougher than a 75 cent steak and ready to fight at the drop of a hat! For practice, they would send their tough Bluejackets ashore to a Honky Tonk beer joint patronized by Army wrap leggings for no other purpose other than honing their fighting skills. Many believed their real purpose for this charade was to keep them from chasing women that were hunting sailors that might be turned into a sea going money trees. It was surprising what some women would do in those days. Actually, they had the gear and desire to do it by being a sweet smelling, eye fluttering', young darlings of the female persuasion.

Those Chief's knew that after a few beers those sailors and soldiers would remember they disliked each other, which would result in a nasty knock down, drag out that would end up with the Shore Patrol's and Military Police's. This resulted in a rapid return to the fleet landing and their vessel before they could make any contact with those sweet smellin' dainty females of the opposite persuasion!

What appears here may sound a little comical or even far-fetched, but in those days the military actually worried about close female contact with their personnel. As an individual safety, the Navy continually warned their young Seaman and Petty Officers to avoid having close intimate contact or marriage that would take their minds off their military skills and duties. Why they even produced movies that required mandatory watching, that explained terrible things that might happen to you if you had intimate contact with certain members of the opposite sex. They must have scared the Hell out of a good many 18 year old kids that were just beginning to have an interest in female companionship!

Men in Grades E-5 and below were not permitted to marry without their Commanding Officers permission. However, this restriction did not apply to higher grades of E-6 & E-7. Actually, there were situations that required special caution. In those early years there were many clever women that used marriage to deploying sailors as a money tree. The government discovered many cases were where money hungry women had married several shipboard deployed sailors who were capable of using their various married names to apply for and receive monthly dependent allotments from several of there numerous "husbands."

Hey, everyone was young once. It's probably true that the company of an attractive, vibrant young female might tend to turn a strong, tough young fighting man into a blithering idiot that would leap to a girls aid, even if she accidentally (?), dropped her nice smelling hanky!!

In the old days a seafaring sailors life was tough. Following a long sea cruise they were ready to welcome formal companionship. It's only natural for that desire to develop between the sexes. Therefore, we pay the price and relaxed and enjoy it whenever possible.

For example, I'm personally familiar with a sailor who met a nice girl on a shore side date in 1940. They eventually took a chance and married months later. They raised two fine sons and are still dating today over 70 years later.

USS MEMPHIS NAVY YARD OVERHAUL 1938 PRE-WW II STYLE

During the Navy's early period our vessels had wooden hulls. Their power and speed depended on the total amount of unfurled sail, plus the power of the wind, and the physical experience of the crew. In those days, it became obvious that the crew belonged to the ship and the ship belonged to them. The care and maintenance of said vessel to keep it operational and ship shape was entirely up to crew. This responsibility extended well into what is known today as scheduled operational overhaul.

As the years passed, he hulls turned to steel and steam engines replaced the sail. Many things now required technical engineering skills to perform maintenance and overhaul of power plants and other items outside the technical ability of the average crew member. However, over the years the Navy trained the various crew members to be able to respond responsible to all underway maintenance that could be performed by trained crew labor.

In relation to all forms of overhaul and repair of Naval vessels, World War II finally brought the U. S. Navy into the twentieth century. Overhaul procedures, prior to our entry into WWII, was a far cry from the type of service required for wartime weapon systems availability and combat readiness. Vessels requiring combat damage repairs had to be committed to short term turn around of weeks and sometime days, rather than the usual scheduled three to six month yard period.

Prior to December 1941 Ships Company performed most repair work manually, which had been standard procedure for many years. Yard personnel were used only for major ship alterations and installing detailed engineering modifications or changes. War suddenly made it mandatory that over 90% of shipboard maintenance and repair work, be performed by trained professionals using specially designed sophisticated equipment, thus eliminating prior manual efforts.

I would like to take you back almost 70 years ago when Ships Company performed a major portion of the scheduled work, mostly by hand labor. Little or no automatic equipment was available unless a pneumatic chipping hammer can be considered special equipment. During this stage of my personal Seaman 2nd class sailor's career, I was a lowly deck hand with more than one whistle blowing Boatswains boot marks impressed on the rear of his dungarees.

The yard effort prior to entering the dry dock was an all hands working party to off load fuel and ammunition. Being one of the lowest paid ratings on board I was caught up in an all hands evolution to unload ammunition. Did we perform this task with our steam crane and cargo nets? Not really, that equipment was strictly reserved for high tonnage jobs. Everything in the area of 100 lb class was a human manpower effort.

Six-inch gun projectiles were block and tackled out of the magazines and positioned on the bluejackets right shoulder. In those days a sailor weighed approximately thirty-five to fifty pounds more than that 6" projectile. Now it wasn't too hard a carry on a level plane. However, unfortunately it was high tide. So, going over the brow from the weather deck to the dock, was at a sharp angle. By the time you got ashore you were moving at a pretty good clip. By your fourth or fifth trip you were hitting land at almost a dead run.

That Boats 2c class at the gangway kept saying, "Move along, pick it up." What went through my mind was "That jackass was going to wear himself out with all that talkin' and tootin' on his little tin whistle."

Eventually, the human body got so numb you lose track of what was happening or how often. By the time the brain returned to normal we discovered we were now handling 6" powder tanks. Empty they were a snap but full they were difficult to handle. Their overall length between 3 to 4 feet made them awkward to control. Then came case after cases of small arms rifle and pistol ammo, 3"-50 rounds, 100 pound aircraft demolition bombs, bomb fuzes, and pyrotechnics. This manual labor took 12 hours per day for 2 days.

Once the fuel and explosive stories were removed, preparations were made to enter the dry dock to refinish the bottom. Several powerful small craft came along side to initiate the move. Placing the ship bottom correctly on the docks support fixtures was a precise technical accomplishment. As the water was pumped out of the dry dock the ship must settle safely on the pre-positioned fixtures. All aboard watched attentively as the ship passed slowly through open gates of the dry dock, or to use the proper name, caissons. Once the ship was properly positioned the small craft departed and the gates moved to the closed position. Manual descending work stages were instantly secured completely around the ship.

All personnel assigned to stages were issued a long handle tool that resembled an oversized garden hoe with the blade bent straight out. It was a scrapper specifically designed for manual removal of the barnacles and other sloppy crud from the sides and bottom of the vessel. The easiest and fastest way to perform this task was while it was still wet. Based thereon, it had to be done as the water level recessed in the dock.

The stages had been swung over the side and prepared for manning. Each stage had a safety line that ran parallel approximately 3 feet above the footboard. In addition, the stagehands were equipped with a waist safety line to be attached to the stage line. As I watched, I quietly prayed for an extra pair of hands, two for manning the scrapper and the extra pair to hang on with. My grandfather, who was a Baptist preacher had often talked about miracles, but I knew perfectly well it was impossible for me to develop anything except cold blooded fear by the time my feet hit the stage.

STAGE FRIGHT—On command I reluctantly went over the side and attached the safety line. As the stage moved down toward the water I grabbed the safety line and almost lost the scrapper. Looking down at the receding water, it appeared murky and ominous, deep too. The men on the stages began the job of scrapping the gunk from the ships side. As I scraped I finally began to feel like I was getting the hang of it. As the scrapping proceeded downward we lowered the stage to keep up with the work.

Everything had gone fine until my foot slipped in the slim from the ship's side. Instantly I found myself half submerged in water at the end of my safety line. The scrapper I dropped had entered the receding water and headed for the bottom of the dock. The other guys on the stage hauled me back on board and I was handed another scrapper by the angry Boats 2c. Being soaking wet and dripping into the sludge on the footboard, it wasn't long before I was again hanging waist deep in the water. Scrapper number 2 was also long gone to the bottom of the dock. It was easy to recognize the red faced angry expression on Boats face. His statement went something like the following, "Get your lazy scared ass back up here on deck so I can put someone on that stage that can stay there."

As our chastised sailor climbed back up the stage lines, he pondered if maybe it wouldn't be better if he just let go and died in the sludge at the bottom of the dock? Hell no, you stupid jackass, you are only 19 and probably have a lifetime of unfortunate errors ahead of you. Some form of punishment would be better. Arriving on deck, it was noted that he had made not one but two enemies, The Boats 2c, and the poor bloke, that replaced me on the stage. It didn't take long for me to find out how severe the punishment would be and how long it would last.

The Boats 2c chewed me up one side and down the other. Part of which I have remembered to this day, "You scared little SOB, I'll teach you to be a sailor. I'm having the Division Petty Officer transfer you to the side cleaning force as of today. Be assured, that every dirty detail that comes down the pike, you will be my first volunteer. Your fear of heights will be broken. You will be painting the mainmast, hauling over stack covers and any other dirty high job I can think up." I remember this as a cure you or kill you system. No mattered how well I performed that Boatswain continued to harass me till the day I received a transfer to new duty.

BOTTOMS UP—Once, the water in the dock was ankle deep, the side cleaning gang, of which I was now a member, plus a group of "selected" volunteers were all armed with scrappers headed for the bottom of the dock. They had been assigned the distinct pleasure of scrapping the bottom of the ship. Now the USS Memphis was a small light cruiser built to conform to the 1922 treaty construction limits. However, when you were underneath her with her exposed bottom at head level she appeared to be monstrous.

Scrapping the glop off her bottom and splashing through it ankle deep was definitely the dirtiest job I ever experienced during my young sailors entire naval career! It was also scary, especially when someone inside the ship hit bottom with a chipping hammer or anything that would make a terrific noise. The sudden sound would scare the hell out of you! Work continued in shifts with short breaks for chow until the job was completed.

Being short of money and unable to purchase a pair of leather work gloves, my hands were raw and blistered from the constant grip on that scrapper handle. It was hard to remember if I walked, or crawled, into the shower. Being completely clothed from my former white hat to shoes, I washed my cloths on my body without taking them off. I then stripped to complete the shower. One thing was certain; it was the final marching orders for his boot camp double-soled high tops. The trash in the bottom of the dock had finished them off. I tossed them into the nearest G.I. can and crawled into hammock roll.

PEAK TANKS & SHAFT SHEETS—The first thing the next day I made sick call. There they plastered my hands with salve, bandaged and taped them up. This made me late reporting for duty. That seemed to please the hell out of Boats 2nd. What went through my young tars mind went something like this, "You little short piece of crap, you may detest me but that doesn't compare with the hate for you building up within me." I never once raised my voice or complained to him. I just kept thinking don't break your day will finally come. What goes around comes around.

The next couple of days they were assigned to scrapping and painting the after peak tanks. These were ballast tanks located in the forward and after section of the ship. They were confined spaces. Ventilation was poor due to the small entry hatches. In those days, it was back in the era before anyone really became concerned about shipboard health hazards. For example, such things like painting with anti-corrosive materials in confined spaces. They just liked to think it was the smell that made the painter sick. Hell, we went in there ourselves not realizing there was a health hazard problem.

Shortly thereafter, the Navy Yard personnel pulled a port screw and shaft for scheduled repair or replacement. Ships Company had the assigned responsibility for maintenance of the shaft sheets that enclosed the shaft. Using a fading memory of over 60 years past, with the shaft removed, the shaft sheet had the general appearance of a sewer pipe twenty or more feet long with the approximate diameter of 30 plus inches. Now that the time arrived to paint the inside of this massive tube, take one guess who was Boat's 2nd's number one selection for the 23:00 to 07:00 shift.

Most people will find it difficult to believe, but be assured it's the God's honest truth. I was one of Seaman 2nd unlucky, so-called, screw-up "volunteers" assigned to this task. Each painter had to crawl into this tube one at a time with a four-inch paint brush and a bucket of anti-corrosive paint and a length of manila safety line tied to his leg. The purpose for the line was to pull him out in the event he passed out.

The instructions were to paint until your eyes burned and you couldn't stand the odor any longer. He could then crawl out and be replaced by the next man. Time in the tube hardly ever exceeded 10 to 15 minutes. This rotation continued until some one got ill and had to report to sick bay. Despite all the obstacles the job was satisfactorily completed. Several of the men ended up sleeping in the sick bay most of the following day. The taste of that paint remained in their throat for days thereafter.

MORE TALES OF MANUAL OVERHAUL LABOR—A couple of months passed and the below water line work had been completed. The port shaft and screw had been reinstalled and tested. The ship sported a new clean spray-painted bottom. It was time to float the vessel, and remove her from the dry dock. It was good to see water under the hull once more. Once removed from the dry dock it was repositioned along side a pier, it was now time for the side cleaners to repaint the sides. In those days we had no pressure paint spraying equipment available to the side cleaning gang. To my knowledge 12" paint rollers, with long handles had not yet been invented. The only tool available was the Navy's famous old 4-inch paint brush. Now the Memphis was 555ft long, with two sides doubling the distance. Forget about the distance weather deck to waterline. This was going to be one heck of a big job for 10 guys armed with those 4" brushes.

The real interesting part was painting the bow. When you lowered the stages straight down, by the time you got to the water line you would be about twelve of more feet away from the ships side. No problem, some smart marine engineer figured that welding pad eyes on the bow about every six or eight feet, we could lash in the stage lines periodically. This system allowed the stage to closely follow the concave curve of the bow. They lowered the stages and tied ourselves in to the side of the ship until we reached the water line. There the painting efforts began, the crew painted themselves back to deck level. This procedure continued the entire length of the ship, both sides, with 4" wide strokes, all 1,110 feet of her.

When the battleship gray sides had been fully coated, it was time to square up and cut in the water line with black paint. This was done with a device known as a camel. The camel was a floating reinforced wood platform. Its primary purpose was fending the ship from direct contact with the pier. In this particular case, we were using one to finish painting the water line.

Next came the circus type job that had been promised. It was time to paint the mainmast. Going up was easy but coming down might be difficult. Working on the vertical portion was fairly simple but the yardarm, which ran horizontal to the mast was a horse of a different color. The yardarm was also supported by steel and wire stays.

Even equipped with a double safety line, a sailor might be more than apprehensive, (scared), having worked his way out on the yardarm. While painting back toward the mast, the bucket of paint, tied to the yard was pulled back in front with one hand while steadying himself by hanging on to the wire stay with the other. Then, painting back toward the mast with the left and hanging on by wrapping the right arm over the stay. However, the closer he got back to the mast, the angle of the stay became greater. Being left handed, I decided to change hands by hanging on with my left and painting with my right. Major mistake, in no time flat I spun around the yard and found myself hanging by the safety lines approximately sixty or more feet above the deck line.

To get back on the yard was unsuccessful. This action attracted quite a crowd of amused watchers at the deck level. Prompt action was taken to rescue me. It was kind of embarrassing to be fished back to the mast by the laughing rescuers. They placed me in the crow's nest to regain my composure. It took a little while to regain courage to face the laughter as I climbed back down the mast.

However, there was one good thing that resulted from this fiasco. Old Boats, my 2nd division leading Petty Officer had become aware of the continued confrontation between Boats 2nd and myself. The decision was immediately made to detach me from Boats 2nd supervision and return me to my regular division duties.

Despite all the problems related to above events, the experience had one positive result. I not only gained weight, but developed considerable upper body strength during this ordeal. I also found that despite the experienced fear and floundering, it definitely improved confidence in my personal ability.

RESTITUTION—Over 10 years later, I was now a Chief Petty Officer, commanding divisions of my own. Between tours I had been assigned temporary duty as a Command Chief Master at Arms. I had suddenly become totally aware that working for me was my old nemesis, Boats 2c, now a BM1c. He never recognized this Chief as that former klutzy kid S2c, and I never reminded him of the fact. Now I would hate say it was get even time, but I'm sure that old Boatswain wondered why his life during that short period of time was so damned uncomfortable. This young Chief was a firm believer in the old saying, "what goes around, comes around."

AND THE BAND PLAYED ON

In the "old" pre World War II Navy almost every vessel larger than a destroyer had its personal official U. S Navy Band. Its sole purpose was to render honors and play during all hands working parties. No one was ever able to explain to any sailor how music was supposed to make hard labor easier. Our Navy bands were excellent, but musically making a 100 lb weight your carrying a single pound lighter is impossible! As for entertaining the crew and making them comfortable, those bands did a great job! They rated special quarters for the purpose of eating, sleeping and practicing. Their only real work was keeping their quarters clean and presentable.

On the USS Memphis CL-13 they were quartered in the after upper citadel, which also housed two 6"53 gun mounts. For a bunch of "fiddle players" and "horn blowers" they were really a great bunch of guys. With our catapult work deck station just forward of their compartment some of our 2nd Division swabbies got to know them pretty well.

During the ships overhaul period at Mare Island Navy Yard, it was noticed that almost every weekend the guys would pack up their instruments and head to the bus station for San Francisco. Some of us wondered what they were doing. After all, it was illegal for them to get a job. So what in the world could be worth hauling a base fiddle all the way to Frisco on a bus? Having worked for them as temporary mess cook for a couple of weeks, I was drafted to find out.

The answer was simple. They were doing it for their own entertainment. They had made a deal with a small hotel in Frisco. They were renting a party room in which to set up their instruments. They even invited us to go with them if we were willing to kick in on the expenses. The following weekend a couple of us took them up on it.

On our arrival in Frisco the first stop was the beverage store to purchase supplies, (Liquor and fixin's). From there it was straight to the hotel where we were welcomed with open arms. It was obvious the band was good for the Hotel business. We moved into the Hotels largest suite. A bellhop immediately arrived with a portable bar fully equipped with ice and mixers. It seemed like everything was happening automatically. Both the band and the hotel personnel were well versed in making preparations, for what?

The band personally selected me to act as bartender, which made sense because I was instrument free. When the band started to play we opened the doors. This was an indicator that a free drinks party was in business. Passers by, especially the ladies, were invited in to enjoy the fun. Some of the guests were also repeaters, spending the weekend at the hotel, because of the bands almost weekly visits. In fact, it was an enjoyable different type of weekend. Not only that, it was a real neat way for lonely sailors to meet nice girls!! With the guys playing, resting, and taking breaks it was a busy suite till the clock struck midnight. That was the time agreed to between the hotel and the band. Any continuation of the festivities was at the discretion of the consenting individuals.

The following morning we had a late brunch, packed up our gear, hit the bus terminal and returned to the Mare Island Navy Yard and our military duties.

RETURN TO THE SEA

At last our good ship the USS Memphis CL-13 was underway again. We had finally departed from the Mare Island yard and headed for the open sea and again majestically past into a cool fall Pacific sea breeze. We thanked the fact we left the odors of the Navy yard in the distant past. There was a distinct rumble of life throughout the entire vessel as we entered the open Pacific by sailing under the Golden Gate Bridge. The sea air became more brisk. It was now early November as we change course south toward our first port of call.

The Memphis had been ordered to visit a small quiet California town with the Spanish name of San Luis Obisbo, which lay approximately 250 miles south of San Francisco Bay. The Navy had made a commitment to provide a vessel to participate in the cities 11 November Armistice Day celebration in memory of the anniversary of the end of World War I.

It was obvious that our light cruiser had the honor of being elected. The ships band and the those assigned to the ship's landing force would have the privilege of representing the U.S. Navy in that small cities annual Armistice Day parade. We were ordered to get our dress blues and a suit of undress whites ready for the selected uniform to be announced based on the prevailing weather

Don't forget the leggings, which was a matter of digging them out of the bottom of the sea bag and giving them a good scrubbing. By now they had changed from a stiff tan to a soft near white tone. Once the uniforms were ready, the only thing left was spit polishing my dress shoes.

The shoreline began to rise over the horizon as the ship turned eastward into the rising sun. Shortly they would call away the special sea detail to guide us into our assigned anchorage. It was also announced that the vessel be prepared to accept visitors during our stay. Visitors hopefully meant groups of curious young ladies that must be catered too. A lot of young sailors would be busting their butts to volunteer for escort duty. It could be a way to work up a date.

The landing force and band received a detailed briefing of our part in the parade. The weather had warmed and it was determined we would march in undress whites complete with rifle, web-belts and bayonets. The band would proceed first followed by the color guard and the colors, and a troop of about 40 men. Now, if we could keep in step without falling over our own feet we might come out of this march looking like a real eye catcher!

The departure time had arrived. At sling arms, we slowly loaded into the launches for transport to the beach. On arrival the Chief's quickly formed us up into a company front four abreast. Once fully formed the Officer in Charge stated "Lets show this town how good the Navy really is. "Sling arms, Squads right, forward March." We were under way. By the time we reached the parade area, we were back in a marching swing moving along like a well-oiled machine.

On the start cue, the Memphis band struck up a lively Navy march song. With a "Right shoulder arms, forward march" we moved out into the parade line. Being on the formation's right outboard side it gave me an excellent view of the people's reaction. The beat of the band mixed with the cheering, flag waving crowd, gave one a good feeling of being a small part of this event. As we neared the reviewing stand, a short halt was called and the order was given to "Fix Bayonets." Once moving again our band broke into "Anchors Aweigh." On the command "Eyes right," we marched stiffly past the stand with our bayonets flashing in the sun. In the front row our Captain and Executive Officer, in their dress white uniforms, stood at attention saluting the colors as we passed by. From that moment on it was all down hill.

The parade was over. There was a short time for mingling with the parade group before returning to the ship. Our best memory was probably about the pretty young ladies that visited the ship that afternoon. Several volunteers escorted our visitors about the weather decks in groups of 5 or 6. We were not permitted to take them below. (We never figured out who they didn't trust. Was it the young ladies or it the poor lonesome sailors?)

CHRISTMAS 1938
ABOARD THE USS MEMPHIS CL 13

The holiday season was in full swing. In fact our Thanksgiving holiday was already history. All hands thoughts had turned to preparations for the up and coming Christmas Holidays. The subject of our married sailors was discussing the purchase of gifts for the wife and kiddies. Many of the men were having deep holiday thoughts of family and love ones in distant areas hundreds of miles away, even our older Boatswain's with their unusual talents with the material they weave their Boatswain lanyards. These were the early days when the Boatswain's were very talented at manufacturing unusual items by hand. Woven and knotted items like Boatswain pipe lanyards, design lace type curtains, table decorations and many other unique items. My friend and boss, Old Boats, our division Petty Officer, had a project in progress but refused to identify what it was.

Some of the higher rated men were hoping for approval of a short leave, but a good majority of the crew, as usual were experiencing a funding shortage or were in debt to our money lender. Therefore, it was obvious a good number of us would celebrate Christmas on board.

The usual holiday work schedules were now directed at brightening ship for Christmas. The weather deck bulkheads rang with the noise of chipping hammers, and the swishing of four inch brushes applying red lead and good old battleship gray paint for dressing ship. Cable rigged with colored lights were strung out beginning at the bow, stretching over the forward gun mounts, the bridge, then up to the foremast. From there it would follow the radio antennas over the four smoke stacks to the mainmast. Then angled down over the after gun mounts and fantail to the stern. Along its length, it was strung with lights and many signal flags. It was especially colorful at night with the lights on and the flags fluttering lightly in a slight breeze.

About 7 days before Christmas, during the late watch, a pine tree of approximate 6 feet suddenly appeared on the Quarter Deck. It was the trophy of a late tipsy returnee from the beach. It had arrived bare but immediately began to develop home made trappings and an occasional ornament. This was followed by colored paper and cardboard holiday symbols strung along the Main Deck. It appeared that the mood aboard had changed with the Holiday in question only a couple of days away.

At 0500 Christmas morning, reveille was much the same as any other day with the familiar piped message, "Clean sweep down fore and aft. Sweep down all decks and ladders!" It was followed on the morning watch by, "Clamp down," and touch up of the shinny brass work on the stanchions and lifelines. However, breakfast was just a preamble. At our twin tables "old Boats" bowed his head and whispered a quiet prayer. When seated, everyone ate lightly to leave plenty of room for the anticipated meal of the day.

At 08:00 the bugle sounded attention, and what was left of the band on board broke into the "Star Spangled Banner" as our ensign sprang to the top of the flag pole on the fantail. Thus ended the workday as the band then began to play Christmas music. Slowly many of the crew members gathered around sitting on deck between the aircraft catapults. Just to listen, humming or singing while silently their minds drifted off to far away places, home and families.

At 12:00 sharp, mess call was sounded. All rushed to their division mess table to partake in the main event of the day! This was the second Christmas meal of my naval career. The turkey and ham and all the fixin's were outstanding. Little did I realize at that particular time, that I would spend over 20 more Christmases before I would clean, press and closet my gold striped uniform for the last official time.

THE USS MEMPHIS CL 13
THE 1938 COAST TO COAST CRUISE

Late in 1938 the mighty Memphis had been designated the flagship for Commander, Aircraft Scouting Forces. This required the transfer of the Memphis Scouting Squadron Aviation Unit, which would be replaced by the Admiral's two personal aircraft and his Command Staff. The first new aircraft that arrived and hoisted aboard was a standard Curtiss SOC-2 float-plane. It was painted the navy standard colors but it lacked the usual Squadron designators.

It was identified as belonging to the Admiral's staff. Once hoisted aboard it was securely stored on the port catapult. The second aircraft to arrive was definitely different. Like an Admirals Barge, which had replaced the Captains Gig in the forward starboard davits, the fuselage was identified as a Flag vehicle by its glossy blue black finish.

Our new Flag Officer Commanded a total of five Patrol Wings, which were located in San Diego, Pearl Harbor, Coco Solo, Seattle, and Norfolk. The aircraft being flown by the Squadrons operating out of these locations ranged from the old PBY-3's to the newer PBY-1 & -2's. Once the Admiral reported aboard, his two star flag was hoisted to the after yard. Our good old USS Memphis had just moved up a notch or two in the world.

On first week in January the USS Memphis called away its special sea detail. As a Flag Ship she had been ordered to participate in the up coming Fleet Problem XX to be conducted on the east coast. As the ship slipped its anchorage in San Diego Bay it backed away and slowly reversed course. The

Naval Air Station and Coronado slipped by on the port side as we headed for Point Loma and the open sea.

Once in the Pacific we added on turns to increase speed as we set a southerly course for our first destination, the Panama Canal Zone. Turns were ordered for 18 knots as we increased our speed. Behind us beautiful California and San Diego disappeared from sight below the horizon. This deployment would carry our vessel thousands of miles to the Atlantic eastern side of the North American Continent.

The pre-planned plotted course would carry the ship along the outer coast of Mexico to Panama and the Canal Zone through the Canal into the Caribbean Sea then north into the Atlantic Ocean. From there, we would sail north along the east coast of North America to Hampton Roads and the Norfolk, VA area. Little did our young sailor realize that several years would pass before he would ever again lay eyes on the sunny coast of Southern California.

The ship bow rose and fell cutting deep into the swollen sea spreading the bow waves side to side while churning a frothy wake to mark our southern passage. As we proceeded further southeast along the outer coast of Mexico the sea began to eventually grow calmer. The sea breezes took on a warmer tropical flavor as the sun rose each morning.

As we closed in on the Pacific side of the Panama Canal, those in the crew who had never traveled the "Big Ditch" began to discuss the efforts of the men who had struggled to build it. To them, it appeared that this endeavor should have been included as the 9th wonder of the World.

It was obvious that they anticipated the future world travel and the large amount of traffic it would draw. To assure the uninterrupted flow of shipping in each direction, east and west, the engineers and builders planned for and considered a duplicate set of lock's to guarantee a continuous flow in each direction. Another problem to consider was the difference in the tidal flow between the two coasts. On the Pacific side the average tidal flow was in the vicinity of about 10 to 12 feet more or less. While on the Atlantic side it averaged approximately one or more feet. This required construction design to compensate for this variation.

Another curious item about the canal was the fact that the eastern Atlantic entrance is further west than the Pacific entrance. This unusual geographic difference was definitely of military importance. Strategically, with any possibility of war, an attack originating from the west, the eastern side would be the most logical target in order to disable this manmade seaward passage. All military planning and the establishment of military facilities were based on this assumption. When World War I began the eastern entrance became the focal point of Central American naval and air defenses.

Land Ho! The tropical western shores of the Isthmus of Panama began to appear on the horizon. On entering the Bay of Panama the city of Balboa lay on our starboard side. However, there was no planned liberty scheduled for Balboa. The good old Memphis went through all the necessary passage procedures including picking up the professional pilots and beginning our passage. The ship slowly approached the Miraflores Locks, which would give our vessel its first lift up to the second row of locks. Electric locomotives, or "mules," as they were called, guided our vessel through the gates and positioned it therein. These electric units, up to six of them, operated on pre-laid tracks running parallel to the lock. The vessels size determined the number of Mules required to position the ship in the lock.

The inside length of the lock was 1000 feet while the width was measured at 110 feet. Because of the locks restricted width, no U.S. Naval vessel built exceeded this width until after the end of World War II. The only naval vessels that had a problem were the Aircraft Carriers. The Lexington CV-2 and the Saratoga CV-3 were able to squeeze through with less than three inches to spare on each side. However, the flight deck overhang had a tendency to knock down standing fixtures like a few light poles!

Once positioned in the lock. We noted that another ship was in the lock with us. Well, why not, we only took up 555 ft, 5in. of the length of the 1000 ft. space available and only 55 feet, 5 inches of width, which was only half the width. When the massive lock gate closed seawater was pumped in to float us to the level of the lake. Once the level of the lake was reached and the gate opened, it was only about two miles across the lake to the Padro Migual Locks. This lock would raise our ship another 30 feet to the Culebra Cut, which was eventually renamed later to the Gaillard Cut to honor the engineer who designed and constructed it.

Our vessel, then under its own power navigated the Cut and Gatun Lake under the direction of the canal pilots. The lake was similar to an enclosed sea surrounded by thick tropical vegetation (jungle), and an occasional small island. As the ship approached the Gatun Dam, speed was reduced to a slow crawl. A series of six locks had been constructed in conjunction with the dam. Passage through these locks would lower the USS Memphis eighty-five feet to the eastern sea level. Here again we moved at the digression of the electric mules operators. Slowly they moved our light cruiser from lock to lock, dropping us about thirty feet as the water was drained out of each lock. Once through massive gate of the third lock, we had finally completed our canal passage.

From there it was just a short run to our off shore anchorage in Colon Harbor. Our special sea detail made ready to drop the hook on command from the bridge. Except for the short period in the locks, once "Let Go" was sounded, the smooth steady beat of our four powerful screws was silent for the first time since departure from San Diego. Many of the off duty sections personnel were chaffing at the bit to hit the beach and relax. Relax, hell, they were really thinking about a hot time in the old town today! The ships shower room was a cheerful place, as they rapidly made ready to hit the beach!

When Liberty Call sounded, it was a spiffy sight to watch that mass of liberty hound's, in snappy clean whites, rapidly approaching the Port gangway of the Quarter Deck. They saluted the Officer of the Deck, requested permission to leave the ship, face aft and saluted the colors, and formed a steady stream of humanity down into the motor launches. There they stacked themselves in like sardines in a can.

What a beautiful sight. It was just a short run in to the Fleet Landing located in the Coco Solo small boat basin. Here this sea of pure white uniform's, with black neckerchiefs erupted out of the launches and over the dock. It was hundreds of shined black shoes that had just returned to solid land! Just outside the station gate was a familiar hangout for those familiar with the area. Many had always assumed that the Knights of Columbus was strictly a Catholic religious organization.

The crew had been advised that we were now participating in the Fleet Problem XX that had brought us to the Atlantic side. At the same time this young seaman had been battling with himself as to whether on not he should take the chance of knocking on the door of the Admirals Flag Lieutenant to question him if a transfer into aviation could be arranged. Why not, the least they could do to him was keel haul him. Why not, nothing tried nothing gained. He was amazed when the officer invited him in. It was a great moment in his short career when he had the good fortune to discuss his desires, and his background for making the request. He permitted me to present my background school records and stated he would review same. In fact, this young sailor was advised he was being given this opportunity because it took a lot of guts for a Seaman 2nd Class to approach an Admiral's Flag Officer for the purpose of making a transfer request. That seaman thanked him but failed to mention how scared he was when he first knocked on the officer's door.

He was finely ordered to report back to the Flag Officer. On arrival at the Flag Officers office, our Seaman was advised he was to be transferred to Patrol Squadron 11 when we reached Guantanamo Bay. The officer stated he noted that I was qualified as a small boat Coxswain. The Seaman thought all that data of qualifications and I'm being transferred into aviation because I can run a boat! Well, can't complain, one way or another I'm finally going into aviation. I thanked the Lt. profusely.

By the time the good old Memphis hit San Juan that seaman was fully packed and standing at the ready for departure. He was to report to the C.O. USS Wright AV 1 for further transfer to the west coast Patrol Squadron VP-11 currently at NAS Norfolk, VA for duty. As I waited departure, Old Boats approached me. He said, "So long kid, I'm glad you are finally getting what you wanted. You done good here and I'm going to miss you in my gun crew. Lots of Luck." I'm going to miss you too Boats as we shook hands goodbye.

The word was passed for him to report to the Quarterdeck because a whale boat was along side for transportation to the Wright. I shouldered my gear saluted the Officer of the Deck and requested permission to leave the ship.

As we pulled away I thought "Goodbye, old girl." Little did I realize that in just over a year I would be back aboard "old girl" working and flying in the SOC's as a member of the USS Memphis Aviation Unit.

THE PANAMA CANAL
&
THEIR OFF SHORE
TROPICAL ISLANDS

Note:—The subject of the Panama Canal has been discussed in our previous story titled "The 1938 USS Memphis CL 13 Coast to Coast Cruise". However, it had been suggested that the canal be covered in detail as a special stand-alone coverage. Short story of the canal has been provided separately.

As the USS Memphis, CL13 approached the Isthmus of Panama's western approach in January 1939 we will try to discuss the Canal and the caliber of men who struggled to build her. For those of us who had experienced a canal passage, it appears to be a construction that should have been included as one of the amazing wonders of the world. It appears today as a monumental tribute to man's engineering ambitions and tenacity. Now that our vessel was about to transverse the "Big Ditch," those of us who served on her would be able to view and admire the results of man's ability to change and improve the world. These men had visions of the future and the major time saving traffic the canal would draw.

Based thereon, they anticipated continuous uninterrupted traffic flow both from the east and west. The engineers and builders planned and constructed a duplicate set of locks to support uninterrupted movement in both directions. Another item of special interest was difference in sea level movement between the Pacific and Atlantic coasts. On the Pacific side the average tidal flow rise and fall exceeded ten to twelve feet. However, on the Atlantic coast the tidal flow measured less approximately a foot. It was necessary that design and construction of the locks had to compensate for this variation.

One of the most curious things about the canal was the fact the Atlantic eastern entrance was geographically further west than the Pacific western entrance. This circumstance was of extreme military importance. Viewing this fact strategically, in the event of war, in theory, the eastern end of the canal would appear to be the most logical target for an enemy wishing to disable our seaward passage. Military planning was based on the same conclusions. Since WW I the eastern entrance has become a major focal point of our Central American naval and air defenses. Our purchase of the Virgin Islands many years ago was a part of this effort. Especially During WW II, canal defense was of major importance. Militarily, The U. S. could not afford the lose of the shorter supply line for the transport of war materials

Of special note, due to the lock width restrictions, no U.S. Naval vessel was built with a beam that exceeded 110 foot until after WW II. The only fleet vessels that presented a problem to canal passage were the aircraft carriers. For example, the original Lexington CV 2 and Saratoga CV 3 were able to squeak through with less than three inches to spare on each side. The problem was the overhanging flight deck and island would damage standing fixtures like the light poles.

When cleared to proceed, our vessel picked up the pilots and steamed slowly toward the Miraflores locks. They would give the ship its first lift up to the second row of locks. Electric locomotives called "mules" guided the ship through the lock gates and positioned it therein. Those electric units, up to about six of them, operated on railroad tracks parallel to the lock. The number of the mules used to guide and position the vessel depended on its size. Plus the fact the lock was 1000 feet long, more than one ship could be positioned in the lock at the same time.

When the massive Miraflores lock closed, seawater was pumped in to raise the ship to the level of Lake Miraflores. Once the gate opened it was a couple of miles across the lake to the

Pedro Miguel Locks. There we were again raised 30 feet to the level of the Culebra Cut, later renamed the Gaillard Cut, in honor of the construction engineer. Under its own power, the ship passed through the Cut and across Gatun Lake.

Speed was reduced to a slow crawl as we approached Gatun Dam. In conjunction with the dam, a series of six locks had been constructed. Passage through this series of locks would lower the ship about eighty-five feet to the Atlantic sea level. Slowly the mules guided the vessel lock to lock lowering us about thirty feet at each of the locks. When the massive gates of the third lock opened, the old Memphis had completed the canal passage to the Atlantic.

Aruba-Dutch West Indies:—Shortly we were again underway. The ship was cruising just out of range of the coast of Columbia, South America. We were advised that the next port of call would be Oranjestad, Aruba. A small island in the Netherlands, West Indies, Oranjertad, the islands largest city was the center of the islands of Arubas major industry, the refinement of Venezueian oil. It was obvious that we knew little about the Dutch people, their culture or life style. As we approached the island from the seaward side, it left no doubt this was an industrial area. There were various size tankers riding high awaiting their turn to take on a load of oil. It gave us the appearance that we had found the home of Shell Oil.

As the Memphis approached its assigned anchorage we began backing down slowly to stop our forward motion as the anchor was let go. Once ashore we found the people very friendly and accommodating. It was probably due to the fact we were the first U. S. military vessel to have dropped anchor here for quite a spell.

Dominican Republic:—It was just a short run to the south side of the isle of Hispaniola, Columbus, which for centuries since 1492 had been known as the discovery of America. In fact Columbus body is buried in the capital city, Cludad Trujillo. It's the largest city in the Republic and is now known as San Domingo. It is considered the oldest city in the western Hemisphere

<u>Goodbye to the U.S. Memphis</u>:—It was a great moment in my aviation career. I had the good fortune to meet, discuss and talk with the Flag Secretary of ComAirScoFor. He stated that the only reason he agreed to review my record books was because as a Seaman 2nd Class I had the guts to approach a Command Flag Officer to ask for help. I thanked him but he never really knew how scared I was when I first knocked on his door.

On reaching Guantanemo Bay I would be transferred to the USS Wright AV-1 for transport to VP-11. They actually wanted me because I was a qualified small boat coxswain.

USS WRIGHT AV 1, Aircraft Tender

This lowly Seaman 2nd Class had recently reported aboard the Wright from the USS Memphis CL 13 at San Juan, Puerto Rico for transportation to Patrol Squadron VP11 currently doing temporary duty at NAS Norfolk, VA. The Squadron's 12 Consolidated PBY-2's had flown from NAS North Island CA via Panama to NAS Norfolk for participation in 1939's Fleet Problem XX, which by the way was still in progress.

Our Seaman's transfer had been engineered by the Flag Command not because of his documented knowledge of Aviation Ordnance but because they needed a boat coxswain. This poor guy had busted his hump at that school and it didn't help one damn bit getting a transfer into a squadron or any other aviation activity. Plus they never let him forget it! Every time they needed someone to coxswain a boat guess who they came looking for! This is kind of getting ahead of the story, but this unhappy thought had been bugging him ever since January 1939! Our Seaman in transfer was currently aboard the Wright seeking transportation to his new duty squadron VP-11.

The Wright was an old Auxiliary launched back in 1920 but received most of it notoriety during the long range seaplane era as an Aviation Command support vessel. Such distinguished Naval Officers as Ernest J. King and Marc A. Mitscher had commanded the vessel. It began life as a lighter than air aviation tender just prior to 1938 when it was reclassified as a heavier than air seaplane tender. It had been Flag Ship for Commander, Aircraft Scouting Force, but when the Admiral shifted his Flag to the USS Memphis in 1938, it then became the Flag ship for The Commander of Patrol Wing 1, (PatWing 1).

Like the Memphis, the Wright departed San Diego in January 1939 to participate in Fleet Problem XX in the Caribbean. Once underway from San Juan the course was set for arrival at NOB Norfolk on 14 March. Upon arrival it was discovered that the squadron was operating out of Narraganset Bay off Newport, R.I. Laughingly the thought went through my mind, if I needed to go to the head I think I would have to go through Newport, R.I. first!

Two days later this new Airdale Seaman 2nd Class was waiting at the Newport fleet landing for a boat to take him out to the USS Childs to meet with his new shipmates.

USS CHILDS AVP-14
IT WAS JUST A SEA GOING
GAS STATION!

As the newest member of Patrol Squadron VP 11, it seemed like this lowly Seaman 2nd Class had been following his wandering "new" Squadron all the way from San Juan, Norfolk, plus further north to Newport, RI. This is a spot I shall always remember because of his initial arrival here in 1937 for recruit training at the Newport Naval Training Station.

As I waited on the Fleet Landing with my sea bag and hammock, a whale boat marked AVP-14 glided into the float. The Coxswain yelled, "You the guy looking for a ride to the Childs?" Our chilled sailors response was tossing his gear aboard and stepping down into the boat. He thought, at long last I have finally reached my original goal. He was now officially attached to an aviation unit, a real "airdale" Squadron. I'm as of this moment a full-fledged member of a U.S. Navy seaplane Squadron. Airdales, that's what the black shoe surface warriors called these elite, fly boys. It appears to me I've sort of entered through the squadron's back door because I could operate a small motor boat.

Patrol Squadron VP-11 was deployed out of NAS North Island, San Diego and was currently participation in Fleet Problem XX being conducted on the east coast. Beginning today I would be tested to determine both my ability and worth. It was Mid-April 1939, Narraganset Bay, off Newport RI, which was its normal gray nasty damp self. A cool brisk wind was blowing the tops off the small waves as the PBY-2 Catalina flying boats of Patrol Squadron 11 bobbed steadily at their temporary moorings. The day was dreary and gray. A

Hell of difference from California and sunny North Island, the Squadrons homeport! The military purpose for this specific location was to conduct hide and seek submarine search and make believe destroy missions.

The support vessel was an old Navy rust bucket, a modified World War I former four pipe destroyer, the USS Childs. Its prior nomenclature was DD-241. She had been converted into a high-speed aircraft tender now identified as AVP-14. Two stacks, boilers and fire rooms had been removed to install an aviation fuel storage system. The Squadron personnel, as the Childs Ship Company referred to them, occupied the ship's forward berthing space.

The space was totally inadequate for all hands. However, in the interest of aircraft safety, sufficient flight crewmen were required to remain aboard their seaplanes at all times. This measure was required in the event a sudden emergency fly away became necessary. The crews were rotated daily in order to get a few "decent" meals, a hot shower and some sack time.

As a former member of a Class "A" aviation trade school, more than a year had been spent as a deck hand, or "swab jockey", on a light cruiser dreaming of getting transferred into a squadron. Did all that aviation knowledge help? Not a damn bit! He got a back door swap because of being a qualified small boat coxswain!! It seemed they needed an extra guy to operate a refueling boat. Well, better late than never!

Now these refueling boats were converted mid-sized enlisted personnel motor launches. Installed just forward of the engine was a fuel tank that held almost 2000 gallons of aviation gasoline. The gunwales were covered with canvas stuffed with padding to protect the thin aluminum sides of the flying boats. The refueling motor launch requires a crew of three, a bow hook, an engineer and a coxswain to man the boat.

When the aircraft returned from their mission, it was the boat crew's job to approach the flying boat on the port side to refuel. Now the fact your fuel tank blocked most of your forward vision it made this job something other than a piece of cake. Once safely tied up along side, the real work began!

Now those Catalina's could hold about 1700 gallons of fuel and they had to be topped off before the next flight! How was this done? With a hand wobble pump manned by the boat crew! The fuel hose had to be passed up to the crew on top of the wing. The gas had to be strained slowly through a chamois to prevent the entry of water and foreign particles! When that three-week tour in the Newport area was over that wobble pump had grown muscles in places I'd never had before or since!!

Damn, it was great to finally be called an airdale!!

LEARNING THE AIRDALE WAY

Patrol Squadron VP-11's twelve PBY-2 aircraft had finally returned to the Naval Air Station, Norfolk, VA from their temporary deployment off the shore of Newport, R.I. They had been participating in an anti-submarine warfare program as part of Fleet Problem XX. The ground crews had returned by ship and were now birthed in the Naval Air Station barracks close to their aircraft parking area. My new shipmates had laughed at my hammock roll stating it was no longer required and trash canned it for him. In a way I hated to see it go. My mind still held a few fond memories of some super sleeping as it swayed with the slow roll of the ship.

However, being able to sleep in a lower bunk again with a four-inch thick mattress was also a pleasure. My uniforms, clothing and other personal gear were neatly stowed within easy access in a six-foot tall steel locker rather than the bottom of a sea bag. Meals were being served in a well organized mess hall without a heavy sea roll that might make your food slide into a single pile on one end of your metal mess tray. This type luxury was reminiscent of the four month tour spent at the Ordnance Class A school in San Diego.

Serving in the Patrol Squadron Navy was a whole different ball game when compared with the shipboard aircraft operational flight plan. The Catalina was a twin engine flying boat equipped with twin side wheels followed by a manual tail wheel steering ability aided either by a tractor or by engine turn up. The beach crew operated under the management of an old time Boatswain Mate 1st Class, Boat's Wheeler. He was in charge of moving, launching and recovering the aircraft from their parking area to the launching ramp and returned. These efforts were accomplished by using a tractor equipped with a towrope and a good size hook. The hook was attached to a large pad eye built into the tail section of the flying boat. It then could be towed stern first toward the launch ramp. Or, if the engines were turning up with the tractor line attached to that same pad eye, the aircraft could be taxied to the launching ramp under its own power.

The beach crew was responsible for the actual launching and recovery of the seaplane. On the clear to launch signal the pilot slowly advanced the throttles to increase the revolutions to start the plane rolling down the launch ramp. Once waterborne the beach crewman who had followed into the water beside them could then unpin and remove the forward wheels assemblies, which are exceptionally heavy.

Therefore, to simplify the crewman's handling the removal and replacement of said wheels, the wheels were kept submerged by filling the tires with water as well as air. The upper section of the assembly has an installed floatation tank filled with air. This unit was attached to the hull with a set of two locking pins. Once the pins are released, the wheels would fall clear and the crewmen could then drag them back ashore. The rear steering wheel was also detached and the hook to the aircraft was released. The pilot was then free and clear to taxi out for take off.

In cold weather the launching crew were clothed in a "boot-suit." This was a full-length suit right up to your neck. To make the new airdale feel good one of the crew warned him not to let the suit fill up with water because he didn't want to see the suit floating across Willowby Spit up side down with the feet pointed straight up in the air.

Returning aircraft preparing to be recovered taxied into the prevailing wind toward the launch and recovery ramp. The pilot made his approach to the beaching ramp under their own power. As the aircraft closed on the ramp, one of the beach crew placed a hook and line through the eye on the inboard wing tip Float. This line was used to spin the seaplane hull to position the tail of the aircraft for attachment to the tractor. Line and hook.

Tension was retained on the swing line and tractor tow line to hold the ship in position until the front wheel assemblies and steer able tail-wheel could be reattached. On a signal from the beach master, the pilot throttle down the engines to idle so the tractor could tow him from the water. Once back and positioned ashore the engines were shut down and the ship was immediately washed down to remove as much salt as possible from the hull.

I finally had my interview with the squadron Commanding Officer, a senior Lt. Commander. He stated he had reviewed my personal record, as well as congratulating me for my services while aboard the USS Childs. Mainly for the purpose of education, for the present he was to work for old Boats in the Beach crew. But, during slack periods he was to report to the Ordnance Chief for familiarization with the squadron's ordnance requirements. I was finally glad to know I would begin working on the equipment for which he had been trained.

All Squadron personnel were anxious to know when they would begin their return flight to the home base at NAS North Island. However, at the same time, there were rumors afloat that two of the Squadrons would remain with Patrol Wing 5 in Norfolk. This was not really happy news, particularly for the married personnel. Coast shifting especially for the married would require breaking up existing homes and planning for the transfer of family personnel and property from one coast to another. It wasn't actually the cost of the effort, because the government picked up the tab, it was more the inconvenience. But being a part of the military it's something that can happen several times in a career. Finally, the word was officially released. VP-11 would remain in Norfolk as part of Air Wing Five and become Patrol Squadron VP-54.

This information went over like a lead balloon with the personnel. But, despite the moaning and groaning that prevailed, theirs was not to reason why; theirs was just to begin to comply. One of my newest shipmates had prayed that he be returned to his girlfriend in San Diego. But that failed to work. In an attempt to cheer him up, it was mentioned that he had been gone quite awhile; maybe his lady friend might already be dating some new sailor she may have met since his departure. His explosive reaction to that possibility indicated that this possibly didn't help make him very happy.

After several weeks of short operations out of NAS Norfolk it was announced the squadron was again scheduled for temporary advanced deployment to somewhere in the Caroline's. It happened over 60 years ago so I've forgotten exactly where. For this project our young hero was assigned as a full time Ordnance striker. We were loaded aboard our support vessel, which was a former "bird" class Navy deep seagoing tug converted into an advanced base seaplane tender. Maybe it might have been the USS Gannet AV-8, which was also attached to PatWing-5. The first ordnance assignment required filling 100-pound water filled practice bombs to be used in low altitude bombing practice.

This was not going to be an easy task. The squadron operating in conjunction with us had not as yet been outfitted with their new PBY aircraft. They were in the final stages of operating the older P2Y-3 seaplanes. These old timers had a great early service record. In 1934 they were the first naval aircraft to make a mass squadron non-stop flight over the Pacific, California to Pearl Harbor, Hawaii.

For the present operation, loading 100-pound bombs on a P2Y was an awkward kind of a problem. Their bomb rack hard points were on the underside of the stub wings. At anchor this placed them very close to the water. To accomplish the loading we had to use a punt. A low square ended boat about eight feet in length. The sailor loading the bomb rack had to lay flat on his back with the bomb on his chest as they snaked the punt under the stub wing. Once in place, the loader had to be sure the racks were cocked and the bomb hooks were open. He could then bench press the bomb up making certain the bomb suspension eyes were aligned with the bomb hooks. He then had to push the bomb up sharply to close and lock the rack hooks. Once he had three bombs loaded and locked and the sway braces down the job was completed. It was a snap once the bomb hooks locked. As the fairly new kid on the block, guess who loaded most of the P2Y's.

On the Squadrons return to NAS Norfolk I reflected on the fact I had been a Seaman 2nd Class for darn near two years. My new Commanding Office had assured me I would be promoted to Seaman 1st Class in October 1939. Just one month before Hitler ordered his troops into an attack on Poland. War had been declared. All America began to wonder if and when we might be involved.

THE PBY-2 CATALINA FLYING BOAT

Following the Japanese 7 December 1941 attack on Pearl Harbor many imagined that the PBY Catalina would have limited value as a World War II combat aircraft. Many stated it was too old, too slow, and too fragile to stand up against modern warfare weapons. I was not surprised in the least that a major mistake was made in the assessment of its value!

This 1930's flying boat design manufactured by Consolidated Aircraft proved to be a sturdy, more valuable, versatile aircraft than many others in the Naval inventory. It was a perfect vehicle for long-range search, patrol, and rescue whose flight range also contributed to its ability to conduct extended anti-submarine and destroy missions. This seaplane had adequate weapons capability, which included low-level torpedo attacks against vessels. Plus during the war, they developed an effective night attack, fly and destroy mission capability.

Early in the war the two-engine patrol bomber was able to demonstrate its versatility as a cargo plane delivering medical supplies and food. It served as an aerial ambulance, a passenger plane, operated as an open sea, rescue vehicle, as well as many other valuable uses. As stated above the flying boat could make open sea landings to recover hundreds of downed aviators saving them from capture or loss at sea.

In fact, PBY pilot, Lt. Nathan Gordon, was awarded the coveted Medal of Honor. Three times he flew his aircraft through enemy fire to rescue fifteen Army fliers downed in the Pacific Ocean. Because of its many valuable uses it was purchased and employed by almost every allied nation for use during World War II era. No other combat aircraft in the inventory ever competed with its various number of mission efforts!

The PBY really hit its stride when some smart flying boat jockey thought up the idea of converting them into night bombers. The aircraft squadrons, assigned this duty, painted their plane a flat black. It makes it almost impossible to detect their exact location in the dark. Because of their unusual finish they were named the "Black Cats."

In the daytime they flew air, sea rescue missions and at night they harassed Japanese vessels and disturbed enemy land operations. The Black Cat pilots understood that night flying might be dangerous, but it was also obvious that to a point the darkness also concealed and protected them. It also covered their approach exercising the element of unexpected surprise.

In their new black outfits it made them almost invisible to surface vessels or to an occasional Japanese night flying floatplane fighter. When a Black Cat aircraft was attacked by an enemy, they would dive and skim low over the water so the enemy attacker was incapable of getting below them for fear of flying headlong into the sea. At that low altitude there was no apparent margin for error.

One of the Black Cat pilots named Jim Cobb took off for Guadalcanal one night for the purpose of harassing the Japanese troops on the ground. His wing racks were loaded with standard heavy ordnance. However, internally his aircraft was loosely loaded amidships with small anti-personnel bombs. For most of the night they flew back and forth over the Japanese positions. The crew would stand at the waist hatches manually flinging these small anti-personnel bombs over the side on orders from the pilots. As Cobb departed the area he sent General Geiger on Guadalcanal the following message, "The Black Cat Flies tonight."

It become fairly obvious that the PBY Black Cat operations would probably be the best remembered combat actions rendered by all their PBY World War II efforts. In fact many unusual records were set. For example, Lt. (jg) William Sumpter and his crew, on the night of 23 Sept. made four direct hits in a single run.

On Davao Gulf off Mindanao he located a 10,000 ton seaplane carrier refueling two destroyer escorts, one on each side. Sumpter flew over the three Japanese vessels at masthead level and released four bombs. The first struck a destroyer, the next two struck the seaplane tender, and the fourth exploded below decks of a small destroyer. The subsequent explosive blast blew the PBY more than 200 feet into the air. The two small destroyers sank almost immediately. Our Black Cat reversed course and came back strafing the seaplane tender that was listing heavily to one side. All three enemy vessel were destroyed.

Another example, Lt. (jg) Robert Schuetz, bombed a transport in Toli Toli, Celebes Island. The Cat had made the attack run through heavy gun fire, which badly damaged the Starboard engine. Schuetz continued his approach and released his ordnance of which two were direct hits on the large vessel. As the plane passed overhead the gunfire penetrated the PBY hull fatally wounding the navigator. The aircraft shook violently as the pilot pulled back on the yoke struggling back to 2000 feet. He shut down the damaged engine and feathered the prop. The crew jettisoned all unnecessary loose equipment while the pilot set his badly damaged aircraft on course back to the tender. That return flight of 550 miles was successfully completed on a single engine.

In the course of only one month PBY Squadron VP-33 had amassed a total score of 43 vessels destroyed or sunk totaling 102,500 tons. Twenty more added up to 53,000 tons, including a cruiser badly damaged.

What is stated above is just an example of the value of this slow, underpowered, fairly good size, cumbersome Flying Boat with the ability to remain airborne for about sixteen hours at a crack. It's also amazing to know that sixty plus years after the war ended in 1945, there were a few PBY's still flying the skyways around the world.

The PBY-2 Catalina Flying Boat

NORTH ATLANTIC NEUTRALITY PATROLS

THE 2nd WORLD WAR BEGINS!! On 1 September 1939, without warning, Hitler's German armor blasted across their eastern border into Poland. The 1918 myth of a "War to End all Wars" crumbled in the dust as the German armor in its power drive charged swiftly toward Warsaw. Per their treaty agreements, England and France immediately declared war on Germany and began to mobilize their forces to aid Poland. But, for the ill prepared allies it was too little to late, the Polish Army fought bravely but their guns were silenced in a matter of weeks.

High level secret discussions were being held between England and the United States. The secret subject matter was directly related to keeping Atlantic sea lanes open, for transport of war materials to England. Despite the fact we were not at war, these talks led to the establishment of an American North Atlantic Neutrality Patrol.

However, the large north Atlantic Naval Air Station under construction at Quonset Point, R.I. was far from ready for practical use. Unfortunately, no formal operational air facility existed north of Norfolk, VA. However, the Newport Naval Torpedo Station R.I. supported a small aviation torpedo test facility on Gould Islands. It was determined that the Gould Island facility could be rapidly modified to accommodate four PBY-2 Patrol seaplanes. This request change in assignments went to the U.S. Navy Patrol Wing 5, based at NAS Norfolk, Virginia.

Patrol Wing 5's PBY Seaplane Command had four Squadron's, which were stretched south down the east coast from Norfolk to the Panama Canal. Patrol Squadron 54, formerly VP-11 of North Island, California had just been repositioned from Patrol Wing 1 to Patrol Wing 5. The VP-54 squadron was immediately issued orders to establish a four plane advanced base detail with sufficient flight and support personnel to conduct patrols which would consider a North Atlantic patrol area that would extend out to the eastern edge of Greenland.

They were ordered to base their operation in conjunction with the Naval Torpedo Stations Aviation Unit based on Gould Island in Narraganset Bay just off Newport, R.I. A two-story barracks building had been hastily constructed and additional concrete pads were paved in the vicinity of the islands small hanger to provide parking space for VP-54's and PBY-2 Catalina's.

Nothing much could be done to improve the existing torpedo test units maintenance hanger on the eastern waterfront of the Island. It was necessary for the torpedo station crew to double up in their work areas in order to provide the VP-54 squadron personnel with working areas. Chief Aviation Ordnanceman "Pop" Sammons being our top-secret bombsight technician, and his three Ordnanceman were the only VP personnel able to operate in their own private space. As an ordnance striker, the former Cruiser sailor, me, was assigned collateral duties with the beach crew and of course, as well as a qualified boat coxswain. For some unknown reason everybody always recalled that I had been a boat coxswain when they needed one.

When you analyze the service we were about to perform, it was obvious the U.S. had chosen up sides even if we hadn't actually declared war. Our patrol areas stretched north and east to Greenland and the open sea. Most of our flying would be conducted between 500 to 1000 feet with an occasional climb to altitude to make long-range visuals. We had been ordered to make armed patrols, which meant our first task was the belting of .30 and .50 caliber ammunition.

Surprisingly, the PBY Catalina flying boat was probably the first Naval aircraft to mount Browning M-2 .50 caliber free guns in their waist hatches. With those old manual hand belting machines it took some time to assemble the necessary belts to arm the two .50's and two .30's in the four seaplanes. Currently the wing bomb racks operation were checked in the event we would be ordered to carry bombs or torpedos. However, during the first year of operation the only shooting and bombing test we performed was for practice.

It soon was obvious winter had arrived. One thing for certain, Narraganst Bay could get mighty mean and nasty in winter. Flying was difficult as well. In those early days the winter flight gear was bulky and uncomfortable because it limited mobility. It consisted of an insolated lined full-length jump suit, sheep skin lined flying boots, gloves and a leather helmet. Once you had all parts assembled and put on, you didn't move around much.

Cold early morning engine starts could be complicated as well. The props had to be pulled through to insure that no oil had collected in the lower cylinders. We even mounted men on top of the wing with manual hand cranks to help start the engines. At the time it was my understanding that getting the system parts in motion prevented the sudden engagement of the electric starter from snapping an engaging spine in the starter system. When the engine caught, it was time to get off the wing before the prop wash blew you off!

The search flights were long; boring operations of up to 16 hours at low-level flight requiring a continuous search scan of the oceans surface for anything questionable or unusual. Occasionally, we would report a vessel and even talked to their radioman. We had a small cooking capability in order to get something hot other that coffee into our system. It was rather rugged duty but the small flight pay did improve the first paycheck each month.

During this tour I passed for advancement to petty officer AOM3c, (Aviation Ordnanceman third Class). Boy, oh boy, that resulted in a six bucks a month increase in pay, $54.00 to $60.00. When you throw in a half set of flight skins at $15.00, it was getting to the stage where our new Petty Officer could rub a couple of bucks together. It even allowed me to take my new lady friend to the movie picture show occasionally! I enjoyed being with her a lot. She made four times the money I did, 60 dollars a week! It was fun kidding her that I wanted to marry her for her money. When I was with her I felt like I hit the big time. Now over 70 plus years later I still think it was a pretty good choice! Our sons think so too!

The only problem was, it did spell the end of my Patrol Squadron duty. The Navy frowned on their young Petty Officers getting married. After all they did have us under contract longer than she did. My transfer back to sea was only a few short months away.

The PBY-2 Catalina's
.50 Caliber Browning Waist Gun

RETURN TO THE USS MEMPHIS

Despite all of old Boat's warnings about getting seriously involved with a young lady early in life, this Petty Officer, AOM3rd Class, couldn't help himself. Actually Boats warnings were valid because he preached that it was insane to get deeply involved before you could afford it. In that respect, this young 3rd Class Petty Officer might have considered himself lucky. His young lady had a good job which paid her four times the amount of money he made. However, he will truthfully advise you that money was the last thing on his mind. This young lady was too perfect to loose just to avoid a Navy transfer.

In those days the Navy was extremely unhappy when their young sailors got hitched. They immediately took action to insure the young lady didn't get more attention than they did. After all they did have me under contract before she did. So within three months and five days I received new orders.

On 27 January 1941 I received my new orders. Report immediately to the Officer in Charge, USS Memphis CL-3 Aviation Unit, NAS Norfolk, Va. I was definitely surprised! It was an unbelievable quirk of fate. I was returning to the identical vessel I had departed in April 1939. Well, at least I would be familiar with the ship. When I checked in a couple of days later our aviation unit consisted of a complement of one, a Lt. Naval Aviator. Our arrival brought the personnel complement up to seven which now included a Chief, an Aviation Machinist Mate 1st Class, a Radioman 2nd Class and two third class Petty Officers, a Ordnanceman and a Metalsmith.

The Lt. recorded our arrival in his personal address book because the unit didn't own a damn thing. Our new Lt. stated we didn't even have a piece of paper to write on or a single screwdriver! Even the little hanger office with the rickety chair and beat up desk was a loaner! Once we all were introduced to each other, the Lt. and the Chief went in search of housing and Messing facilities.

The rest of us knew one thing for sure; you can't do anything without transportation and a telephone. Our first move was to officially become operational. The first thing we accomplished in the office was get a phone installed. We then checked out a truck from the motor pool. The Aviation Supply Office was kind enough to provided us with a series of Shipboard Aviation Unit allowance lists to figure out what we were authorized to draw from supply. The 1st Class and the two thirds started filling out supply requisitions. We elected the Radioman unit yeoman who bummed paper and writing materials from another office in the hanger.

On our first load from supply, we returned with office materials, chairs, a typewriter, and a file cabinet. The next load consisted of tools, and tool kits for all hands. We even began to draw spare parts, flight gear and jackets. Cruise boxes were ordered from the Carpenter Shop. In the interest of safety and extended ownership we even drew several large locks to keep the moochers, who were watching us unload all these new goodies from pulling midnight Small Stores. While all this hard work was going on another Lt, (jg) Naval Aviator showed up. We were just beginning to look like an operating unit, just one thing was missing, a couple of airplanes.

The aircraft we would be flying would be single engine Curtiss SOC-3 Seagull biplanes equipped with 36 foot folding wings. A Pratt Whitney 600 horsepower R-1340-18 engine powered them. On floats, their cruising speed was approximately 130 knots with a cruising range of about five hours, or a distance of about 700 miles. The Max-speed was estimated at approximately 140 to 150 knots. That was if we were flying down hill, with a good tail wind.

Finally, the first aircraft arrived equipped with wheel landing gear. It was either new or just out of major overhaul. I have forgotten what the flight log stated. For some damn fool reason we were all happy it arrived. In the next couple of days we all began taking turns flying in it and at the senior aviators suggestion even received some back seat stick time. A few more days later the second aircraft arrived, also on wheels. Shortly there after our centerline and wing tip floats arrived. But the boss stated we would wait to install them until we received orders to report aboard.

Some time was spent aboard the Memphis as well, checking out our spaces. The ship had made a lot of modifications since my departure. They were now feeding cafeteria style. No longer did the mess cooks race back and forth to the galley for tureen refills. The Main Deck hammock netting and folding cot storage area had been replaced by overhead to deck folding steel bunks and lockers

The former Memphis sailor, me, who had departed this vessel as a Seaman 2nd had returned as a Petty Officer 3rd Class. Curiosity had me wandering back to my old familiar 2nd Division spaces. I was especially looking for his old boss, Boats 1st Class. However, I was told by those who remembered, they thought Old Boats had finally made Chief and had either transferred or retired.

We were kept busy getting ready to move aboard, but had left the Center Line and Wing Tip Floats as the last item to install. We did this so we could keep flying the aircraft so everyone would become completely familiar with it prior to arriving aboard. I had installed and bore sighted the combination telescopic gun and bombsight through the armored windscreen. I surely would have liked to install the guns. In particular, the synchronized fixed forward firing gun. It sure would have been easier to install ashore than on the catapult aboard. However, all the armament equipment was boxed and stored on the ship. So it meant we would do it the Navy way, which naturally was the hard way.

Our Senior Officer called me into the office and said, "Gunner your free right now. I'd like you to go over to the parachute loft." The reply, "Yes Sir, what do you want me to get?" He stated, "I want you to get a set of parachute packing tools and while you are there you better learn how to pack a chute." The response, "Hey Lt., I'm just a B-B stacking gun cocker not a qualified chute rigger." The Lt. said, "Our complement doesn't call for a rigger so somebody has to do it and you're my selection." "I sure hope you know what your doing Lt." As it turned out it wasn't as complicated as I thought, just very precise. However, this kid was smart, every time we pulled into San Juan I would rush over to their loft and get the chutes repacked there.

Before we moved aboard we had to replace the wheeled gear and reconfigure with a centerline main float and the two wing tip floats. Once the word was passed to move aboard, we raised the aircraft by chain fall and dropped the wheeled gear. The main struts and retainers for the centerline float were attached to the fuselage. The centerline float on the wheeled stand was rolled under the aircraft for attachment. The alignment of the float with the aircraft centerline was a tricky job requiring two men, and a 50 ft. measuring tape! When everything was properly aligned all attachments were locked down and safety wired. Attaching the wing tip floats to the wing hard points was a snap. The wheeled float unit now became the means for delivering the airplane down to the ship for hoisting aboard.

With the wings folded back and locked both aircraft were ready to be towed from the Air Station to the Naval Operating Base where the USS Memphis was docked. Upon arrival the port side aircraft was hoisted aboard and secured on the port Catapult Car. Immediate following a cargo net was lowered to take aboard our cruise boxes and other paraphernalia. To complete the loading our second aircraft was then hoisted aboard and locked down on the starboard catapult car.

As we were packing things away in the wing storage, our crews attention was brought to the bronze plaque stating that the USS Memphis had returned Charles Lindbergh and his aircraft, The Spirit of St Louis, back to the states after his historic solo Atlantic flight to Paris in 1927.

Several other changes had been made to the vessel to improve her besides the instillation of bunks and the Cafeteria system. The foremast and main mast and a bit of the heavy superstructure had been removed or modified to compensate for the weight of the additional armament and protective splinter shields that had been installed around the 3 inch guns.

The aviation Units birthing space was on the Port side opposite the Ward Room Galley. This arrangement proved to be very handy once a mess attendant was assigned to care for our officers. It didn't take long to draw the ire of the surface sailors. We had been placed in a special privilege category. The mere fact we were eligible for special flight pay didn't sit well. But much to their chagrin they disliked most the fact that flight operation schedules gave us head of the line meal privileges.

Our working area was rather constrained. In reality such a space didn't exist. The only working area that actually belonged to us was the aircraft themselves. Even the catapults belonged to someone else, the torpedo gang. Top that off with the fact the catapults were mounted on property belonging to, the 2nd Deck Division. As a former 2nd division member we would get angry with the Airdales when they would get a newly swabbed deck dirty.

The Aviation Unit did own a tool stowage locker on the Port side just aft of #4 stack just to the right of the Catapult. That's where we laughingly kept our workbench. A 4 inch vice mounted on a weighted 30 Caliber ammo Box. At least when working on ordnance materials, like our Machine Guns, we shared space with the ships armory personnel.

Once our gear was completely loaded the ship was now underway headed north for Narragansett Bay and Newport, R.I. This time I didn't mind because it would give me the opportunity to visit with the wife who was working at the Naval Torpedo Station. On the way we got our machine guns installed, plus the forward firing guns synchronized to fire through the propellers. All our Senior Aviator asked was, "Have you ever done it before?" The reply was, "Once a couple of years ago." How it was accomplished is not really important to the story at hand. When completed both Cats were trained outboard, the engines started, and each gun was test fired. Sorry, Didn't damage a single propeller!

We were now lying off the coast of Newport R.I. It was time for the pilots to qualify for catapulting and underway recovery. To get airborne we used compressed air Catapults that operated on the principle of an oversized mechanical slingshot. When released the catapult car raced down the track where it was stopped instantly by plungers mounted on the end of the cat. Centrifugal force, and the thrust of the aircraft engine, plus the quiet prayers of the pilot and crewman, gets the aircraft airborne. Certain conditions must be taken into consideration. Due to the fact the catapults were only 16 feet above the water line all Cat Shots had to be made on the up roll. If and when they were accidentally fired on the down roll I'm sure the occupants of the plane were glad they were wearing inflatable life jackets.

Aircraft underway recovery was performed by what use to be called Cast Recovery. Once the aircraft landed the pilot taxied up to the sled towed by the ship. When the hook on the centerline float caught in the sleds net, the pilot would reduce the throttle to Idle. The sled towing the aircraft could then be maneuvered in close to the ships side. The rear seat occupant of the aircraft then climbed out, straddled the pilot, opened the upper wing compartment and removed the planes hoisting sling, which he must engage with the hook of the hoisting crane. This could be a dangerous job. Most aircrewmen performing these hookups would immediately count his fingers to make sure he didn't leave any in the hook up.

NOTE:—The above two paragraphs have been limited to the basics. A detailed description of the catapulting and recovery cycle has been explained in detail in the Story, "Famous Cruiser Aviators and Their SOC's."

For several days' operations went well without incident but occasionally accidents do happen. One day in the process of attempting a Port side pickup, the sea was running high hampering the recovery. The pilot had made a perfect landing and hookup to the sled. As the plane was drawn closer to the ships side, the sea was rising and falling about 6 feet which made it difficult for the Aircrewman to make the connection with the pelican hook of the ships crane. Suddenly the sea surged bringing the aircrafts Starboard wing tip against the ships side before the crane hook could be engaged with the aircraft-hoisting sling. The force was so great approximately one foot of the upper wing tip was badly damaged.

The plane was recovered on the very next try but the inspected damage forced the trials to be completed with a single aircraft. Once the ship returned to the Naval Operating Base, Norfolk, Va. we unloaded the damaged aircraft for return back to the Overhaul and Repair Department. A few days later we received a replacement aircraft. We were really lucky; it had already been fully configured for sea duty. All we had to do was inspect and test to insure everything was satisfactory. The plane was an SON-1 model. It was identical to the SOC 3 except the Naval Aircraft Factory in Philadelphia manufactured it.

In addition the Unit gained two more personnel, another Naval Aviator, an Ensign and another enlisted man, a mess Attendant. The ship also received new orders to join the South Atlantic Neutrality Squadron. This would require combat configured patrolling with Guns, Ammunition and loaded Bomb Racks; we would be on the constant lookout for submarines. German subs and their supply vessel's that is! But that adventure will make a good follow up story.

"THE LADY WHO WAS LEFT BEHIND"

Despite the current World War II situation we can't have it interfere with the passing of a Mothers Day. This is the time when we pay tribute to the lovely mothers and wives who are left behind when their loved ones are deployed during times of international conflict.

The young lady I personally have in mind is typical example. She married her husband a year before the U.S. was forced into World War II when the Japanese first bombed Pearl Harbor. Prior to the war the Navy wasn't especially happy when their Petty Officers under 2nd Class decided to get married! Usually, a sudden change in orders for the wayward male solved their problem. The Navy required the sailors concentration to be 100% on Navy matters.

This particular lady in question was one in a million. She was both ambitious as well as smart. She had a good job and a paltry fifty bucks a month allotment from her deployed mate! She was well aware her funds were inadequate to build the home she desired. Having good credit and a 2nd position would help in supplementing her income.

She was able to be with her husband only on occasional leave. So when war erupted she applied for and obtained a job at the U. S. Naval Torpedo Station, Goat Island, Newport R.I., just a short government ferry ride from the Navy Fleet Landing. During the war the torpedo station worked around the clock which meant working shifts. In addition she also maintained one of her other jobs by negotiating shift arrangements with her boss.

On the torpedo station job she was trained as a machine operator to manufacture precise torpedo detonator casings. She became very proficient at this position receiving an award as a top level WOW (Woman Ordnance Worker). During Congressman Sheppard's of California inspection of the station, he interviewed her on the job. All this was published in the Newport newspaper the following day, (the paper sold a large number of extra copies that day!)

All work and no play make's a lady a dull girl. Shortly thereafter, her husband received new orders. He was reassigned to duty at the Naval Air Training Station, Pensacola, Florida. Based thereon, the Torpedo Station released her with the understanding that she report to the employment office at Pensacola for new assignment. However, this never happened, she decided to quit manufacturing and take up the job of raising a nice family.

This represents a small sample of one ladies effort to support her man in the service. For everyone's information, it takes a woman with a lot of intestinal fortitude to successfully manage and maintain a military family. She was not alone. There were, and still are, thousands of women who have worked and worried alone in support of a loved one who had placed his life on the line in defense of this Nation.

FAMOUS CRUSIER AVIATOR'S and THEIR SOC's

Having served with the Navy in uniform for over twenty-two years and twenty years with the Department of Navy, I often reminisce about events experienced during that time period. The mind often drifts back more than 67 years to early aviation experiences a few years prior to our entry into World War II.

Based on that mental drifting, this article will attempt to introduce the reader to a young man's early aviation beginnings with Cruiser/Battleship style aviation during the 1930's. Prior to the invention and introduction of the long range electronic radar scanning systems, special shipboard aviation units personnel performed many fleet hours, flying scouting, search and find, and weapon spotting missions. In reality, these shipboard aircrews were the human radar that flew ahead of the surface forces to search out and warn the ships of distant pending danger. These were the flying, flashing, dashing, helmet and goggled sailors of the Cruiser and Battleship Navy.

My personal cruiser flying experience was obtained aboard the light cruiser USS Memphis CL-13, one of the ten commissioned four stack Omaha Class vessel's. These noble ships entered naval service between 1923 and 1925. They were fast little ships, 555 feet long and 55 feet wide, with a gross weight of over 7,050 tons and a maximum speed of about 30 knots. They were armed with a main battery of ten to twelve 6"53 rifles and six dual purpose 3"50 anti-aircraft guns, two triple 21" torpedo tubes and two 60 foot compressed air aircraft catapults mounted on the flush deck just aft of the #4 stack.

By the middle to late 30's these catapults mounted a pair of Curtiss SOC-2, SOC-3's, or their equivalent Naval Aircraft

Factory manufactured SON-1's. The SOC'S, named Seagull, was a single float biplane with fabric-covered wings and tail surfaces. They were powered by a 600hp Pratt & Whitney R-1340-18 radial engine that gave it a cruising speed of approximately 100 plus knots. Under full power, (while flying slightly down hill with a good tail wind), it might have squeezed out almost 150 plus knots.

Their armament consisted of two .30 caliber Browning M-2 machine guns. One fixed gun mounted under the right cowl just forward of the pilots seat synchronized to fire through the propeller arc. The other, a free scarf-ring mount in the aft seat. The aircraft was also capable of carrying a wing mounted bomb load of up to two 325 lb depth charges. Vouching for this is easy because I was a participating "volunteer" during the initial shipboard test launches with aerial depth charges on board. What the Hell, in those days, as a 3rd Class Petty Officer they paid us fly boys the big bucks to fly in these famous sea going flying machines. Thirty dollar's extra a month for a full set and fifteen bucks a month extra pay for a half set of flight orders!

To best describe cruiser mounted compressed air catapults, we referred to them as the equivalent of an oversized slingshot! Once we unfolded the wings and locked place for flight, we then turned up the engine and fully checked the aircraft for a catapult launch. The catapult was then trained out 30+ degrees. The catapult car, on which the aircraft was mounted, was drawn to the rear and locked to the catapult by a hold back key. This hold back key was designed to break once sufficient air pressure was attained for the plane's launch. The catapults were only 16 feet above the shipboard water line. The ship would increase speed and make a slight turn to face the catapult into the prevailing wind.

In the aircraft, on the signal the pilot would advance the throttle to full power and indicate when he was ready. The launch valve was then opened at the precise moment the vessels began an up roll. When the hold back key parted, the catapult car would plunge down the track. As the car hit the recoil plungers at the end of the cat the plane would be launched into the air with an estimated speed of approximately 60 knots per hour. Often the pilot and observer felt like flapping their arms like a humming bird to make damn sure they got airborne. Launching on the down roll was a no-no. It could, and sometimes did, result in the plane being shot directly into the sea.

In those days airborne search and find missions were flow on a prearranged plot. Normally about a four hour inverted triangular flight. In the event of radio silence communication back with the ship was done at low altitude and low speed with the use of bean-bags! Now this was not exactly easy. Especially, on a ship with four stacks as big in diameter as those old light cruisers! To deliver the message the pilot would open the leading edge wing slots and approach the ship slowly from an angle to avoid as much as possible the stack gas. It was hoped the rear seat passenger was an ex-ball player. Hitting the deck between the cats would have been a tough job for a Yankee 20 game-winner!

Once the mission was completed the idea was to get the plane and its crew back on the vessel safely. Aircraft recovery underway was a rather complicated procedure known as Cast Recovery. This system of retrieval required the dedicated concentration of almost all the deck divisions on the ship.

The recovery device was a towed sled equipped with two special vanes mounted on it underside to keep the sled riding away from the side of the vessel. The towing was performed by a bowline that ran forward to the forecastle where it was controlled by the 1st deck division. It was their responsibility to keep the sled riding parallel to the catapult. A breast line handled by the 3rd deck division managed the outboard distance of the sled from the ship's side. Attached to the rear of the sled was a large manila net similar to a cargo net. When the aircraft returned from its flight and was ready to land, the sled would be streamed.

The ship would then perform a wide continuous turn into the wind to create a smooth landing surface by forming a slick on the water. The pilot would make his landing approach on to the slick and rapidly taxi up to the sled to engage the towing hook attached to the forward underside surface of his center float. Once engaged the pilot would retard his throttle and be towed by the sled.

Concurrently the 1st and 3rd deck divisions would begin taking in the bow and breast line to keep the aircraft in general proximity to the catapult. As the plane was eased in toward the ship's side, the vessel itself would straighten its course into the wind. The 2nd division who operate the hoisting crane rigged it outboard to wait for the aircraft to be drawn in close enough to permit the engagement of its pelican hook into the planes hoisting sling which was stored in the center of the aircraft's upper wing panel. The breast line had to be taken in slowly to bring the plane in close to the ship's side for hook up. Currently the bowline was retrieved to maintain its position parallel to the catapult. The signals to control these actions was passed on the Boatswain's Pipes.

The crewman would climb from the rear cockpit, straddle the pilot, place his feet in the stirrups, open the hatch in the wing center section to break out the hoisting sling. The crane operator would then lower the pelican hook to the plane crewman who's job it was to engage the hook with the hoisting sling. During this part of the operation, aviation unit personnel stood by on the deck with long bamboo fending poles to keep the aircraft wing tip from contact with the side of the ship. Once the crane hook and the plane's hoisting sling were engaged, the crane operator could raise the aircraft clear of the water. The pilot would then shut down the engine.

Aircraft being towed by sled waiting to make
Hoisting contact for pick up

Aircraft being hoisted aboard for placement on
Port catapult

As the crane operator raised the aircraft, the aircrew man counted his fingers to make sure he hadn't left any in between the hook and the sling! Once the aircraft was swung inboard it was placed back on the catapult car where it was locked in place. Upon recovery of the sled the entire operation was complete. During the recovery process the vessel had continued to maintain its same course and speed.

Once again locked back in place the aircraft was immediately washed down with fresh water to remove as much salt as possible. The wings were then either folded back or have the storm struts installed. This was a very intricate sequence of events that takes lots more time to explain than to perform.

Recovery underway is especially dangerous when performed in a heavy sea. With the sea rising and falling several feet it complicates the hook up between the rising and falling aircraft's extended hoisting sling and the crane's hook. The plane crewman must be quick to engage the hoisting hook in the sling without leaving part of his hand between the two! There were also limits to the fending crews ability to keep the plane from contacting the side of the ship. Occasionally, the surging sea might thrust the wing toward the ships side. In these circumstances the fending poles were utterly useless in preventing wing damage. If the damage wasn't too severe you might see one of these birds cleared to fly with the wing tip slightly crunched and patched over with some doped down fabric.

The main problem involving aviation duty at sea with the SOC Seagull was the total lack of space to perform maintenance. Maintaining these aircraft was a real chore. The aircrews working space was the plane itself and the deck space just aft of #4 stack. Further, this space was shared with the torpedo gang, who was responsible for servicing the catapult, and the 2nd division who were responsible for aircraft recovery and the area in which the aviation group worked.

There was a steel aviation tool locker about 4 to 5 feet square and about 7 feet tall aft of the stack. Our workbench consisted of a weighted .30 caliber ammunition case with a 4 inch vice mounted there on. The aviation crew itself, was often amazed at how it was able to keep two planes in up flight status capable of each flying 80 to 100 hours a month. Especially, if the ships Executive Officer was a non-aviator with the idea you couldn't make mandatory periodic checks or take the plane "apart" without first getting his permission!

Guns, especially those that had to be installed in the plane for extended periods, were subjected to a vigorous maintenance program. To combat rust generated by salt-water landings, the receiver and barrel of the forward firing fixed gun had to be coated with a special preservative. The muzzle barrel bearing surfaces were heavily lubricated and covered with rubber sleeves to avoid internal rusting that might prevent charging and firing. Believe it or not, condoms worked perfectly in this capacity!

The free gun, in the aft cockpit, was better protected from the elements. It was stored under the turtle back aft of the cockpit area. Once the gun was pulled out and locked into firing position on the scarf-ring, the turtle back could be folded down. This gave the rear gunner free firing access from wingtip to wingtip. He just had to remember not to shoot up his vertical and horizontal stabilizers, which were less than three feet aft of the muzzle of his gun! Despite its location, the free gun also required periodic visual inspection and maintenance

Synchronization of fixed guns to fire through the propeller arc began to disappear during WWII in favor of the intense, concentrated firepower of four to six wing mounted guns. However, it is interesting to note that during WW I it was the first modification to coordinate aircraft control and firepower accuracy by aiming the aircraft to properly align the guns with the target. As already stated, the SOC Seagull had one fixed synchronized gun. Firing guns through the propeller arc sounded like a complicated procedure but in reality the installation was quite simple.

The firing is timed mechanically with the propellers revolutions. The synchronizing generator was mounted on the aircraft's engine. An impulse cable was connected to the generator and fed to the trigger motor mounted on the gun. The generator had high and low lobes that rotated at the engines speed. The rotating lobes sent impulses through the cable to the guns trigger motor. However, the impulses were not physically aligned with the sear and firing pin of the guns bolt until the firing switch was on and the trigger mechanism of the pilot's control stick was closed.

To assure the clearance of the propeller, it was necessary to manually set the "zero shot". The propeller had to be turned by hand and the trigger motor on the gun adjusted to release the firing pin a prescribed distance behind the propeller blade. Once this position was determined, the trigger motor was locked and safety wired. Upon completion of each installation, the catapult was trained outboard, the engine turned up and the gun fired to make certain we would not shoot holes through the propeller blades!

Until the rapid improvement in sighting equipment developed during WW II, the airborne weapons aiming devices from the 20's to the 40's were primitive holdovers from WW I. Most aircraft pilot gun sights, including that of the Seagull, was a telescope mounted and bore sighted through the center of the windscreen. Despite its problems, it was amazing the amount of accuracy some pilots were able to attain with this inferior equipment. The scope represented a multi-purpose unit for gunnery, strafing, and bombing. Most flyers disliked the use of the scope. It limited visibility as well as the loss of depth perception. In the interest of safety, the aft seat crewman usually mounted the spare control stick during bombing and strafing runs. The reason being to remind the pilot it was time to pull out of the dive!

The gun sights on the free gun in the aft cockpit were even more primitive. The rear sight was a fold down ring sight approximately four inches in diameter. There was a smaller inner ring, these rings were supposed to aid the gunner in determining lead. The guns front sight could be either a single post and bead or a newer version called a wind vein post. This sight had two opposing veins that were activated by the aircrafts slipstream. When the gun was moved from one position to another the angle of attack of the slipstream over the veins changed the position of the post. In theory this was intended to aid in determining a change in lead. If it worked most of the back seat drivers never noticed. Experience, practice and instinctive judging of the angle of the targets flight line and speed estimate was a bigger aid than those old iron sights!

Our Seagulls also had a capability of delivering expendable stores. A single external bomb rack was mounted at hard points under each lower wing. Weapons release was controlled by the pilot through the use of a manually operated toggle mechanism mounted on the left side of the cockpit forward of and below the throttle quadrant. Attached to the release mechanism was a cable system running from the fuselage through the wing panels to the racks.

Proper operating tension was adjustable, maintained by turnbuckles. Four options were available to the pilot, armed right, left, salvo and safe salvo. Prior to the authorization to carry aerial depth charges, the normal bomb load was two 100-pound general-purpose bombs with instantaneous impact fuzes. Releases either armed or safe was controlled by the use of arming wires connected to the bomb rack, lead through the safety pin hole in the bomb fuze and retained by two safety clips. Dropped armed, the wire remained with the rack thus permitting airflow on the fuze propeller to arm the weapon. Dropped safe, the wire went with the store insuring the bomb would not detonate.

The final ordnance items on board were the pyrotechnics, two high intensity parachute flares. The flares were carried internally on the port side of the fuselage next to the observer rear seat. Their release was cable controlled to unlock the spring-loaded door and flipped the flare outboard. A ripcord attached to an internal frame member released the parachute and actuated the flare. In the interest of safety the pilot normally started a slight turn to the right to insure the flare clears the tail section. There have been known incidents when the flare chute passed over the horizontal stabilizer strut while the flare went under. This problem is disturbing to the flight crew because it leaves the burning flare beating a tattoo on the rudder surface!

This has been a rather long, detailed rendition of the general structure and capability of an old warhorse, the SOC Seagull. Even though this stretched the writer's memory back over 67 years, fond memories exist of early experiences serving in this capacity. In those days operating conditions and maintenance requirements were both dangerous as well as difficult to perform. Spotting shipboard firing practice and scouting and search missions were necessary and responsible functions but lacked the glamour and rewards of the fighter and attack Navy.

Top that off with the fact that aviation personnel were not always popular with the surface sailor. The aviation group's maintenance efforts conflicted with that of ships deck force often causing a lot of extra hard work. Further, operational mission assignments sometimes lead to special privileges like sleeping in, head of the chow line, and flight order extra pay which was resented by some personnel. Despite operating problems and the so-called lack of glory, the aviation officers and men who served a couple of years working and flying in the cruiser and battleship Navy received a valuable education that served them well in future naval aviation endeavors.

Despite all its dangers and associated problems, to a young sailor of the mid 1930's it was not only a great experience; it was one hell of an enjoyable experience! You were able to honestly lay claim to the fact you were serving your Country. You were able to enjoy many of the worldly sights while at the same time you were able to enjoy life experiences that many of the average citizen would never have the same opportunities.

THE CURTISS SOC-SEAGULL

In the early days of the 19th and 20th century the world's Navy's sailed from place to place strictly by the wind and compass but still operated pretty much in the blind. When traveling in areas of possible danger they area of observation was conducted I using human lookout in a crows nest high in the rigging, scanning for the dangers ahead. Their distance vision capability was totally limited to the focal power of the long glass.

In 1903 a couple of bicycle mechanics, who some people considered slightly off their rocker', had inserted a small combustion engine in an object that resembled an oversized kite. This they took down to Kitty Hawk where they assumed the wind might be of help. The driver of this odd machine sat in the front end of his vehicle and started the engine. In a matter of a few minutes he was off the ground and was in the air. After hundreds of years of struggle and disaster man had finally discovered his ability to fly!

Like any successful discovery there was a rush by possible builders desiring to make a buck on the deal. One such individual was Glenn Curtiss, an engineer who had also been tinkering with aircraft building ideas, began to prepare construction of an improved version of the Wright Brothers model.

As progress continued many nations took an interest. They began to wonder how this new flying machine might be adapted for military purposes. There were a few young U. S. Naval officers that immediately became interested. Most individuals included these young sailors. However, their Superior Officers of the big gun click considered they were all off their rocker. What possible use could the Navy have for these flimsy kites? What possible value could they be to deep-water combat vessels?

Well, to begin with, how about the capability of an extended reconnaissance? If there was a way to keep an aircraft aboard a ship, that sailor could stop wearing himself out climbing that mast with a long glass!

Those interested young officers had a real friend in Glenn Curtiss. Working hard they finally disproved the negativities and began discovering advances in the construction of seaplanes and flying boats. By the early 1930's the Navy had two Curtiss built aircraft aboard the battleships and cruisers. That airplane was the Curtiss SOC-Seagull (Scout Observation Curtiss).

The addition of catapults and a pair of aircraft extended the beam and forward visual capability on a clear day by approximately three hundred miles depending on the planes altitude. The Navy placed their first contract for the Curtiss SOC in 1933. The first aircraft entered service almost two years later in 1935. Order number one provided 135 SOC-1'S models followed by a request for 40 SOC-2'S and 83 SOC-3's. The Naval Aircraft Factory in Philadelphia also produced a mirror image version of the SOC-3 which was designated SON-1.

The Seagull was a 3600 lb empty weight, single centerline float biplane, which was capable of being switched to a two-wheel landing gear when used ashore. Combat loaded its total weight was approximately 5300 lbs. Most were powered with a Pratt & Whitney R-1340-22 550 HP radial engine rated for a high speed of 165 MPH.

Experience indicated maximizing out at about 130 plus knots if traveling in a slight down hill direction. The aircraft was fitted with 36 ft fabric covered folding wings that could be locked opened and supported with safety struts, or stored with the wings locked fully folded. Each position could be used depending on weather condition.

For handling the aircraft once he had landed on the slick produced by the vessel the pilot taxied up on to the recovery sled to engage the floats locking tow strut in the tow net attached to the rear of the recovery sled. Once engaged the sleds two control lines could be drawn in to keep the aircraft positioned in close proximity to the catapult control car.

Concurrently the rear seat crewman could climb up, straddle the pilots cockpit, open the storage hatch in the center section of the upper wing, extract the hoisting sling and prepare to attach same to the cranes hoisting hook. Once completed the plane was hoisted out of the water and returned to and locked back onto the catapult car.

For its lifespan aboard our Naval vessels the SOC-2&3 Seagull did an excellent job for what it was designed for as a scout observer. Plus during its operations during WW II it made a considerable number of rescues saving the lives of downed Naval Aviators. It had also been known to engage in light combat particularly against enemy submarines,

Its combat ability rested in two .30–06 caliber Browning M-2 machine guns. One fixed mounted under the right side cowling forwarded of the pilot. This gun was synchronized to fire through the propeller arc controlled by a lobed generator mounted on the right rear engine housing. The gun was fired by the pilot and aimed through the use of a telescope mounted and bore sighted through the forward cockpit windscreen. The Aircrewman that flew with the pilot was also armed with a scarf ring mounted free firing Browning that was stored beneath the aft turtle back just forward of the vertical stabilizer and rudder. In addition, two bomb racks were mounted at hard points outboard of the fuselage. These racks were capable of loading explosive stores weighting up to 325 lbs each. Weapons release was controlled by the pilot through a manual bomb release quadrant mounted on the left side of the cockpit just below the throttle quadrant. Releases could be selected armed left, armed right, safe right on left, or salvo armed or safe

The personnel that manned the aviation units aboard our combat vessels were in a separate category from the more visible carrier pilots and crewman. There was little to no glory extended to the personnel that manned the combat vessels flying machines. However, their jobs were not only important acting as the human radar, but flying off the older vessels landing and being picked up underway amidships was a very dangerous operation.

The SOC-2 type Seagull Aircraft flown
from Battleships and Cruisers
During the mid 1930's and 1940's

USS MEMPHIS CL-13
SOUTH ATLANTIC NEUTRALITY
PATROLS

It was early 1941 when it was determined the Omaha Class light cruiser USS Memphis CL-13 would not be returning to the Pacific Fleet as the crew had anticipated. There were many moans and groans, but ours was to follow issued orders, not to determine our operational schedule. Since the beginning of World War II in Europe, operational emphasis had been placed on keeping the Atlantic sea lanes open between the States and England, with a tight system of sea and air neutrality units. We had not actually declared war, but there wasn't any doubt who Roosevelt was routing for. As a result, something called lend lease was putting U.S. industries on a wartime schedule. As a result, the German Navy's submarine service no longer gave a tinkers damn who's ship they slipped a torpedo into.

Our Light Cruiser and two flanking destroyers had been directed to gear up for neutrality patrols to play a ready alert role, but at the same time be capable of self defense in the event it became absolutely necessary. After all, we were not at war; we were just playing a waiting game. As far as our Aviation Unit was concerned, we had been ordered to fly with a full combat load of ammunition and two 100lb general-purpose bombs hung under the wings. Guns and weaponry carried on board seaplane aircraft operating in close proximity to salt water require an intensive maintenance system.

Routine daily operational salt water landings can result in rapid accumulate of rust and corrosion unless a continuous maintainability program is conducted. Therefore, the fixed gun parts had to be coated with a special lube to assure the moving parts would remain combat ready. Special sleeves were placed over the muzzles to prevent internal rust from preventing the gun from being charged and fired. Believe it or not condoms worked perfectly.

As we took in our mooring lines the horn blasts signaled we were underway. I'm sorry to say it would be quite some time before any of us would see the United States again. We steamed out of Hampton Roads escorted by a pair of slick new destroyers. The first port of call would be San Juan, Puerto Rico. As we steamed south, the sea seemed to get smoother, the sun brighter, and the sea breezes warmer.

Most of our workload was readying the planes for the patrol work in the South Atlantic. We had already received orders to completely repaint the aircraft a solid non-reflective light gray when we reached San Juan. Goodbye to the classy slick silver finish and the bright yellow upper wing panel that had been a navy trademark for over twenty years. Actually, the yellow upper wing had little to do with the color scheme. It originated when naval aircraft had floatation gear. The bright yellow color assisted in locating downed aircraft at sea.

Arrangements had been made at the San Juan Naval Air Station in advance for the repainting of both aircraft. The air station had been operated previously by the Pan American Air Ways flying the Clipper flying Boats. We were really lucky to be able to take the planes ashore to paint them. It definably assured a much neater job than if we have been forced to do it with the planes on the catapult. Plus the fact our senior aviator, would be the boss.' Our short term experience had already taught us he was much more flexible than the ships Executive Officer.

We also had another plus, if my memory is correct one of our junior officers family's operated a plantation a short distance outside the city. All of which lead to good working relations, liberty, and living conditions. The unit with its limited number of personnel turned with an all hands working party to quickly finish the painting effort. Once the transformation of the planes was completed, we were back to flight operations.

With a $15.00 half set of flight skins as an incentive, as the weapons specialist it was my privilege to instruct the pilots and crews to the secrets of aerial gunnery. One pilot who had some prior experience, wanted to know how, as a third class, I knew so much about the subject. As a joke I stated I learned a lot by watching World War I aerial combat movies. In reality, much was learned on the working end of a .50 Caliber Browning M-2 mounted in the waist hatch of a PBY-2. All the pilots and crews enjoyed the chance to practice on a towed target sleeve before we returned to the ship.

Liberty was delightful in this tropical paradise. Beautiful beaches, warm sea breezes and just enough rain each afternoon to keep things cooled off. Local prices were inexpensive, the food was very good and the tours at the Bacardi Rum Plant always ended with tasty free drinks. The people at that plant were exceptionally generous with the American Sailor in uniform. However, Uncle Sam didn't hire us to enjoy a tropical holiday, so we were at sea again with our two sharp flotilla leader destroyers as our escort.

We were on a southeasterly heading making turns for a cruising speed of about eighteen knots headed in the general direction of the Cape Verde Islands just off the west coast of Africa. During the trans-Atlantic crossing most of our time was spent getting the aircraft prepared for their daily neutrality patrols. Ammunition was belted, and their loaded magazines stored in the aircraft. During our break period's this Ordnanceman wrote letters home and studied for advancement to 2nd class Petty Officer.

When the Cape Verde's began to rise on the horizon, the ship made a sharp course change to the southwest and headed for the Port of Pernambuco, (Racife) Brazil. As we approached the Equator, preparations were made to conduct the shellback initiations. As we crossed the equator, his royal Majesty Neptune Rex, ruler of the Raging Main mounted his dais to convert all pollywogs into shellbacks. Seated with him was the Queen of the Main and her Royal Baby. Facing the Throne were two backward dumping chairs where the charged pollywog's would be tried before being dumped into a four foot deep pool of raging maniacs to be ceremoniously baptized, or in fact half drowned, before being thrown out on deck for additional treatment as well as some maniac's enjoyment.

On 8 May 1941, the mayhem began as we crossed the Equator at Latitude 0000, Longitude 34 Degrees W. The royal sheriff's men dragged each accused before Rex, his Queen and the Royal Baby. And despite having kissed the royal baby's fat hairy belly, were immediately pronounced guilty, stripped of most, or all clothing, placed in the tilting chair, worked over by the Royal surgeons, given a shot of electricity through the bottom of the chair, then dumped unceremoniously backward into the pool. After half drowning they were then tossed out on deck.

But that wasn't the last of it. You were then made to crawl on your hand and knee's through a wind-sail full of ripe garbage while other maniac's beat the hell out of you through the canvas with paddles. Boy, we sure had a great time. We know we did because they said so! A few days later we received a beautiful certificate signed by Captain Parrish. It stated we were now worthy shellbacks. I have retained this old dried up document into the 21st century. We were now eligible to beat the devil out of the next bunch of shipmates who had never crossed the line. As an additional thrill we airdales had the special opportunity to fly across the equator in our SOC's!

We were now operating on station below the equator. The dawn to dark neutrality flights would now begin. Because of the heavy German submarine action in the north Atlantic against neutral vessels, shipments to allied ports were beginning to be made by the longer, almost safer, southern routes. A good part of our mission was to see that those routes remained open.

The aircraft were now fully armed, even to a demolition bomb loaded on each wing bomb rack. As to what purpose they served was beyond me. The only bomb fuzes we had on board were the contact variety which would call for a very close, or direct hit to be of any value. The workday now began about 0400 in the morning. In the pre World War II era electronic radar systems didn't exist. We the shipboard fly-boys were the eyes of the fleet, the human search radar. If we detected anything it was our duty to rush back with the warning!

Both aircraft were subject to pre-flight checks the prior evening and repeated in the morning to be certain that one would definitely go on time. Once catapulted, the pilot would fly an inverted triangular course plotted for competition at the ships actual location four hours later. Once advising he was completing his sortie the on board plane was, manned, engine turned up, and catapulted prior to streaming the recovery sled to pick up the returning flight.

With recovery completed and locked back on its catapult, it was completely washed down to remove all salt, refueled, and immediately worked off any yellow sheet discrepancies noted by the pilot during the flight. The pilot and crewman were also rotated to insure we were putting fresh alert personnel in the air.

The only respite was when we made Port in Recife, Brazil to refuel ship and take on necessary stores. It also gave the crew the opportunity for a little shore leave, or to just relax and take life easy. In just a couple of days, with our necessary stores replenished the mighty Memphis and its escorts would again be roaming the south Atlantic. To date we had good luck, and were doing a great job maintaining the flight schedule. Up to this point all launches and recovery's had been made successfully. But true to form everything can't work perfect every time.

On this particular day, the sea was running pretty heavy. For reasons unknown, the launch timing, or a defective hold back link on the catapult car, resulted in the port side aircraft being accidentally launched on a sharp down roll. The pilot made a valiant effort, but the aircraft had been moving too slowly to attain the necessary lift for a safe recovery. The aircraft entered the sea at about a 30-degree angle with a mighty splash! The impact caused the centerline float struts to pierce the float bringing it closer to the fuselage. The propeller chopped into the float stalling the engine instantly. In addition the wings were badly damaged. Luckily, the aircrew had anticipated the water entry and braced themselves, thus surviving the crash.

As we watched they both climbed out onto the upper wing, which by now was almost down to water level. Suddenly we saw the pilot reenter the submerged cockpit! In a few seconds later he popped out again. One of the Destroyer escorts slowly approached the sinking plane, lowered a whaleboat, and recovered the two rather damp aircrewmen. As the crew was rescued all we could see was part of the upper wing and the tail surfaces. Slowly, the badly damaged plane slipped out of sight beneath the rolling sea.

The Memphis lay dead in the water as the destroyer's whaleboat came along side to return our flight crew. They were immediately sent below to sick bay for a medical check up. With the exception of a few bumps and bruises, it was lucky neither suffered major damage. Everyone was curious as to why the pilot went back into the cockpit. He stated that he suddenly remembered the 7x50 binoculars he had carried in the plane where given to him by family and he didn't want to lose them.

The accidental loss of government property creates considerable workload identifying items for survey. But rules in place before our declaration of war had to be followed. Shortly after the accident we again sailed north of the equator, stopping at Port of Spain, Trinidad and a couple of stops in the Windward Islands. At one of these locations, a young Ensign showed up with the replacement aircraft. As we hoisted him aboard and locked the plane on the catapult car, the young officer pulled off his helmet and goggles and replaced them with what looked like an army garrison cap. It didn't escape the notice of our Executive Officer who yelled, "Young man, what the hell is that thing on your head?" He responded, "It's new issue Sir." The Exec. "I don't give a damn what it is. It's the only one on this vessel. I don't want to see it again."

When we again reached the equator we made a quick turn and headed west directly along the equator. We immediately executed a zigzag course, which had us crossing the equator every 8 minutes. This effort continued for 2 days. By high school math, this equated to 7 ½ crossings per hour, 180 per day, or an estimated total of 360 crossings during the two-day period. This particular operation has to be some form of military, and civilian record.

As a change of pace and an effort to give the anti-aircraft gunners a test of their reaction time somebody got a bright Idea called "Surprise Fire." Plus, they felt we, the fly-boys, were the only ones that could set it up. Who else could get a target in the air at 500 or more feet? The idea was that we could perform this feat on one of our returns from playing human radar. Now the target suggested was a parachute flare. We would eject the flare from the plane, then get the hell out of the way and let the .50 calibers Brownings bang away at it.

The air boss says with a big smile, you're the flare ejector so I guess I would have to earn my 15 bucks. On returning to the ship, we had quietly finished our four hour search and destroy mission. On the down wind the pilot yelled, "Lets do it." With an abrupt 180 over the ship he shouted, "Eject the Flare!" I pulled the release and away it went. "Has it lit up?" he yelled. The response, "I don't see a damn thing." "Take a good look. See it NOW?" "Oh yea, we are towing it. It's lit up real good and beating on the rudder. You should be able to feel it on the stick." The pilot yelled, "Do something to get rid of It. We don't want to catch fire". The reply, "I don't think that's going to happen. The chute went over the horizontal stabilizer strut while the flare went under it."

The pilot, "Lower the turtleback and crawl out there and see if you can break it loose with the stick." "You got to be kidding" was my retort. But, I removed my chute, rotated the rear seat to face aft. The gun was swung out of the way and locked, the gunners safety belt was put on and the turtleback lowered. As I leaned out over the turtleback, my comment, "Have I gone nuts? What the hell am I doing?" Lucky for me, there with a loud pop and the flare burned out. With a sigh of relief, my comment was, "There isn't much of the flare body left, I think you can land safely now." The .30 caliber returned under the turtleback. My chute was replaced and I sat down shaking like a puppy trying to pass a peach seed. We made a perfect landing on the slick and prepared to be hoisted aboard. Surprisingly, "Surprised Fire" was never repeated again.

Once back on board the question was, "What are we going to do with that parachute?" My response, "We are going to wash the salt out of it, hang it up in wing storage to dry, and then "we" are going to store "it" in my locker. After all, I was the guy out on the turtleback." Later, after the return home, my spouse made a lot of nice things out of that nylon chute!

Following the above incident, we were back in port for a little relaxation and recreation. This trip we were into Bihia, Brazil's oldest city. It was the fourth largest city in the country. But while there I received some excellent news. As of 1 July 1941 I had been advanced in rating to AOM2nd Class. In reality, making second-class in this time warp, before the completion of your first cruise, could be considered an unbelievable outstanding accomplishment. It was real luck, right time right place. One rate available, one sailor being tested!

Having logged several thousand hours of flight time during a career, experiences indicated that flying off old Cruiser's was probably the most dangerous. Especially off older vessels like the Memphis where the aviation program was an after thought. In these cases catapults had to be installed on space available. In some cases the catapults were mounted on towers because there wasn't any deck space to mount it. Later vessels specially designed to carry aircraft; the aviation unit occupied the stern where fewer problems existed. In the opinion, of many, cast recovery amidships was the most dangerous part of any flight

Landing on the slick created by the recovery vessel was a piece of cake. But once hooked to the sled trouble could begin and the aircrew had only limited control of the situation. In fact, sea conditions were really the controlling factor. A heavy sea could instantly destroy the aircraft by a sudden surge into the side of the ship. Or a sudden vertical surge could raise you up where the hook or cable of the hoisting crane could make contact with the idling propeller, other aircraft parts or even a member of the aircrew. The following sample was the latter.

After one of our four-hour flights we made a perfect landing on the slick and approached the sled. The crewman left the cockpit climbed over the pilot, put his feet in the stirrups and readied the hoisting cable for hook up. We were riding in a six to eight foot swell, which definitely indicated a difficult hook up! A sudden swell brought the crewmans head in direct contact with the crane's pelican hook. He was stunned, lost vision, and the pilot grabbed his upper legs to keep him from falling. He shook his head, cleared his vision and made the hook up on the next try.

Even opening and closing the eyes made his head hurt. Once the aircraft was aboard, he was helped to the deck from the plane, then rushed to the Sick Bay. The doctor claimed he had a big tennis ball bump but appeared to be OK. He was put on the sick list for observation and released back to duty the next day. Terrific headaches were experienced for a couple of weeks and it left a dent in my head. Approximately 25 years later he required to have two vertebra in his neck fuzzed to take the pressure off a nerve which was causing my left arm to shrivel.

The ship was again patrolling above the equator between the Windward Islands and the Cape Verde's. We were experiencing bookoo flight hours but was having little to no action other than routine maintenance. We were actually amazed at how well the aircraft had remained almost constantly in an up status. For relaxation we did visit a few small islands and St. Thomas in the Virgin Islands. However, Charlotte Amalie was a tourist trap not a sailor town.

Again we dipped below the equator stopping in Racife to refuel and take on stores. As we departed for the west coast of Africa it was advised we would be escorting a passenger vessel. Two thirds of the distance was the same old routine. Suddenly we began to increase speed as well as steering a zigzag course. General Quarters was sounded. A pilot raced aft yelled to me, "Get in, we are going sub hunting." Grabbing a helmet and goggles from the storage locker we climbed aboard as the catapult car was moving aft to the launch position. Immediately the catapult began training outboard.

In nothing flat we were airborne climbing out. My question, "What the hell is going on?" "One of the destroyers seems to have reported a possible torpedo in the water." If it was, it sure hasn't hit anything yet because there was no explosion. The destroyers were also gaining speed. Suddenly, one of them rolled two depth charges. The explosion made one hell of a boom and the eruption of water lifted the can's stern several feet.

We began making tight circles at about 500 feet in the general direction of the destroyer making continually wider circles. The aft .30 Caliber Browning machine gun was trained out and the first cartridge charged into the chamber while we continued to circle. The sea was fairly calm and the water appeared clear so we figured we might be able to see it if it was at periscope depth. Suddenly we spotted a long dark under water shadow. The pilot stood the plane up on one wing in a quick circle to get a better look.

At my suggestion, "It could be a sub, lets make another run over it and salvo the two 100 pound bombs. With contact fuzes we probably can't hurt him much but if he's there maybe we can ring his bell!" As we made the run the pilot's eye was glued to that stupid telescope. He then released the bombs, which made only a double bang and a good size waterspout compared to the destroyers depth charges. As I watched over the tail surfaces the destroyer now moving at flank speed, charged over our drop area and let go another pair of depth charges. There was a mighty boom and an exceptionally large geyser of water thrust into the air. We swore we might have seen the top of a conning tower and expended some random shots at it, but while the destroyers dropped a couple more depth charge's it was obvious we no longer had any contact. The destroyers continued to search but drew a blank. If he was still down there he was either sunk or satisfied with a draw!

It was again time to head for San Juan. Just a short while ago my enlistment had expired. So I was prepared to again say goodbye to the USS Memphis CL 13. Because of my enlistment expiration, the ship dropped me off at the HQ 10th Naval District in San Juan for further transfer to the Receiving Ship, New York. Little did I realize we would be at war on my arrival in New York. One thing for sure, I would find I was still at the beginning of my naval career not the possible end as originally anticipated.

USS MEMPHIS CL 13
ITS SERVICE LIFE

Over the years a lot of information has been written about the Omaha Class light cruisers, and a good part of it has been negative claims that the design of these vessels was obsolete prior to their construction. Granted they were designed in 1916. But, whoever did the designing was a visionary. In reality the results was a high-speed overgrown destroyer that performed as an outstanding light cruiser. The ten ships in this class served this nation well between the years 1923 and 1947, a total of 24 years.

The reason the USS Memphis was selected to be eulogized over the other nine vessels is due of having served two tours in this particular ship between 1938 and 1941. It is believed that you would appreciate knowing that in the past, your writer became very familiar with the subject vessel. Naturally, I didn't originate everything that will be stated herein. The subject matter had to be researched to be sure that the written information presented is both truthful, as well as accurate.

The United States placed the original order with Wm Cramp and Sons of Philadelphia on 24 January 1919. Which, by the way was the year I was born. (Information only, not really important to USS Memphis history). Her keel was laid on 14 October 1920. The launching ceremony was conducted 17 April 1924 and the service commissioning took place 4 February 1925. Under the command of Captain Henry Lackey the vessel departed almost immediately on a shakedown cruise to the Caribbean. I didn't blame them one bit; it's mighty cold in Philly in February!

The newly Commissioned Memphis was slickly built in the same basic mold of a speedy oversized destroyer. Its displacement was 7,050 tons, was 555ft.6in in overall length, with a beam width of 55ft.6in and a draft of 20 ft. Its 4 mighty screws could drive it a snappy speed close to 35 knots. The vessel was highly maneuverable due to a specially designed hydroelectric rudder control system. Its personnel complement was almost 800 officers and enlisted men.

Upon completion of its shakedown, she transverse the Panama Canal into the Pacific. In June the Memphis joined a scouting fleet off Honolulu for a cruise to the South Pacific. There they spent three months visiting Australia and New Zealand. She then returned to the Atlantic for operations in the West Indies prior to returning to her home Port, New York City.

Orders were then issued to relieve the USS Pittsburgh CA-4 as flagship of Commander U.S. Naval Forces, Europe. She continued to operate in European Waters until 1927. In August 1926 during a visit to Santander, Spain, the ship was host to Spain's King Alfonso XIII.

On 3 June 1927 the Memphis embarked an American National Hero. At Southampton, England Charles A. Lindbergh and his aircraft were taken aboard. The Memphis was to be his taxi home after his famous non-stop flight from Roosevelt Field, New York to Paris. The Memphis departed Cherbourg, France the next day arriving in Washington D.C. on 11 June. Their famous passenger and his aircraft were disembarked at the Washington Navy Yard. A bronze plaque honoring this event was mounted in Wing Storage atop the midship's deck-house. Every time I enter that space I had to stop and admire that plaque.

During January 1928 the Memphis was assigned escort duty for President Calvin Coolidge on a West Indian cruise. After 4 months of Caribbean operations she was ordered to transfer to the eastern Pacific. In early June the Memphis arrived off Balboa, Canal Zone for duty along the Central America's coast. There she remained on peacekeeping duty until May 1933. This included being highly visible during the Corinto, Nicaragua

Inauguration of President Juan B. Sacasa in 1932. For the next 5 years her duties were alternately operating between the west coast and the West Indies troubled areas

After a good will cruise to Australia early in 1938 she returned to the San Diego area where on 25 September 1938 one Seaman 2nd Class, fresh out of Ordnance School, climbed the port gangway with his shouldered sea bag and Hammock roll. This was a very important event in the USS Memphis history because that was me! In a very short period of time I studied seamanship. That involved how to polish brass, swab decks, use a 4 inch paint brush, load a 6" 53 gun and how to scrape the nasty crud off a Cruisers bottom at the Mare Island Navy yard. It was a tough year for a kid trained for aviation. But in that year I learned more about the real Navy than I'm willing to admit. Much of which was taught with the aid of a size 10-regulation shoe!

On 12 July 1939, with most vessels attached to the eastern Pacific fleet, we were waiting at anchor in San Francisco for President Roosevelt's review of the Fleet. We manned the rail in full dress uniform. Would you believe I don't remember seeing the president that day. Did you? I sure hope somebody saw the President!

On January 1940 The Memphis became flagship to the Commander, Aircraft Scouting Force, (ComAirScoFor). As a result, the ship departed San Diego for the Panama Canal and the east coast to participate in Fleet Problem XX. It was a lucky break for me. On arrival at San Juan I had finally received my transfer to Patrol Squadron 11, but there was a joker in the deck. Neither the USS Memphis, nor I, knew that like General MacArthur, I would soon return to the Memphis. A vessel that had never been requested in the first place!

The Memphis according to her historical log book, never again returned to the Pacific Ocean. For the remainder of her career she served mainly in the South Atlantic. When the Flag of Commander Aircraft Scouting Force departed the Memphis a new Aviation unit had to be formed for assignment to the ship. By now your scribe had been promoted to Aviation

Ordnanceman 3rd Class. You can't believe who was nominated by the Bureau of Navigation, Department of the Navy to fill the Ordnance spot in that Unit. You're right, really smart. Can't you just see some young shore bound Officer at the Department saying, "Look guys here's an AOM3rd who has served on the Memphis before. He could be a big help to the New Senior Aviator and the unit getting them acclimated to the ship!"

When reporting to the Senior Aviator at NAS Norfolk, it was obvious we didn't even own a screwdriver! I'll not bore you with the efforts of the unit to prepare two aircraft and all its accessory equipment and materials for deployment at sea. That's another story. We reported aboard prepared to depart for aircraft shake-down and qualifications.

The ship had a major face-lift since I departed. The hammock and folding cot birthing system was no more. The Main deck now sported triple deck birthing and a blower system to make the spaces more livable. I assumed this same effort also applied to other living areas. The messing had also been revised by a change to a Cafeteria system. A sound power system was also now in place but the boatswain mates still used lung power with their little tin whistles to insure the passing of the word.

We finished the aircraft qualifications at Newport R.I. on 24 April 1941. Per operational orders, the ship cruised south to participate in the South Atlantic Neutrality Patrols. Somewhere on the way out of Hampton Rhodes we picked up two new destroyer Flotilla leaders as escorts. The patrol triangle would be Trinidad, Cape San Roque, and Cape Verde Islands, to Recife, Brazil. On the way to Recife we crossed the Equator on 8 May 1941 where all the non-shellbacks received their just reward.

In July 1941 I was promoted to AOM2nd Class and was raised in salary to $72.00 a month base pay. Shortly thereafter I was transferred to the Receiving Ship New York for discharge. But the Japanese screwed that up. They deliberately bombed Pearl Harbor just to keep me in the service.

The Memphis continued the South Atlantic patrols after the Japanese attack on Pearl Harbor and did so for most of World

War II. In March of 1942 she escorted two Army transports in convoy to Ascension Island where the Army's 38th Engineers General Service Regiment constructed an airport staging point for flying planes from the U.S. to Africa. By May she was on patrol near the entrance of Fort de France, Martinique.

In January 1943, The USS Memphis again flew the flag of the President of the United States, Franklin D. Roosevelt off Bathurst, Gambia. This was during the 14 to 24 January Casablanca Conference where Roosevelt and Prime Minister Churchill discussed plans for the invasion of Sicily and Italy. From February to September 1943, The Memphis went back to patrolling off Bahia and Recife Brazil looking for blockade runners. In January 1944 Uruguay's President Amenzoga and Brazil's President Getulio Vargas toured the ship even though both their countries were rendering valuable aid to the enemy in blockading the "Atlantic Narrows".

The following year the Memphis was again ordered to Europe. On arrival at Naples, Italy she raised the Flag of Admiral Harold R. Stark, Commander of U.S. Naval Forces, Europe. She then got underway for Valletta, Malta, which was the scene of the preliminary Allied Conferences prior to the February Yalta Conference. Before the end of January the Memphis hosted visits from Fleet Admiral Ernest J. King and General of the Army George C. Marshall.

On 18 February 1945 the Memphis arrived in Algiers for President Roosevelt's last Allied Conference prior to his departure back to the United States. For the following eight months she continued to host many distinguished allied leaders. In addition, on 15 August 1945 she was assigned to participate in the first anniversary celebrations of the Allied landings at San Raphael and St. Tropez in southern France. On 27 October 1945 she was in Naples, Italy to represent the United States at the Italian Navy Day festivities.

Late in November 1945 the USS Memphis CL 13 made her final voyage home from Tangier to the Philadelphia Navy Yard. On 17 December 1945 the old girl was struck from the Navy's inventory. With little to none fanfare, on 8 January 1947 she was sold for scrap.

Many young sailors, both Officer and enlisted, really began their Naval careers, by working and studying the Navy's basic seamanship requirements while serving in this noble old vessel. This duty may have been the original building blocks on which many built their lifetime careers. How do I know this? Because I was one of them, on my first tour I boarded her directly from boot training and Class A service school. When I departed her after the 2nd tour, I had been promoted to E-5 Aviation Ordnanceman 2nd Class. I was lucky to be in the right place at the right time. In those days, making 2nd Class in less than 4 years almost fell into the miracle category.

AOC Harry L. Keneman USN (Ret.)

USS Memphis CL 13

PEARL HARBOR
07:55 HOURS, 7 DEC. 1941

Over sixty-nine years has passed, but each year on the first of December many old sailor's thoughts drift back to Pearl Harbor and the Japanese "surprise" attack on our ill prepared Fleet anchorage. Despite the fact our Military had been placed on a war alert, no specific direct order had been issued warning Pearl of a possible attack, nor, was any special form of defense stipulated in the event such an attack did occur. At this moment I would like to express a personal opinion developed over the years as to the reasons why our military completely failed to be ready to defend against what transpired. Having spent close to fifty years of my life in Naval service, and having studied extensively what happened that infamous day, I'm certain my opinion may be just as valid as any other.

Nothing much about life, peace and war, has ready changed over the years. Down through history wars have emerged over something one nation needed to become an international power. In this particular case, President Roosevelt, plus other international leaders, had sanctioned the Japanese prohibiting the possible sale or trade of oil to Japan. These sanctions were originated because of the continued expansion of Japanese conquests in China.

When you can't purchase what you require, it becomes necessary to find another avenue to obtain said product. Without the easy availability of oil the Japanese were unable to further their ambition to expand their desired national world position. Therefore, they were willing to use war as the basic method of gaining control of the oil fields in Southeast Asia and the East Indies. This fact in itself appeared to be ample warning to do more than just increase our defense posture.

It had also been a well-kept secret, that our joint military intelligence in Washington for quite some time had been doing an excellent job of analyzing and breaking down Japanese Naval Military codes. The capability of being able to decipher Japanese intercepts permitted our military to monitor Japanese Naval intentions, which should have given us a major advantage. These intercepts were being analyzed daily and discussed with President Roosevelt. This also should have resulted in Direct Orders from high level military to immediately increase our defense posture at selective high-level military positions, such as Pearl Harbor. Increasing early defense postures in a way might have offset the fact that their secret plans to attack the United States was never mentioned in their naval movement transmissions.

For reasons unknown, the President expressed a wish to review the raw intercept data. Based thereon a secret delivery pouch was established marked "Operation Magic" it was designed especially to transmit the raw information directly to the President. However, it appeared as if this process might have inadvertently reduced the availability of vital information concerning Japanese Naval movements to certain military personnel.

No specific secret operational warning orders or instructions, which should have been transmitted directly by Secret message traffic never materialized. General information ended up being transmitted via standard message traffic with vague, confusing suggested actions rather than by the release of direct defensive orders. Despite the release of a possible war warning, no direct order stating take what ever action considered necessary pertaining to Japanese movements, no specific Joint military defense plan for protective action was established. In fact, Adm. Starks's message of 28 November stated, "take whatever action considered necessary pertaining to Japanese movements, but restrict any efforts that might alarm the islands civil population."

In fact, it specifically stated not to take any offensive action unless the Japanese committed an "overt" act.

That order directly handcuffed any possible offensive type action by the Pacific fleet unless actually attacked. However, it certainly did not prevent defensive preparations. Adm. Kimmel followed standing orders received to the letter but later took the blame for failure at Pearl Harbor. Several other warning signs were received. For example, the Army had established a newly constructed radar early warning system north of Pearl. The operators actually detected the incoming first wave of Japanese attackers and reported their approach. The duty officer that received the telephone report told the radar personnel to go to breakfast that the incoming aircraft were probably a formation of B-17's coming in from the states. In addition, one of our destroyers also reported the sinking of a Japanese miniature submarine outside the entrance to Pearl but that reported "overt" act was also ignored.

The first attack wave of 213 Japanese fighter, bomber and torpedo aircraft arrived over Pearl at 07:55 just as our vessels bands were making ready to render colors. The Japanese immediately began making low altitude bombing and torpedo runs on their assigned targets. It became obvious we were totally unaware that the Japanese Long Lance torpedoes had been modified to operate in Pearl's shallow water. Less than an hour later the Japanese second wave of 170 additional enemy aircraft arrived to continue the attack.

Of the eight Pacific Fleet battleships moored adjacent to Ford Island, 2 were destroyed, 2 sunk, one beached and three slightly damaged. Ten other vessels were also damaged or destroyed. Of the 359 Army, Navy and Marine Corps aircraft that had been stored closely packed out in the open to prevent sabotage became easy targets for strafing fighter and attack aircraft. Only 47 of over 300 aircraft survived undamaged. At the final personnel count, 3,681 fine Army, Navy and Marine personnel died or were wounded that day because of the failure to receive possible warning intelligence information and the lack of a planned defensive policy. It appeared that despite the small number of early reported warnings all hands were just looking forward to enjoying a quiet pre-Christmas Sunday atmosphere rather than an one sided naval battle.

The Japanese losses numbered 29 aircraft and 5 miniature submarines committed to the attack. The only real American break was the fact the vessels they most wanted to destroy was our three aircraft carriers but luckily the carriers were "safely" at sea.

The Japanese success at Pearl and the war in the Pacific that followed would prove that the Aircraft Carrier would eventually replace the Battleship as the new capital ship for naval warfare. Vessels supporting combat aircraft were sounding the demise of the big gun vessels.

The worst thing that could have happened to the Japanese that day did happen. They had planned to have an official Declaration of War delivered to the United States prior to the first release of a weapon at Pearl. The fact was this never happened. The war began without benefit of an official Declaration of War. In the United States, the mere thought of a sneak attack actually generated a hate outrage that carried all the way across the Pacific Ocean back to Japan. Like most diplomatic offices, that fatal Sunday morning the Japanese Embassy in Washington was short handed operating with only duty personnel. This unfortunately caused them to take an unusual amount of time to translate the Declaration of War into English. In the movie version of the attack, "Tora, Tora, Tora," Adm. Yamamoto stated, "All we have done is awaken a sleeping Giant." In reality, his actual statement was, "It does not do to slit a sleeping throat."

Most individuals wondered how this disaster could have possibly happened. Were we not supposed to learn something from past tests and experiences? During Fleet Problem XIX in 1938, the U.S. Fleet also launched a simulated successful surprise attack on Pearl. Was it possible this was where the Japanese got the idea? As stated previously, for quite some time U.S. Cryptanalysts had been deciphering Japans most secret radio traffic. Despite being on a war alert, Adm. Kimmel and Gen. Short Commanding the Hawaiian sector had not received any positive warning which might have suggested a surprise attack, especially on Pearl.

For what reason were these senior officers not privy to available information? Reviewing the situation several theories had concluded that the Pacific Fleet was the victim of a conspiracy of silence. Some factions suggested that President Roosevelt and his supporters were anxious to enter the war against Germany and her allies. However, at the time, the American public disagreed and was not interested in being involved in the European War.

Therefore, it was intimated that the President required some sort of outrage to anger the public in order to support his desire to declare war with Germany. Did he and his supporters intentionally set up the Pacific Fleet by withholding intelligence that would have alerted Kimmel and Short to the fact that a Japanese attack was a dangerous threat? A book titled "Day of Deceit" authored by Robert B. Stinnett suggested that the President did.

Having personally been educated in the State of New York where Roosevelt had been Governor before becoming President, I will admit that President Roosevelt was not one of my favorite individuals. However, it's impossible to believe that Mr. Roosevelt would stoop so low as to sacrifice the lives and injury to 3,581 American human beings. He was a fairly intelligent person and would surely have found a much simpler method to attain his objective.

In a one man's opinion, our military's failure to adequately prepare for the defense of Pearl that Sunday morning was due to a series of factors, a lack of understanding of the seriousness of the situation, fear of making a major mistake, or, of senior reprisal, distrust of subordinate personnel, possible political ramifications, the lack of believable intelligence availability, ineffective inter-service cooperation and last, but not the least, pure human stupidity.

For the Japanese, they were slightly better off, but it was not the total victory they expected because they missed hitting the aircraft carriers. Their task was also compromised by a fatal mistake. They failed to complete the job. The Japanese Air Group Commander Mitsuo Fuchida demanded that Adm. Nagumo launch a third strike. But the Admiral, who had always considered the attack a foolish gamble, refused and decided to withdraw. For the Japanese this was a major error. However for the United States it was a piece of luck.

The attacking pilots concentrated on the destruction of ships, aircraft, and personnel units. They made no attempt what so ever to destroy the vast oil storage area, the major repair facilities, or the submarine base. Destruction of these facilities would have set the United States back approximately another additional year, or even longer in the resurrection of the Pacific Fleet.

As stated previously our losses that day were the unbelievable failure of defense coordination efforts between the various elements of our government. As we scan today's newspapers each morning, the reader is not at all surprised to find that this governments problem may still exists 67 years after the Japanese released the first bombs and torpedoes that fatal morning in December 1941. When it comes to our nation at war, we are definitely subject to disastrous failures if the elements of our government are not all operating on the same page. The civilian gentleman that occupies the desk marked Secretary of Defense, should definitely be knowledgeable about the military and be able to intelligently explain things when facing Congress.

This nations elected officials are busy individuals that do the voting on the floor, however, there isn't sufficient time in a year, let alone a day, to be knowable of all the subjects under consideration, nor in today's world they are almost incapable of being totally responsible to their constituents at home. In an attempt to get the work done each has at least two elaborate staffs that performs their studies, does their research and actually advises your officials a recommendation on the way they should vote. Another consideration, if you intend to make it big with your political party, on the tough ones you better vote the party line, or else!

It pains me to say this, when it comes to military issues, Representatives and Senators who were knowledgeable military veterans no longer dominate the Congress. Most of these sharp old cookies have long ago retired to a peaceful bed in Arlington. Today when it comes to military strategy the Defense Department is the number one authority. The appointed Secretary of Defense has at hand, some of the most knowledgeable military minds in the business, The Joint Chiefs of Staff. Here all the various military elements are represented as a group.

These military gentlemen and their various services have been specially trained in the development of military strategy. Now the Secretary and Congressional members should ask questions related to the military's strategy but they are not paid to develop it, because that's the Joint Chiefs job. Once they understand what the military wishes to accomplish, it their job to find the necessary funds and equipment to support it. In reality it's a rather simple procedure when everyone sticks to his own tasks.

CPO JOHN FINN, MEDAL OF HONOR

At the Naval Air Station Kaneohe, Hawaii it was a clear, bright Sunday morning, 7 December 1941. At the John Finn quarters, Chief Aviation Ordnanceman John Finn and his wife were quietly enjoying a Sunday Morning sleep in. Suddenly there was the roar of diving aircraft engines rudely awakening them. John thought, "This is unusual, what was scheduled for Sunday?" It got even more unusual when he heard the static of attacking machine gun fire and the first explosion.

It didn't take much thought to realize that we were suddenly at war. Leaping out of bed and grabbing a few cloths he drove madly toward his hanger area, where he saw that some of our aircraft were on fire. Japanese aircraft were strafing and bombing the airfield. Bullets and shrapnel were flying everywhere! Without much thought, he dragged a mount of a Browning M-2 .50 caliber machine gun out of the hanger into the aircraft parking area. There he began firing at the incoming attacking aircraft.

Being out in the open, returning fire, he immediately began drawing fire from the incoming aircraft. Projectiles began hitting all around him. He was also taking some hits, but probably due to an adrenaline rush he barely noticed. He continued to concentrate fire on the aircraft that appeared to be zeroing in on him personally.

With the help of someone hauling .50 caliber belts, he was able to continue to maintain constant fire through the attack. However, he was finally forced to go to the sick bay to be patched up. All hands, including John, were astonished to discover he had suffered over 20 wounds. In reality it was a miracle that he had survived the attack. Despite his wounds he was back on the job the following day. Cleaning up and preparing for a possible follow up attack. ACOM John Finn was one of 15 personnel recommended for, and receiving the Navy Medal of Honor for his valor and dedication to duty. Of the fifteen only 5 lived to actually receive the medal. A year later one of that five was killed in action.

Shortly thereafter he was recommended for and promoted to a commissioned officer. In 1943, while attending the Air Force aircraft turret school at Briggs Manufacturing Co. in Detroit Michigan, I had the pleasure of meeting John for the first time. For a guy with the Medal, who rated a salute from EVERY individual in uniform regardless of rank, he was the most modest man I ever met.

John eventually retired from the Navy as a lieutenant. However, he continued to be invited to speak about the war. During the 60th anniversary of the Pearl Harbor attack, he made the keynote address at the ceremony at the USS Arizona Memorial. In his late nineties, pushing toward the age of 100 he was the sole surviving Pearl Harbor Medal of Honor recipient.

John had been actively supporting the National Museum of the Pacific War at Pearl. The latest information I had seen was a newspaper report indicating he attended the latest Pearl Harbor Memorial service on 7 December 2009. However, in May 2010 information was received that John had died at his home at age 100 a couple of days prior to our Memorial Day ceremony. I immediately destroyed my presentation for that service and instead, without need of writing on paper, I eulogized the passing of a national hero. We had lost the oldest living recipient of the Navy version of the Medal of Honor Lt. John William Finn, U.S. Navy Retired.

"WHY TWO WHEN ONE WILL DO?"

While serving on the Staff of Commander, Naval Air Force, Atlantic Fleet, (COMNAVAIRLANT), Staff during the late 1950's there served a very unique character. Our Missile Officer was Commander "Chubby" Lyons, Naval Aviator. I believe my friend "Chubby" was the Navy's only Aircraft Carrier qualified, one-legged aviator.

Prior to World War II, Chubby was an enlisted 1st Class Petty Officer. He had successfully graduated from the flight training school at the Naval Air Training Station, Pensacola, Fla. and received his Wings of Gold. In those early days officer graduates received the designator of "Naval Aviator." Enlisted Pilots who graduated from the exact same course were designated, "Naval Aviation Pilots." NAP'S.

Chubb's claim to exceptional fame began on the morning of 7 December 1941 where he was serving with a Ford Island Patrol Squadron at Pearl. He had just reported for duty that morning when the Japanese began their sneak attack. He found himself in the middle of the first day of the war. Unfortunately, he was badly wounded which required the removal of his left leg just below the knee. He spent several months in the hospital and when released he had to appear before a survey board for review and possible discharge.

He fought his release from active duty all the way to the Washington desk of Four Star Admiral Ernest King, Commander In Chief, US Fleet. He claimed he was just as effective a sailor with one leg as two. By then he had all ready been promoted to Chief Petty Officer and won his battle to remain in service.

He then began his efforts to return to flight status. His request again went all the way to Washington requesting return to flight status. However, it was approved with the stipulation that he fly with another qualified pilot when airborne. He then applied to be qualified to fly single cockpit aircraft. The Navy finally agreed to schedule him for a special check ride to determine his aerial performance capability. The assigned check pilot's report comment was, "That guy flies better with one leg than most pilots do with two."

Shortly there after he was commissioned as a Lt. (jg) and performed active aviation assignments despite his disability. One of which was the air controlled drone business. During the Bikini atomic tests he was part of the effort flying drones though the atomic clouds. Flying off the carrier during this period, some pilots didn't believe he flew with an artificial leg. I'm not positive, but it was stated that on one of his landings, he climbed out of his aircraft and handed his leg to a non-believer.

Finally, a medical problem having nothing to do with his leg eventually grounded him. He was reassigned limited duty and retrained as a missile maintenance officer. On AirLant Staff he and I shared the same office and became good friends with similar hunting and fishing interests. When Commander Lyons was transferred I purchased his Norfolk home. He finally retired from the Navy as a Captain. Pretty darn good for a former one legged white hat. A real hero!

A CAREER IS BORN!

In the year of our Lord 1937 a young man 18 years of age graduated from a small town high school in Sea Cliff, Long Island with fairly decent grades. Now in those days, if you hadn't been lucky enough to be born with a silver spoon in your mouth, it was obvious you were not making preparations to depart for college. But there were obvious alternatives. Being in love with salt water and being fascinated with our Navy, it was suggested I try to get an appointment to the Naval Academy with the assistance of our local Congressman.

When that effort failed a nice Navy recruiting Lieutenant visited our house claiming that on joining the Navy, it would be possible to get an appointment directly from the President of the United States! Boy, did we bite on that one! I then enlisted in what is now known as the "OLD" Navy. In the Mid 1930's the Newport, R.I. Naval Training Station with its age-old field stone buildings actually looked more like a penitentiary than a Naval Base.

But the Navy itself was modernizing. We were now powering most of our warships with oil rather than coal. After all the black gang had to get liberty once in a while. Further, we were now loading our long rifles from the breech end vice the muzzle. Some big shot gun cocker down in Dahlgren Va. figured out it was a lot safer to do it that way. I will admit I learned to holy stone teak wood decks on an old 3 mast wooden ship called the USS Constellation built in the 1850's!

After a few months of training I went down to file my application for the Academy. Woops! One thing that nice Naval Officer didn't mention, first you had to serve so many months before making an application and you had to be under 19 years of age the April prior to entry into the Academy! Can you imagine how I felt at age 18 and being too old for anything!

In three years and a butt I can gracefully back out of this Navy. I didn't have to reenlist. My Navy hope of an occupation was resolved shortly after I applied for Aerial Photographic School. The Navy's analysis had determined to enter me in Ordnance School to make a gun cocker out of me. While there, I settled my interests in Advanced Aviation Ordnance.

Military Aircraft really seemed to be the up and coming thing. Our F3F biplane fighters now had retractable landing gear. Even if it did take about half the flight time cranking the wheels up and the last half of the flight to crank them back down again. They flew at unbelievable speeds over 200 knots and fired twin Browning 30 Calibers though the propeller arch without hitting the same. At least the pilot hoped they didn't. On graduation, I applied for duty on the USS Saratoga CV-3, which my Dad helped build in the New York Ship Building Corporation located in Camden, NJ. However, my luck still hadn't improved. I ended up swabbing decks in the 2nd Division of the Light Cruiser USS Memphis CL-13. That just had to be my lucky number!

About a year later that old Cruiser became the Flagship of the Naval Aircraft Scouting Force. With luck I was able to present my credentials to the Flag Lieutenant and asked for his aid to get transferred into aviation. Several days later he called me back in. He questioned, "I understand You're a qualified small boat coxswain!" I was astonished, reams of pages on my aviation knowledge and a one line statement that he knew how to run a boat and I became an Airdale!! Talk about backing into a job!

Actually, being a former Yacht Club member, I already knew how to operate a boat long before joining the Navy! A few weeks later I was glad to find myself refueling PBY-2 flying boats at anchorage off, where else? Newport, R.I. It seems to have become my favorite small town. The Aircraft Tender was an old converted four pipe destroyer. The USS Childs AV-14 now with only two stacks, because two fire and engine rooms had been removed to provide aviation fuel storage space.

We completed the fleet programs then moved back to NAS Norfolk and was advised the Squadron would be repositioned on the east coast. Now working ordnance, I finally qualified for and was promoted to AOM3C (Aviation Ordnanceman 3rd Class). But they never forgot about that boat coxswain.

When the war started in Europe in 1939 part of our squadron returned again to, where else, Newport R.I. I ran a fuel boat again from the storage tanks at Melville to our aircraft flying out of the Torpedo Station's Gould Island.

Newport had always felt like bad luck until I met a girl named Josephine. After 70 years of marriage we sometimes reminisce as to my Newport luck. But that's another story. Actually the Navy didn't really approve of my marriage. In less than three months I again received orders back to sea. Report to NAS Norfolk Va. for duty with the new Aviation Unit of the USS Memphis CL-13. From her we would fly in Curtiss SOC-2/3's, a biplane with fabric covered folding wings with a speed capability of a little over 130 knots going slightly down hill. The catapults were compressed air units mounted amidships approximately 16 feet above the water line

Because of the short distance to the waterline, the catapult crew, who were actually the ships torpedomen, not aviation personnel, always tried to shoot us off on an up roll to keep from shooting us into the water. That actually happened on a couple of occasions! In a windless condition it was necessary for the ship make turns close to 30-knot crosswind so the aircraft would be headed into prevailing wind. Once we signaled the catapult shooter, the pilot with his left hand on the throttle full forward and his right on the stick partially back, we departed the catapult at about 60 miles an hour. All the poor guy in the back seat could do was wave his arm like a humming bird trying to help get us airborne!

Returning to the vessel was the real fun. The ship launched the aircraft recovery sled then made a fast running circle into the wind to create a smooth water slick for us to land on. We then taxied up on to the sled to engage the tow hook on the bottom of the float. The pilot then reduced the throttle to idle. Using the sled towlines, they worked us in close to the side of the ship while she was still making pretty good steerage. The back seat airman straddled the pilot, opened and removed the hoisting sling from the upper wing and engaged the boom hook safely without losing any fingers. He hoped! Once hooked up, hoisting the aircraft and locking it on the catapult sled was a piece of cake!

The ships crew sort of hated us because three Deck Divisions worked their butts off getting us off and on the ship for which they didn't get any special pay. At the same time they knew we were making the big bucks because we were flyboys. Big bucks my foot! We might have to fly a hundred hours in 2 weeks for an extra 15 bucks a month.

By the end of my cruise I had been lucky enough to make AOM2C. Actually, that was quite an accomplishment, particularly in that particular time warp. The Memphis put me ashore in San Juan, Puerto Rico. The 10th Naval District put him on an Army Transport headed for New York. Two days prior to our arrival we listened to the radio reports of the surprise Japanese Attack on Pearl Harbor. Can you believe that? The whole damn Japanese Navy had deliberately planned that attack to screw up our plans for a 90 day vacation before Josephine and I determined if I should ship over.

Well, he figured it was going to be a long war. So what the Hell, we finally decided to make it a career!

ANOTHER KIND OF WAR

It was the end of December 1941 and our nation had been at war for less than a month. As I had previously stated, it had been my intention to accept my honorable discharge, so the wife and I could take a 90-day vacation to get to know one another again. However, that beautiful idea went down the toilet drain when the first bomb or torpedo exploded at Pearl Harbor on that fateful morning 7 December 1941.

Four years of naval service had made me intelligent enough to realize it was my duty to ship over immediately and accept the 14-day leave I was being offered. Where the wife and I went has no bearing on this story. On responding back to the Receiving ship, N. Y. I immediately checked to discover which of my three possible assignment requests was selected. Per usual I remained at zero. The Lt. stated I was to report to the Naval Air Station Argentia. My response, "Never heard if it, where in the Hell is it!" Nervously the Lt. responded. "We didn't know either until we questioned the Bureau of Navigation at the Navy Department! Its in Newfoundland!"

My new orders read, "Proceed to the Charleston Navy Yard, Boston for further transport to the Naval Air Station Argentia for duty. Think man, is there someone in the past 4 years that I really Pee-Ode?" Actually, things could even get worse. Two weeks later as an assigned draft Petty Officer, I was marching at least 40 Newport recruit trainees aboard the USS Pyro (A-1) an Ammunition Ship bound for our new duty station NAS Argentia.

Just think about it, in the month of January 1942 I had just been transferred from warm breezes south of the equator to the frosty dark, dreary coast of Newfoundland. There was no welcoming brass band either. Just a single truck whose driver, a Navy Chief Petty Officer who did mention, "Welcome Aboard, How many white hats did you bring?" When I stated 40 plus, it surprised the Chief. He replied that would more than double our current Ships Company.

The Chief said lets get loaded up and we can head for the hanger "The Administrative Building hasn't been finished yet and neither has the barracks. The Administrative Office is on the second deck of the hanger and you will be bunked in the empty hanger offices for a short period till the barracks are completed."

I had the draft line up in two ranks outside the Administrative Office. Entering the office I handed over the case of personnel records to the Yeoman, saluted the Lt. (jg) and stated, "Harry L. Keneman, AOM2nd Class and draft personnel reporting for Duty." "Welcome aboard Petty Officer things are going to be tough for a while. We are at the mercy of the contract construction crews who are doing their best to get us to the point of possibly calling ourselves operational. To begin with, you're advised that you are the only Ordnanceman on board. Therefore you are now the head, as well as being the entire Ordnance Department. Once you get settled we will assign you a guide and a civilian contractor to show you the Ordnance area and its buildings."

I stated I had a question, "Where is this so called Ordnance maintenance building I was supposed to operate?" The officer laughed and stated if you look across the street it will be built on one of those lots. He laughed again and stated the Chief will take you and your sailors down to the galley and see every one gets fed. I laughed and replied, "Thank God the galleys operational at least we won't starve to death!"

Once temporally settled in, I was introduced to my guide, an Aviation Machinist Mate 1st Class who had been on board a couple of months. The Building Contractor Personnel had been aboard for several months and based construction on the order of priority. Their first target was the aircraft runways. This wasn't easy because they had to move 60 some feet of packed Peat Moss in an effort to locate solid ground to pour concrete.

However, it did leave deep trenches of peat, which were real snow collectors.

In order to permit proper servicing for the PBY Flying boats during the HA! Summer HA! Season, the waterfront and the beaching ramp also required early construction. Oh yes, don't forget the Hanger, which I believed was the first "completed" structure. Across the ramp from the hanger was the Machine Shop completely finished and housing some of most beautiful brand new power tools of all shapes and sizes but not a single technician. Why bother, No electricity!!

Speaking of electricity, what juice we were using to work with was being supplied by the USS Prairie AD-15. This sea going vessel was not only here to service the destroyers, it also provided our only connection to the U.S. of America for mail service, the Ship Store, Gyp Joint, clothing supplies, etc. as well as the stations electricity, last but not the least the bases sick bay!

Now of minor interest, the station had one assigned aircraft. A utility flying boat JRF-2; which was jacked up and lacked a set of wheels. I tried hard but never discovered where the wheels went. I kind of felt they probably graced some proud Newfie's truck trailer. Actually, we never worried about them because we didn't have an airdale pilot to fly it anyhow.

We did have one active combat Flying Squadron on board and it was one of my jobs to service them with any required Ordnance they might need. This was Patrol Squadron 82 which was charged with locate, chase & destroy submarines that might be trying to sink cargo vessels trying to haul war supplies to aid the English. They were equipped with Lockheed Hudson PBO-1's built for the British and bummed by the U.S. for this specific job.

It was now time I took a look-see at the specific areas that fell under my personal responsibilities such as the weapons magazines, inert weapons storage buildings. The Chief had told me I would need a proper vehicle for the long term to perform necessary routine inspections and visits to weapons storage areas. The normal bomb or open truck would be overkill and cumbersome for the job. What you need is a Jeep. I agreed but remarked I hadn't seen any in the motor pool.

The Chief removed a key from his pocket and handed it to me. "The Army guys got lots of jeeps in their motor pool. I would suggest you visit their Rec Hall tonight, have a couple of beers. On your way back pass by their motor pool, choose a jeep and just drive it back to our side." I had to admit, it worked like a charm. A couple of days later it departed the hanger decked out in a coat of Navy gray complete with a navy number.

Our weapon magazines proved to be of Quonset style metal construction fronted by a solid concrete wall, which allowed the passage of a 6 by 6 truck, plus no plans for internal electricity. This indicated all storage would be stress and strain on the backs of the strongest young sailors amongst the recruits from the draft I escorted to this miserable country. We used battle lamps for lights and bummed some pipe from the contractors for movement across the concrete floor. It meant stacking crated 500 & 1000lb bombs in piles three to four high with human backbreaking efforts that rubbed the wrong way. The Kids never complained much but I'm positive these fine kids hadn't planned to serve their country as common Laborers.

When we ran out of indoor space we laid out dummage and stacked the incoming weapons out doors up to about five feet high. I never figured out who was expected to use all these weapons. The aircraft of VP-83 were limited to the depth charges they carried on anti sub patrols and they were lucky to sink a couple during the period I was attached.

Actually, this duty wasn't all bad. The Navy Department automatically promoted me to Aviation Ordnanceman 1st class for services rendered.

THE GROUNDING!

Veterans learn quickly about the horrors of war. However, not all casualties happen on the battlefield. Over one quarter of the casualties during World Was II were from incidents other than combat. It's proof positive that you didn't necessarily have to fall in battle in order to die for your country! Such incidents rarely see the light of day, due to being deeply buried in Ship's Logs or hidden closely in official military reports.

Some time later a curious historian might accidentally discover it. The events I'll try to report on here is a story of long forgotten bravery, suffering and survival involving a tragic incident that happened over 68 years ago. First, please understand, I was not personally involved until after the grounding, therefore, some of what has been describe herein might be what was assumed happened in certain situations or events rather than the exact sequence of occurrences.

Early morning 18 February 1942 three naval vessels, the old four piped destroyer, USS Truxtun DD 229 and another destroyer was escorting a cargo vessel, USS Pollux AKS-2 toward Placentia Bay, Newfoundland, bound for the Naval Air Station that was under construction there. The vessels were bucking high winds, extremely heavy seas and, inclement blizzard type weather, which had obstructed visibility. Due to storm conditions and excessively high winds, they had veered slightly off course, which had unfortunately positioned them very close to Newfoundland's rocky coastline.

Too close in fact, suddenly there was the crushing grind of steel on rock as the two vessels, less than a mile apart, almost simultaneously made direct contact with the shore line. Last minute efforts by the vessels crews to clear the shore failed. The combined power of the wind, the surging sea, and the jagged rocks began to sound a death toll for the two stricken vessels. The emergency alarms sounded by both vessels had sent damage control personnel to their stations to access the situation. Almost immediately both vessels had begun to take on seawater. The only alternative left, their skippers was to pass the word to abandon ships to the mercy of the sea and attempt to get the crews safely ashore.

It was immediately determined that power had to be maintained as long as possible to provide necessary lighting for working parties. Initial volunteer attempts to make shore were disastrous. In addition, men exiting the flooding heated fire and engine rooms below that jumped over the side, disappeared almost instantly after entering the icy waters. An effort to launch lifeboats was also unsuccessful due to the boats being destroyed by the surging sea and the rocks. Initial attempts to get grappling line to the beach also failed. Finally, two brave sailors in a small life raft were able to make it to the beach with lines. Once ashore they began rigging the raft as a rescue device by running the raft back and forth to the stranded vessel bringing in ten or more crewmen with each trip.

While the work went on to get more men ashore, an 18 year old Apprentice Seaman named Bergeron with less than four months naval service, and a Chief Petty Officer named Peterson were able to climb the 200 foot ice covered cliff hand over hand in a desperate attempt to locate Newfoundlanders ashore. On reaching the top they located a hay shack where they rolled themselves in hay to retain warmth, and took a brief rest. Shortly, the young Seaman regained his strength and struck out alone in search of help. After traveling for over two miles he finally discovered a small mining camp. The miners were shocked when they saw the condition of the exhausted bedraggled young sailor. They jumped into immediate action once they heard the tale about the disaster.

Telephone calls were made to St Lawrence and Lawn. Everyone capable rushed to the sites of the two stranded vessels. They arrived with food, clothing, blankets and tools to be used in assisting the rescue of personnel from the stranded vessels. On their arrival some of the local islanders lowered themselves down the cliff to the beachfront to assist the ships personnel in aiding crewman from the vessels. Survivors were being moved to higher ground to be attended to and fed food. The efforts took most of the day and part of the next with special attention being given to the more seriously injured. Thanks to the islanders response to this catastrophic disaster those that reached the shore had the natives to thank for saving them from death from exposure. But by this time some of the rescuers were in almost as bad a shape as the survivors!

Immediate action was taken by the navy to provide on site personnel at the grounding area. With the help of the native population, medical aid was administered to the living. Concurrently, the grim task got underway to recover and identify the dead and missing. Total losses from the two vessels numbered 203 personnel. A total of 48 bodies were recovered in the next few days. As expeditiously as possible the deceased were transferred to the naval station for identification, medical examination and preparation for burial. They were buried at NAS Argentia with full military honors. For several weeks other bodies were being found on the shore and in the coves. The remains of the Commanding Officer of the Truxtun, Lcdr Hickcox was later found still aboard his vessel.

A total of 158 survivors were extracted from the stranded vessels and the pounding sea. Of this number only three officers and forty-three men were from the Truxtun. For several weeks after the disaster additional bodies continued to be found along the shore and in the coves. These individuals were interred in the St. Lawrence Church yard in ground donated by the Parish Priest.

President Roosevelt sent a personal message to the residents of Lawn and St. Lawrence thanking them for their outstanding work in the rescue efforts. None of the natives died during the rescue efforts. However, several suffered weeks later from injuries, frostbite and some later died of pneumonia.

In 1953 the U.S, Government built a hospital in St. Lawrence. In the lobby of said hospital, displayed under glass is the national ensign of the Truxtun, which was salvaged from the vessel by one of the rescuers. On the opposite wall is a plaque presented by President Eisenhower. The last paragraph reads; "The people of the United States is presenting this hospital to express the gratitude for the fortitude and generosity of the people of Newfoundland that night. It is hoped that this Hospital will serve as a memorial of the 203 officers and men of the United States Navy who lost their lives in the disaster and a vital reminder of the inherent courage of mankind."

Each year on 15 February, the anniversary of the grounding, a memorial service is held on the Hospital grounds for the American sailors who perished that fateful night.

"SIGHTED SUB—SANK SAME"

My prior writing related to the Naval Air Station, Argentia, Newfoundland has been highly critical and often derogatory. You will be surprised to find that, this story is different. In fact, it's highly complimentary. Maybe that's because our story began and ended at NAS Argentia, and the remainder of the story happened over the North Atlantic Ocean.

You may remember that I had previously advised that a very unusual military base had only one fully operational combat activity. That happened to be Patrol Squadron VP-82 who's Commanding Officer was Commander W. L Erdmann. VP-82 was a resident activity assigned the specific duties of anti-submarine protection of military supply convoys crossing the eastern North Atlantic. Having personally flown a goodly number of hours on similar missions they usually can be rather boring with only an occasional swift heavy action moment or two.

On 28 January 1942, aircraft 82-P-9, a Lockheed Hudson PBO-1, piloted by Patrol Plane Commander Donald Frances Mason Aviation Machinist Mate 1st Class (NAP) (Enlisted Naval Aviation Pilot), taxied out to the only active runway at 10 minutes after 01:00 pm. He took off between the peat bog cliffs on each side of the runway. His plane crew included Co-Pilot Algia Baldwin, AMM-1c (NAP), Plane Captain Albert Zink, AMM-2c, and Charles Mellinger, RM-2c. Their mission was to make an anti-submarine sweep aft of convoy HX-172. Their armament consisted of the usual Machine gun ammunition and 2 each 325lb Mark XVII Depth Charges set to detonate at the depth of 50 feet.

While on station at 3:15 pm, their attention was drawn to a target. It was a submarine periscope just to the left of their flight path. Their aircraft was flying at a speed of 140 knots at a altitude of 800 feet. The submarine was operating in a slightly rough sea and was leaving a very visible wake. Mason made a quick turn and dove his aircraft toward the target from a slight angle astern.

It was obvious the sub had been completely surprised because there was no indication of its beginning to submerge. The depth charges were released at an estimated altitude of 250 feet or more at an air speed of 165 knots. The charges entered the water astraddle the target. The explosions erupted on either side lifting the hull of the target, which brought the conning tower well clear of the water. It was a definite kill. The submarine was seen vertically slipping under and out of sight. Within minutes oil began to bubble to the surface and continued for several minutes.

While the pilot flew the aircraft, the Co-pilot had released the armed charges with the manual release. The plane captain attempted to take photos but there wasn't sufficient lighting to get a clear shot. The pilot then reversed course and headed back toward Argentia due to the fact the newly constructed runway had no lighting system. To the radioman Mason directed the following message be sent "Sighted Sub, Sank Same." The radioman was surprised at the unusual verbiage of the message but sent that exact wording over the air as instructed.

Squadron Commander Erdmann's official report of the attack was submitted via the required system but do to the fact the sinking was never officially confirmed an official release was withheld. However, Vice Admiral Ingersoll, Commander in Chief of the U. S. Atlantic Fleet's response, with the recommendation the pilots be promoted and an award; As directed Mason was promoted to Chief Petty Officer and received the Distinguished Flying Cross.

The Navy did not officially release the news until 1 April 1941. When they did his short radio message, "Sighted Sub, Sank Same!" caught on with the general public and will stand alone with other Navy expressions like "I have not yet begun to fight!" and "Damn the torpedoes, full speed ahead!"

On 1 March 1942 another VP-82 pilot, Ensign William Tepuni sank a "confirmed" German U-boat, which was released as the "first" actual sinking in the North Atlantic area. Two weeks later on 15 March 1942 Chief Petty Officer Mason attacked and sank another German submarine with almost the same crew he had aboard on 28 January. This sinking was officially confirmed. As the result, he was promoted to the Commissioned Rank of Ensign and awarded his second Distinguished Flying Cross. The members of his crew also received awards, probably the Air Medal.

On his return to the states he was requested to assist with the war bond drive. Here in the states, the general public gave him a warm welcome. After all, wasn't he the young sailor that sent that proud radio message, "Sighted Sub, Sank Same!?"

FIGHT FOR SURVIVAL

On 1 February 1942, over 69 years ago, a lone torpedo bomber, with a faulty engine was trying to make it back to its Home at sea aboard the USS Enterprise CV 6, when they were struck by a heavy squall. In the cockpit was an old timer, an enlisted Chief NAP (Naval Aviation Pilot) named Harold Dixon fighting hard to keep the plane airborne. At the radio, trying to keep a bearing signal on the air by signaling their position was radioman 1st Class Gene Aldrich. The bomber, gunner was Aviation Ordnanceman, my future shipmate Tony Pastula. However, their efforts went for naught, the squall finally forced them to ditch the aircraft.

Once in the water, they broke out the rubber life raft, inflated it and collected what they could. As they bobbed around in the four by eight foot life raft they watched sadly as their aircraft slowly disappeared below the surface of the rolling sea. When the squall subsided they inventoried their items. Besides their raft they had their flight gear, clothing, a .45 Caliber pistol, a couple of clips of ammo, a pocket knife, pliers, and a length of ¼ inch manila line. Chief Dixon used the manila line and one of the life jackets to rig a sea anchor for the raft. This was day one of their unbelievable adventure.

By dawn of 2nd day they had talked themselves silly while scanning the sky in hopes the search plane they saw in the distance would turn in their direction. But it never did. The following day Aldrich was able to stab a fish with his pocket knife. They consumed everything but the bones. On the 5th day it rained again. They drank all the water they could and stored water in the rafts oar pockets for later use.

As they floated along the only sound was the lapping of the water against the raft. They had definitely ran out of things to say. Suddenly an albatross lighted on one end of the raft. Aldrich and Pastula scrambled for the gun, one picked it up and shot the bird, which fell back into the water. Dixon, who happened to be the only one of the three who could swim dived into the water and retrieved the bird. I imagine the feathers really flew when he got back in the raft. Again they ate everything but the bones.

Day 7 they were lucky again, it rained. They drank their fill and again stored water in the oar pockets. A shark swam up and bumped the raft. Quickly Aldrich was stabbing it with his knife, then flipped it into the raft on top of Pastula lying in the bottom. Tony wrestled the four-foot shark to the bottom of the raft and started ripping him open with the pliers. They ate as much as they could; especially the liver which one of them stated was good in circumstances such as theirs.

By then they were beginning to forget, was losing track of time and were having trouble keeping things straight in their mind. By day 10 they had killed another shark with the gun. By now the gun had corroded and would no longer work properly. Chief Dixon decided to find something for them to do. He tied their shoes to their hands and had them start paddling the raft.

On day 13 they caught and killed a tern like bird and ate every bit of the birds flesh and internal parts, which they claimed, tasted almost like chicken. Time passed slowly for several days with nothing to do except save a little rainwater and paddle with their shoes. On day 21 they spotted a floating Coconut and overturned the raft retrieving it. Once back aboard they cracked it open. The milk was slightly tainted but they drank it and ate the solid meat of the nut anyway.

A few days later they were overtaken by a terrible hurricane. They had plenty to do trying to keep the raft afloat. They had removed their clothing and were using them for bailing. The more water they through out at one end the more rolled in from the other. A large wave flipped them over which they righted. Twice more they were flipped over and righted the raft before the hurricane subsided. The three failed to understand how and why they were all still alive.

By now they had lost all their possessions including their clothing. Totally naked they lay in the bottom of the raft exposed to the burning sun. On the 33rd day they were again subjected to the capsizing of the raft. It was a miracle they had sufficient energy to climb back into the raft. On day 34 Dixon and Pastula lay resting in the bottom of the raft when Aldrich shouted, "There's a corn field." As they reared up thinking he had finally lost his mind, they saw the shore and greenery of an island! "Paddle, Paddle" yelled Dixon.

There were white breaking rollers on the shore as they finally rode the raft in on to a sandy beach. One of the trio mentioned they hoped there wasn't any Japanese on board. There the natives found them on the beach and immediately began taking care of them. Aldrich laughingly mentioned, "All we needed now was a Dorothy Lamour." The following day, they found there were quite a few.

Physically the three men had lost considerable weight and overall were in pretty bad physical condition. In reality, it was a miracle that these men had lived through a 34 day ordeal where winds, water currents, just drifting and shoe paddling had taken them almost a thousand miles from where they had ditched their aircraft. However, the natives knew exactly what had to be done to aid them back to good health.

Eventually, their position was finally located and an aircraft arrived to return them back to the Navy. Chief Dixon even stated that when the war was over he would retire and return to that island. I often wondered if he kept that promise!

THE WORLDS LARGEST MEMORIAL Lcdr. Edward H. "Butch" O'Hare, USN Medal Of Honor

While dozing in my aircraft passenger seat, a flight attendant's announcement came over the speaker system, "Please raise all seat backs and connect all seat belts. We are on our final approach to Chicago O'Hare. We will be landing shortly." On the name O'Hare, my mind rushed back over 67 years to the Aircraft Carrier USS Lexington, CV-2 in the western Pacific on 20 February 1942.

Chicago O'Hare International Airport is probably the world's largest memorial dedicated to the memory of a single World War II hero! This Chicago Airport bears the name of Lt. Commander Edward H. "Butch" O'Hare a recipient of the Navy's most prestigious award for combat bravery, The Medal of Honor.

"Butch" O'Hare's naval career began with his entry into the U. S. Naval Academy as a Plebe in 1933. At the Academy he spent four years training to become a Naval Officer. He graduated with the class of 1937 as an Ensign and reported aboard the USS New Mexico BB-40. He served aboard her for two years prior to his selection for Aviation training at NAS Pensacola, Florida.

During flight training at Pensacola Butch took to flying like fish to water. It was obvious that he was born to be a Naval Aviator. On 2 May 1940, the Commanding Officer of NAS Pensacola signed his certificate designating him as Naval Aviator #6405. He was then assigned to Fighter Squadron VF-3, of the USS Saratoga with orders to report by 1 July 1940 to VF-3 at NAS San Diego, North Island for duty involving flying.

Here his progress fell under the trained eye of an expert aviator, LCdr "Jimmy" Thach, The Commander of Fighter Squadron VF-3. Jimmy soon figured Butch showed definite potential as a combat wingman. Therefore, Butch fit in well with VF-3.

By now the Japanese sneak attack on Pearl Harbor had given the U. S. a special invitation to join with them in WW II. Butch had worked closely with LCdr Thach in the development of special night fighting procedures and the soon to be famous "Thach Weave". This flight procedure permitted the Grumman F4F "Wildcat" pilots to combat the Japanese "Zero" fighter on an equal footing.

On short notice Thach was advised his squadron VF-3 was to replace VF-2, the famous Flying Chiefs, on the USS Lexington CV-2. In a short period of time the Lexington was operating in the south Pacific. Off Bougainvillea in the late afternoon of 20 February 1942 the Japanese had scheduled two bomber Air Groups of twin engine "Betty" heavy bomber's to attack, and destroy the U. S. Aircraft Carrier Lexington. Upon the Lexington's radar detection of the incoming Japanese, the carrier immediately launched their strike fighters to meet said attack while the bogies were still about 45 miles out. Butch, and his wingman, had been assigned high level CAP (Combat Air Patrol) over the ship. On reaching altitude Butch had loaded and test fired his wing mounted .50 caliber machine guns.

While observing the distant air-to-air battle progressing toward the ship, Butch noted the approach of a separate formation of nine undetected Japanese Betty bombers just below him headed directly for the carrier Lexington. Singly, without further thought, he dove his aircraft and made an initial pass with guns blazing. With perfect aim, he destroyed one aircraft and badly damaged another. Pulling up again he dove for a second pass at the enemy formation from the opposite side. His blazing gun fire downed two additional bandits. Again, he reversed course for a third pass that resulted in the destruction of another enemy aircraft. On his fourth and final run he flamed the Betty he damaged in his first dive.

The three remaining Japanese aircraft, one of which was damaged, jettisoned their ordnance and headed for home. Only one of which reached his objective, one of the Betty's crashed on the way to base as the result of battle damage received and one other was shot down by another pilot, Butch O'Hare, without any assistance, had accomplished an amazing feat. He had thwarted a direct attack on his vessel, and in a matter of about four minutes, he had broken up an attack by destroying a total of 5 enemy aircraft and one probable.

Back in America, after over two months of negative war news, Butch O'Hare's heroic exploit was well received by the home public. On returning to the states for reassignment he was advised to report to the White House for presentation of the Navy's Medal of Honor. The presentation took place 21 April 1942 in the Oval office with President Roosevelt. It was the Presidents first opportunity to decorate a WW II hero. He also signed Navy Secretary Knox's recommendation to promote Butch to the rank of Lt. Commander. As a follow up result, he was also subjected to personal appearances in support of recruiting efforts and bond sales. This was not his style; he wanted to return to duty.

However, this story has a tragic conclusion. Butch eventually returned to sea to carrier duty. One dark night he turned up the engine of his F6F "Hellcat", released his brakes and roared down the carrier deck. Butch disappeared into the darkness in search of a night combat target, never to be heard from again. Over the years, there have been numerous discussions regarding his disappearance. One of which was the possibility of his being the victim of friendly fire. However, that possibility was never proved.

As I strolled though the hustle and bustle of the Chicago O'Hare airport I watched the hurried passing of the travelers. As I watched a thought passed my mind. There must be thousands of travelers that hurry through this edifice each day. A good portion of them hustle through ignoring the airport memorabilia display about its namesake, while the other portion that rushes by, never heard of Edward H. "Butch" O'Hare and probably cared less. Well, there still existed a small group of WW II Navy aviation types who care. To them Butch O'Hare will always be a special bright star memory in our nation's Naval aviation history. However, daily, as time passes many of these same shipmates are rapidly reporting to Butch's squadron in the great beyond.

"OPERATION SHANGRI-LA"

It was early January 1942; our citizen's morale was somewhat down in the dumps. They were still trying to recover from the shock and the reality of the Japanese 7 December sneak attack on our Naval Base at Pearl Harbor. It was hard to believe that the battleship Arizona had been totally destroyed with the loss of over a thousand crewmen and that a good part of the remaining Pacific battle force was sitting on the bottom or were badly damaged.

At the conclusion of a war conferences in Washington it was determined that something special had to be done immediately. Not only to resurrect and repair our battle fleet, but some form of military action had to be initiated for a strike back shock effect on the Japanese in order to boost the morale of our own citizens. It was brought to the attention of our top military, that a famous air racer, Colonel Jimmy Doolittle had a good idea but it sounded kind of far-fetched.

When asked to explain he suggested rather bluntly, "The only answer is to bomb Tokyo as soon as possible." The reaction was amazement. How could that be possible? Doolittle replied, "Just load as many B-25's as possible on one of the Navy's carriers, escort it within flying distance of Japan then launch the strike." How do the planes and crews return? "They don't, once they make their bomb drops they continue west and land in China. You may be assured of two results. It would notify the Japanese we were on the rebound. Plus it might force them to return home some of their deployed forces to bolster their home defenses. Our national response should improve morale and be well worth the loss of a few aircraft."

The first proposal on this recommendation received a flat negative response, but after thought they reversed their position and the plan was approved. The carrier USS Hornet commanded by Vice Admiral "Bull" Halsey was selected as the launch vessel. It was also determined that the USS Enterprise should accompany the Hornet to fly air cover for the Hornet's packed deck load of B-25 bomber aircraft. It was also determined that a maximum of sixteen B-25's could be brought aboard and still have sufficient deck space for the launch run. At that point in time no armed twin-engine aircraft of that size had ever been launched from a Carrier flight deck. Therefore, crews had to be selected and specifically trained for carrier takeoffs.

The B-25's, Mitchell's, were twin engine medium high wing bombers powered with 1700 hp Wright 2600-29 radial engines with a max speed 0f 275 MPH and a range of 1350 miles. For carrier take off training, the selected crews flew their airplanes to the Naval Air Station Pensacola, FL. Here, qualified Naval Aviators for carrier take offs secretly trained the aircraft and crews. The take offs were repeated over and over until they could get the B-25's airborne in the prescribed distance.

As the aircraft were loaded aboard the Hornet anyone viewing the effort knew the planes were too large to be able to land aboard, therefore everyone would automatically assumed that the Hornet was about to ferry them somewhere. Once at sea the radio was used only once to ensure contact rendezvous with the Enterprise. This message was intercepted by the Japanese intelligence unit who now knew that an American task force of two or more carriers was at sea but was not really concerned because their so called warning picket lines extended out 700 miles from the home islands. They assumed this would provide them ample time to respond if considered necessary.

After 10 April the Hornet and Enterprise proceeded westward with total radio silence toward the determined launch point. On the morning of 18 April the two carriers and their task force crossed the Japanese picket line and were eventually spotted by a picket vessel. Halsey then assumed that their position had now been revealed. The decision was made to immediately launch the 16 B-25's and withdraw the task force.

The Japanese had no idea that any aircraft aboard could be successfully launched 550 miles from their home islands.

Actually, the approaching B-25's were spotted and reported, but the warning was disregarded because the Japanese knew the U.S. didn't have twin-engine carrier aircraft. There was also patrolling fighters in the air at 10,000 feet but they never saw the incoming bombers that were flying at approximately 150 feet off the water. As our bomber aircraft crossed the Japanese shoreline they headed directly for their designated targets. As determined, they bombed Tokyo, Yokosuka, Nagoya, and other locations. However, not much damage was rendered, but their sudden appearances caused considerable alarm. Not a single aircraft was shot down but all aircraft were destroyed in the China landings or crashed resulting from running out of fuel. One plane landed in Russian territory where the crew was arrested.

Two crews had the misfortune of crash landing in Japanese occupied Hankow. They were returned to Japan and prosecuted for the death of school children. Three of the crew was eventually executed for the deaths of those children. Many Americans considered our losses in aircraft and personnel was way too expensive for the slight amount of damage and the minor concern on the part of the Japanese. The spread of targets was also a mistake. It was realized later the effort would have been far more effective, and gained more attention, if all the mission's weapon releases had been concentrated on the Imperial Palace grounds which would have definitely made a greater impact on Japanese Military thinking.

The bombing raid did result in a Japanese task force searching for our carriers without success. The raid did generate Japanese concern for the Emperor, which lead to a major change in naval defensive strategy and placed a greater strain on naval operations for the rest of the war. A perfect example was the exceptional impact placed on future operations like the Coral Sea and the Battle of Midway.

There was no doubt that the bombing raid put a strain on U.S and Chinese relations. Chiang Kai-shek had objected greatly to the plan because he knew our planes landing in China would cause Japanese reprisals against the Chinese. He was absolutely correct. The Japanese launched attacks against the Chinese Provinces of Chekiang and Kiangsi that killed hundreds of people.

After the raid the White House Correspondents questioned President Roosevelt from where the attack on Japan was launched. As I understand it, he smiled and replied, "Shangri-La".

B-25 Mitchell aircraft aboard the USS Hornet

THE BATTLE OF THE CORAL SEA
3-8 May 1942

Following the Japanese so called victory at Pearl Harbor their Naval Commanders were basking in the glow of superiority and the sunshine of successful accomplishment. That however, was not the case of Admiral Chester W. Nimitz, Commander in Chief, Pacific Fleet. The Admiral, his subordinates and allies were in constant tactical meetings trying to determine methods and procedures which might be used by their reduced Pearl Harbor combat capability currently available to them to successfully curb further advances by the Japanese Imperial fleet.

On 9 April "Magic" intercepts of Japanese transmissions revealed information that the Japanese were planning new advances into the Southwest Pacific in their quest to gain control of an urgently needed product not available in the home islands, OIL! Follow up transmissions lead the Nimitz team to estimate that the Japanese would commit at least three Fleet and one Light Carrier to the proposed operation. It was also assumed that their immediate objective's would be Port Moresby and the island of Tulagi.

Adm. Nimitz was also aware that the USS Enterprise and USS Hornet who were rapidly steaming back from the launching of the Doolittie raid on Japan might possibly arrive in time to increase his Fleet Carrier force to four. Based on the hopes of that probability, Adm. Nimitz immediately ordered R.Adm Fitch's USS Lexington's Task force 11, the only Carrier task force in the Central Pacific to rendezvous with R.Adm Fletcher's USS Yorktown Task Force 17 the only one in the Southwest Pacific, The consolidation of forces was for the purpose of increasing fleet strength for the possible destruction of the advancing Japanese forces. The third element joined with them was the U.S. and Aussie Cruiser and Destroyer Task Force 44, Commanded by R.Adm Crace R.N.

There was defiantly high hopes that the USS Enterprise and Hornet Commanded by V.Adm "Bull" Halsey, would be able to arrive in time to join forces and double the allies Carrier capability to four. There was however, a slight timing problem. There was a good possibility the coming battle could be underway before the Enterprise and Hornet might be able to participate. Adm. Halsey who was just arriving from the Tokyo raid, offered to give it a try. He immediately began to refuel his Carrier Task Force and prepared to set sail for the Coral Sea area on 30 April.

Conducting the operation without their added strength was considered a big risk but Adm. Nimitz determined the risk had to be taken. When the two allied Task forces merged R.Adm Fletcher immediately combined all Commands into one enlarged Task Force 17.

Being aware the Japanese force were on its way, as of 1 May R.Adm Fletcher had began refueling his force in anticipation of the possible coming battle. R.Adm. Fitch did likewise, but advised Fletcher it would take till noon on 4 May to complete refueling his vessels. Based thereon, Fletcher determined to move his Force further to the Northwest and immediately signaled Adm. Fitch of the revised rendezvous point.

The approaching Japanese fleet had organized their vessels into two separate landing forces, each with its own support force, one to attack Tulagi and the other to strike Port Moresby. The main attack force consisted of the light Carrier *Shoho* and a Carrier Strike Force of fleet Carriers, IJN *Shokaku* and *Zuikaku* commanded by V. Adm. Inoue. On 3 May the Japanese began their operation with the seizure and possession of Island of Tulagi, which proved to be not defended.

Fletcher on receiving notice of the Japanese landing on Tulagi and being in a good position, on 4 May launched a total of three Yorktown carrier air strikes against the enemy vessels located off Tulagi. By the end of the day the strikes had sunk a destroyer, a transport, and 3 smaller vessels. Bad weather suddenly set in which prohibiting both sides of the ability to maintain knowledge of each others location.

On 7 May the Japanese accidentally made contact with the U.S, fleet oiler USS Neosho AO-23 and its escort the destroyer, USS Sims DD-409. The enemy sank both vessels. The same day U.S. forces found a part of the Japanese Main Body Support Force and clobbered the *Shoho* with 13 bomb and 7 torpedo hits, which sent her to the bottom. On the morning of 8 May the opposing carrier forces finally made contact. Both sides lunched strikes against each other. On the flights to their target the two opposing air groups passed each other but never noticed the other due to the very heavy cloud cover.

The first strike contact favored the U.S. forces. Just before noon the American aircraft attacked the carrier Shokaku. The vessel was able to dodge the torpedoes launched at them but received serious bomb damage which destroyed their capability to launch and recover aircraft. This problem for all intents and purposes effectively put her out of action. The Yorktown suffered minor bomb damage from a single bomb hit and several near misses. At the same time the Lexington was attacked by the Japanese air group receiving two each torpedo and bomb hits. At first it appeared it had not really caused too much damage. However, about an hour later she suffered a series of internal aviation gasoline detonations and fires, which necessitated the order to abandon ship and required the decision of having to sink her.

By then all combat ceased and the battle was over. Neither side tried to launch a follow up strike. Historically, the battle did take place prior to the arrival of the USS Hornet and the Enterprise. During the engagement the Japanese carrier Strike force lost a total of seventy-seven of its one hundred eight operational aircraft. Despite their aviators false claim of having sunk both Allied carriers the Japanese chose to withdraw due to the fact they had insufficient air cover to continue their planned operations. The withdrawal also cancelled the Port Moresby invasion efforts, and appeared to have stalled southwestern expansion efforts.

When comparing tonnage loses, the sinking of the *Shoho* in comparison to that of the Lexington it might appear as a Japanese victory. However, for the U.S. it was definitely a strategic victory. For many months, the Imperial Japanese Navy was deprived the use of about one third of its Fleet Carrier forces because of the time required to repair the carriers damaged during the Coral Sea conflict. It was also the beginning of serious losses to the cream of the Japanese Air Group flying personnel.

The most interesting item about the Coral Sea battle was the fact that it was the first time in naval history that competing vessels faced each other in combat where not a single round was fired by either side. It was important to note that from this point on use of aviation combat tactics would take a front row position during the follow up sea battles.

ADM. JOHN S. "JIMMY" THACH

John Smith Thach was born 19 April 1905 in Pine Bluffs, Arkansas a long way from the salt water, and Navy he loved. He was selected to enter the U.S. Naval Academy in June 1923. On graduation in 1927 he was commissioned an Ensign and reported to the Battleship USS Mississippi, then to the USS California prior to his selection for flight training at the Naval Air Station Pensacola, Fla. On graduation in 1929 he was designated a Naval Aviator.

Ensign Thatch proved to be a natural for the privilege of wearing the Navy's Wings of Gold. He was not only a good pilot, he also proved to be the developer of combat flight and gunnery tactics that established him as one of the Navy's exceptional top aerial gunnery experts. In just a few years his consistent performance qualified him both as a flight instructor and as a test pilot. In 1940 he received a formal written Commendation which stated he had demonstrated "exceptional skill and technique in aerial gunnery and bombing, efficient and the meticulous operation of a gunnery department, and demonstrated a marked ability to train other pilots in fighting plane tactics and gunnery."

When the Japanese attacked Pearl Harbor in 1941, Thach had advanced to the rank of LCdr. He had been selected as Commanding Officer of the USS Saratoga CA-3 VF-3 Fighter Squadron. At that time his squadron was flying what was considered the Navy's Number 1 fighter aircraft, the Grumman F4F-3 Wildcat. This Fighter was a good solid aircraft. Being the Navy's leading authority on combat aircraft and aerial tactics, Thach was completely aware the light Japanese "Zero" fighter's performance and maneuverability was superior to our own aircraft. However, he was also aware of its faults. Its light weight construction, lacked body armor and self sealing fuel tanks which would make it highly susceptible to proper delivery of accurate 50 caliber gun fire.

The Grumman F4F-3/4 also had some good qualities of its own. It's tougher, more serviceable construction, plus body and equipment armor, self-sealing fuel tanks, and the firepower of its Browning Machine Guns and plenty of ammunition with .50 caliber projectiles. All of which impacted on the Wildcats speed, climb rate, and maneuverability. Therefore, Thach started to use his extensive knowledge of the subject to develop flight combat tactics that would give the Wildcat pilots an equal fighting chance against the Zero jockeys. Believe it or not, he designed a new combat tactic at his kitchen table with a hand full of matchsticks. This newly devised flight tactic became known as the "Thach Weave".

This tactic eliminated World War One's well know three-plane V formation and has the pilots operating as combat pairs. The pilots would attempt to maintain an altitude advantage, weave back and forth when encountering the zero. The weave not only provides the lead pilot an opportunity to take his shot, it permits his wingman to shoot at a zero that might be on his partners tail and vice versa. The tactic proved extremely successful in air to air combat during the Battle of Midway.

The Navy was well aware that the fighter plane was nothing more than an aerial gun. The zero deflection tail chasing of WW I combat became a dangerous sport when the enemy began to put gunners in their planes to fire aft at the attacker. Based thereon, since the early 20's the U. S. Navy was about the only military organization that preferred to train their pilots to use attack procedures that required the use of the deflection shot.

From the time the first shot was fired, it became fairly obvious that beginning an attack with an altitude advantage was a plus. Another fact you had to fire your projectiles at a particular empty spot in the air that would be filled with an enemy plane when your bullets got there to assure to score positive hits and a victory. Cdr Thach spent considerable time teaching pilots of all ages to use his various attack techniques and his two fighter weave. The percentage or degree of offset deflection depended on air speed and the angle of attack. As proof of the pudding, the total result of Japanese losses of the so-called superior Zero aircraft actually became greater than that of our Navy fighters.

Cdr Thach remained on active duty following the war. He Commanded the USS Sicily during the Korean police action followed latter by C.O. of the USS F. D. Roosevelt. CV-42. He was promoted to Rear Admiral in 1955, Vice Admiral in 1960 and Admiral when he was designated Commander in Chief, U.S. Naval Forces Europe and remained in that position until his retirement in 1967. Adm. Thach died 15 April 1981. During his more than 40 years of service he received numerous medals and awards. Some of which were the Distinguished Service Medal, two Navy Crosses, two Legion of Merits and a Bronze Star. He was quite a special individual.

As a final note, today jet pilots are still using the famous Thach Weave when participating in aerial combat.

THE BATTLE OF MIDWAY
4 June 1942

The Imperial Japanese Navy felt the first real sting of the U. S. Navys aerial military capability during the battle of the Coral Sea because of combat damages they suffered, the operational loss of two fleet carriers for several months to come and the sinking of a light Carrier. Their aerial capability was also severely damaged by the loss of well over three quarters of their aircraft as well as their on sight air group personnel.

It might definitely have a serious impact on their Central Pacific offense against Midway and the Aleutian's until such time major repairs could be completed and the repaired vessels might be returned to the fleet. However, their battle loss failed to slow the determination of Fleet Admiral.Yamamoto's desire to begin his previously planned Midway operation.

It was his intention to extend the territorial range of the Japanese defense perimeter by the capture and occupation of the Midway atoll located a little over a thousand miles Northwest of Pearl Harbor. An additional objective was the seizure and occupation of the Aleutian islands of Attu and Kiska. Yamamoto was convinced that control of these properties, especially Midway, would reduce the possibility of further bombing of the home islands similar to that of the Doolittle raid.

On Japanese Navy Day, 27 May 1942, the First Strike Force departed their Hashirajima anchorage and set a northeasterly course for Midway. Unknown to Japanese intelligence, the U.S. Navy's "Magic" Operation had been intercepting Japanese message traffic. One intercept translation provided Nimitz with the knowledge of the Japanese basic combat intentions. However, the exact objective had been identified only as AF. The Intelligence Officer of the Pacific Fleet Layton had concluded that AF meant Midway. Therefore, to confirm his suspicion's, a plain language dispatch was released stating that the Midway water distillation plant had broken down.

Two days later a Japanese message indicated that AF was running out of fresh water. Thus confirming the Japanese target was Midway. Nimitz immediately began planning defensive action based on an estimate that the Japanese position might be sighted approximately 06:00, 4 June, about 175 miles Northwest of Midway. A PBY search aircraft reported the sighting of the Japanese approach, which confirmed the enemy's approach on that very same course and time.

The miraculous repair of the Coral Sea damages to the USS Yorktown's by Pearl's repair facilities permitted Admiral Nimitz to deploy three fleet carriers for Midway's defense. These vessels were divided in two task forces. Rear Admiral Fletcher Commanded Task Force 17 with the Yorktown. Fletcher was also in Tactical Command of both Task Forces. The Enterprise and Hornet were assigned to TF-16 Commanded by Rear Admiral, Spruance. Who had been a quick replacement choice for Vice Adm. Halsey who had been hospitalized with an acute skin infection. The U. S. forces were ordered to take a defense position about 300 miles northeast of Midway and be prepared to launch a surprise attack against Japanese units as they closed on Midway from the Northwest.

Adm. Yamamoto's forces deployed a total of 113 surface vessels and 16 submarines against the Pacific Fleet's 47 naval vessels and 26 submarines. For carriers the count was 8 against 3, battleship's 11 to 0, and cruisers and destroyers the total was 73 to 44. The Pacific Fleets only advantage was the Navy's Operations Magic intelligence. In theory, it appeared that the overall advantage rested with the Japanese while the home team might possibly go down in defeat.

Fortunately for the U.S., the Japanese forces were divided into separate approach formations. This division of power reduced their overall strength and precluded instant mutual support. Also their advanced Submarine Force arrived on station too late to intercept, or be aware of, the arrival of the two U.S. Task Forces, which included the three U. S. aircraft Carriers. The new enemy Fleet Carrier *Junyo* and the light Carrier R*yujo* had been assigned to conduct the Aleutian operation. The light Carrier *Zuiho* was escorting the Midway Invasion Forces and the light Carrier. *Hosho* was assigned to Adm. Yamamoto's Main force. None of the above attack formations were accurately positioned to be in close support range for the remaining 4 Fleet Carriers attached to V.Adm Nagumo's First Carrier Strike Force. The planned division of attack resources actually reduced the Combined Fleet Carrier superiority to a 4 to 3 difference of only a single Carrier.

The Japanese began their attack at 04:30 am on 4 June with Admiral Nagumo 108 aircraft launch toward Midway. At that exact moment neither side knew for certain that the other was in the vicinity. At slightly before 06:00 am a PBY Patrol aircraft notified Fletcher of the sighting of one of the enemy formation. In addition Adm. Nagumo's cruiser reconnaissance aircraft had been unable to locate or report the presence of an opposing U. S. force until almost two hours later. Plus they failed to advise Nagumo that their sighting included a Carrier until an additional hour had passed.

However, the presence of U.S. Carrier's became very apparent when three squadrons of TBD Devastators, arriving without a protective fighter screen, made their heroic independent low, altitude torpedo attacks against the Japanese Carriers. Less than half the torpedo planes were able to release their weapon's because they were swarmed upon by Zero fighter CAP (Combat Air Patrol) swarming in from high altitude'. None of the torpedoes dropped by our slow Torpedo aircraft were able to obtain a scoring hit. Of the 41 Devastator Torpedo Aircraft engaged in the attack, 35 were destroyed. All 15 of the USS Hornet's Torpedo Squadron 8 aircraft were totally destroyed with only one pilot left alive.

Adm. Naugmo's Carriers first strike aircraft had been recovered following their bombing attack on Midway. Said aircraft were in the process of rearming their planes for a second launch. On notification of U.S. carriers in the area, there was an order to change ordnance to a carrier attack. This resulted in the flight and hanger decks to become abnormally scattered with the vast exchange of live ordnance. They were trying as swiftly as possible to shift weapons loads from a land-bombing mission to a Carrier strike force. At approximately the same time the U.S. carriers Douglas SBD dive-bombers arrived on the scene. Lucky, for the Dauntless dive-bombers, the Japanese Combat Air Patrol Zero fighters were still at low altitude where they had been scoring heavily on our torpedo squadrons.

With their new opponents arrival the Zeros, in a panic, were scratching for altitude. Unfortunately, for the Japanese vessels, all 48 of the Enterprise and Yorktown SBD Dauntless aircraft had pushed over their noses, opened their dive flaps and took dead aim on the helpless Japanese Carriers. In just a few minutes the SBD's dive-bombers had scored deathblows to three Fleet Carriers, *Akagi, Kaga, and Soryu.* These vessels received numerous hits, which were detonating scattered live ordnance and starting fires, which were turning their vessels into flaming infernos. The only IJN Carrier left intact was the *Haryu.*

In retaliation *Haryu* launched the first of two strikes on the U.S. Task Force, which incidentally, would finally lead to her own destruction. As a result the USS Yorktown was seriously damaged, laying dead in the water with all but one of her fire rooms out of commission. The smoking hulks of the Japanese Carriers were slowly headed for Davy Jones locker. The *Soryu* slipped below the surface about seven that evening. The *Kaga* followed her under a short time later. The *Akagi* was finally sunk by an IJN destroyer at sunrise on 5 June. The *Haryu,* which had burned through the night, went down around 09:00 the morning of the 5th as well. Based on the results Adm. Yamamoto ordered an immediate withdrawal. The Japanese Midway losses cost their navy almost half their Aircraft Carrier force as well as some of the best of their Air Group personnel.

The following day the Japanese submarine I-168 sunk the badly damaged USS Yorktown with a spread of four torpedoes.

Unfortunately, the destroyer Hammann DD-442 that had been tied up along side the Yorktown rendering help was blown in two and went down with the carrier.

On 7 June the Japanese Alaskan invasion forces landed without opposition on Attu and Kiska in the Aleutians. But their position was short lived there. The U.S. Navy was exceptionally lucky, the battle of Midway proved to be an exceptional victory for Adm. Nimitz and the Pacific Battle Fleet. Plus it was a significant turning point because it signaled the beginning of our military's western march back across the Pacific.

"A MOMENT IN TIME WW II"

The sky was dark and the night air was moist. Our aircraft bomb bays had been loaded for the mission. The engines had been warmed up and were turning up slowly in anticipation of flight. The pilots settled into their flight deck seats and engaged their shoulder straps and quickly ran through their checklist. The intercom crackled, the pilot questioned, "Chief, everybody settled on board ready for flight?" The response, "Stations manned and ready." "We have a go signal," stated the co-pilot. The brakes were released and throttles slowly advanced as the aircraft slowly taxied out. As the Fight Commander lined up on the runway for takeoff, the mission details flashed through his mind. This mission was a high-level three plane annoyance bombing sortie. It was a standard quick drop and run strike without benefit of fighter cover. The purpose was nothing more than the usual effort to keep the enemy awake while rendering as much physical damage to the target as possible.

The intercom snapped, "All ready for takeoff?" The pilot's throttles were advanced as the brakes were released, the forward speed rapidly increased as the plane sped down the dark steel runway. As the aircraft lightened, he eased back on the control yoke lifting the plane into the dark night air. The only visible light was the flashing bluish glow from the engine exhausts. The copilot actuated the wheels up switches bringing the wheels to the closed and locked position. The three aircraft steadily climbed till they hit 12,000 feet. Leveling off, the pilots eased their throttles back to cruising speed. They shifted into cruise formation as they settled on to their predetermined flight path. The intercom crackled, "Report". Each crew station reported manned and ready. Again the intercom relayed, "Clear your guns." The order was followed by short bursts of flame and the sharp rapid sound of our .50 caliber guns mixing in with the drone of the engines.

"OK, Take it easy guys. Stay off the air, we have almost two hours to the target." As they droned on through the night, the dawn began to be visible to the east. From the intercom, "Stay alert, keep watch, we are approaching the target. Chief, get down in your hole with the bomb sight." Suddenly, a waning voice from the upper deck turret "Looks like bandits, 9 o'clock high." "Watch em." "Roger that, there are three of them. Looks like their planning to hit us with a high-side run." The tail gunner was the first to open fire, quickly followed by the upper deck turret and port waist gunner. The sound of gunfire rose over that of the engines as .50 caliber empty cartridge cases rattled around on the metal deck amidships. The enemy aircraft dove under the flight and away. Reforming again they rapidly climbed for altitude. From the upper deck came, "Looks like we might have scored on one of them, he's beginning to trail smoke."

From the pilot, "Target in sight. We're starting to make our run, the *SBAE is active. Bomb bays doors are open. Chief it's your airplane." The Chief crouched over the sight making his adjustments. Gunfire again broke out as the two remaining enemy aircraft made another desperate diving run. "Bombs away" shouted the Chief as a stick of four 500lb *GP's departed the bomb bay. From the tail gunner, "Chief, looks like you might have hit a small tanker, it's starting to burn. Also there's something on fire ashore and one bomb landed smack on the runway."

From the pilot, "Chief, I again have control. Reversing course, will line up for another drop run on the way out. Salvo all remaining weapons on the target as we depart." From the upper deck, "Looks like number 2 aircraft has scored on one of those bastards. The last one is spiraling away. Appears to have given up." As they made the reverse turn and lined up, the pilot again notified the Chief he again had control. The chief's eye was glued to the bomb sight as he calculated the drop "Bombs away" he yelled, "All stores away, close bomb bay doors and let's get the hell out of here." No one bothered to access the damage as they quickly departed the smoke covered attack scene.

"Anyone hurt, damage report?" asked the pilot. The intercom replied, "A few bullet holes to repair but no injuries greater than skinned knuckles from a recoiling 50." The return flight was uneventful and the debriefing on landing was boring. The crews were happy to be back, have a bite to eat and hit the sack. Like they said in "Gone with the wind". Tomorrow is another day.

(*SBAE—Stabilized Bombing Approach Equipment:
*GP's—General Purpose Bombs)

THE F6F "HELLCAT" FIGHTER

Leroy Grumman, better known about Long Island, N.Y. as Roy, was the Manager and Chief Engineer of the Loening Aircraft Engineering Corp. When the owners decided to merge Loening with the Keystone Aircraft Company and move it to Pennsylvania, Roy decided he didn't want to leave Long Island. He and a few friends pooled their funds and despite the 1929 stock market collapse, they purchased Loening and renamed it the Grumman Aircraft Engineering Corporation. It was a struggle at first but at the time they didn't realize they were developing one of the most famous aircraft factory's known as "The Ironworks."

Roy Grumman was sort of partial to the U.S. Navy having graduated from the Naval Air Station Pensacola Flight Training Program in September 1918 as Ensign Leroy Grumman Naval Aviator #1215. Therefore, when they first opened for business 2 January 1930, I'm certain their planning look forward to eventually doing a lot of business with the U S Navy. Their first break through had them manufacturing special floats with retractable wheels for use on the Vought O3U-1.

Grumman Aircraft was well aware the Navy was interested in installing retractable landing gear on fighters. However, the fuselage designs of active duty aircraft prohibited their installation. This gave Roy the idea of designing a fighter around his retractable gear system. The result was the first Navy fighter Aircraft the FF-1. This was the beginning of a long series of Grumman fighters from the FF-1 to the modern jet F-14 Tomcat which had recently began withdrawn from active service.

However, this particular article wishes to discuss the Navy's most superior fighter aircraft of World War II. The Navy had requested Grumman design an updated version of the F4F that would be superior to our enemy's lightweight zero fighter aircraft. With the aid of F4F combat pilots and the Navy's request for replacement of the original engine with the eighteen cylinder Pratt and Whitney R2800-16 engine with a Turbo Supercharger, which resulted in the design of the most comprehensive fighter aircraft produced during the war. The first F6F-3 (with the P & W engine), provided a 25% increase in power, more fuel capacity, greater range, more safety features, added body armor for both pilot, and equipment, increased firepower and weapons delivery capability.

The first production F6F-3 was flown on 4 October 1942 with first fleet deliveries going to VF-9 on the USS Essex only 18 months after the placement of the first order. The first combat operational use was by VF-5 flying off the USS Yorktown during the attack on Marcus Island. As the Hellcats came off the assembly line they immediately began replacing the squadrons F4F's during 1943 and 44. Their superiority as a fighting machine was well demonstrated by their victories over Japanese aircraft in the battle of the Philippine Sea.

As production continued certain modifications were made to further increase their capability. Provisions were incorporated to provide a 2000-pound centerline bomb capability. In some installations .50 caliber Browning wing guns were replaced with 20 MM cannon, and installations were incorporated to arm each outer wing with six 5 inch HVAR Zuni rocket launchers. Official Navy records indicate that carrier Hellcats were credited with air-to-air combat destruction of 4,947 enemy aircraft. An additional total of 209 were downed by land based F6F's. These totals indicate that in excess of more than 60% of the total enemy aircraft destroyed by U.S. aircraft was credited to versions of the F6F Hellcats.

During their production cycle 12.275 F6F Hellcats came off the assembly line. For an aircraft built in such a massive quantity it's amazing to know that despite the number of modifications it was pretty much the same basic design as the first group to come off the line.

After the war the F6F for a good period of time remained operational with Navy and Marine Reserve Units. Quite a number were also converted to drones to be used as targets in various test programs. Many of these famous birds remained in service until 1961.

Today a F6F Hellcat is on display at the National Museum of Naval Aviation at the Naval Air Station, Pensacola. It appears in the battle dress of Medal of Honor recipient Commander David McCampbell complete with his 34 Japanese Flag symbols indicating the number enemy planes shot down during a single combat tour.

U.S.S. SARATOGA CV-3

The keel for the Battle Cruiser #3 the USS Saratoga was laid down 25 September 1920 at the New York Shipbuilding Corporation, Camden, N.J. It was scheduled to become the sister ship of the Battle Cruiser #2 the USS Lexington. Both vessels were named after famous Revolutionary War battles. As Battle Cruisers it was expected they would eventually become the two largest combat vessels in the U.S. Navy's Fleet.

However, an international Washington Naval treaty agreed to in 1922 for the purpose of neutralizing the build up of large hull navy's by placing tonnage limits on various combat vessels. This agreement placed the partially completed hull of Battle Cruisers #2 and #3 illegal. What could possibly be done with them, scrap 'em? I don't think so! I wouldn't swear to it, but I'll bet a few of those nutty visionary flyboys got to the ears of the Admirals stating that the treaty never referred to tonnage limits for Aircraft Carriers.

Once the decision was made to redesign the two vessels as Aircraft Carriers, it put the steel benders, riveters and welders at the New York Shipbuilding Corporation back to work. As I recall, my Dad had something to do with the riveters that helped build that ship. From 1922 till her launching in 1925, the construction configuration effort shifted toward the conversion to an aircraft carrier. Now, what might make this story seen odd was the fact during my naval career I twice attempted to be assigned duty in that vessel. However, the only time I was ever aboard was at the tender age of 5, the day before its second launching on 6 April 1925.

The Saratoga CV-3 was officially commissioned as our third Aircraft Carrier on 16 November 1927, Captain Harry E. Yarnell Commanding. On 6 January 1928 she departed the

Philadelphia area for her first shakedown cruise. Cdr Mark Mitscher, the Saratoga's first Air Officer and future WW II Task Force Commander, made the first underway landing on board 11 January. In a special experiment that was only attempted once, on 27 January 1928, the U.S. Navy airship Los Angeles made a mooring to the Saratoga's stern, to take on fuel and other stores. The exchange was successful, but was never attempted again.

On the same day the Sara sailed to the Pacific via the Panama Canal. It was a really tight squeeze. There was only three inches to spare on either side. Plus her flight deck took out a few standing light fixtures. On 21 February she finally joined the Battle fleet off San Pedro, California. In January 1929 she participated in her first Fleet Problem No. IX. During the exercise with a single cruiser escort she made a high speed run south and performed a successful "surprise" air attack on the Panama Canal zone even though it was being defended by her sister ship, USS Lexington CV-2 and the combined fleet. Thus proving conclusively the future value of a task force centered around the carrier and its air power. The tactics were then included in fleet doctrine and continued to be tested in future fleet problems.

In 1936 she was again involved in a Canal Zone fleet problem. Then returned to Hawaii for additional fleet operations before returning to the San Diego area. After various training cruises off Diego she again steamed to Hawaii to participate in Fleet problem XIX. During the 2nd phase of the problem, Saratoga launched a very successful surprise air strike against Pearl Harbor from several 100 miles north of Hawaii. Might it have been possible that's where the Japanese got the idea for the 7 December attack in 1941?

In January 1941 the Sara was scheduled to enter Bremerton navy yard for modernization conversion that included the flight deck widening forward, fitting a blister on her starboard side and, installing additional small caliber anti-aircraft guns. When the Japanese struck at Pearl she departed San Diego the following day as the central vessel of a third Task Force headed for Wake for the purpose of reinforcing their aircraft complement. She stopped at Pearl just long enough to refuel. However, the Task Force was delayed because of the low speed capability of the fleet oiler. Once word was received the Japanese had landed and secured Wake the relief effort was scrubbed.

On 11 January while headed south to join the USS Enterprise she sustained a deep running torpedo hit made by Japanese Submarine I-16. Six crewman were killed and three fire rooms were flooded. Despite the damage she returned to Pearl under her own power. While the ship was under repair the 8" turret gun mounts, which were utterly useless on an Aircraft Carrier, were removed. She then returned to Bremerton for installation of more effective rapid-fire anti-aircraft batteries.

Based on an enemy intelligence intercept, the Saratoga was ordered to make a speed run to Pearl to participate in the pending Midway battle. However, she arrived two days after the battle was over. She then refueled and departed Pearl on 11 June transferred 34 new aircraft to replenish the Hornet and Enterprise's depleted aircraft compliment. The three carriers then headed north to engage Japanese activities in the Aleutians but the operation was cancelled due to the Japanese withdrawal. The Saratoga again returned to Pearl Harbor.

On 7 July she sailed for the southwest Pacific where she provided close air cover for the Guadalcanal landing rehearsals in the Fiji Islands. These events coordinated cooperation between the surface and air units covering for the Guadalcanal landings. As Rear Adm. Fletcher's Flagship, on 7 August, the Saratoga air group opened the Guadalcanal assault with an early morning launch which resulted in a continuous two days of air cover for our Marine landings.

On day one of the invasion, the Japanese air attack was routed before it was able to reach the covering carriers. Fearing further assaults, the powers that be, ordered allied carrier forces to withdrawn on late afternoon of 8 August to make a refueling rendezvous with the oiler. This spelled disaster for four allied cruisers that were sunk during the 35 minute Battle of Savo Island shortly after midnight.

As anticipated the Japanese counter attack was finely detected on 23 August. Saratoga immediately launched aircraft but due to a low ceiling they were unable to make contact with the enemy vessels. Therefore, their aircraft landed on Henderson Field and spent the night on Guadalcanal. As they returned to the ship the next day, the first contact report was received on the enemy attacking carriers. The Saratoga immediately launched another strike, which resulted in the Japanese carrier *Ryujo* being destroyed and sent to the bottom.

Another group of incoming aircraft detected resulted in our subject vessel launching still another strike which caused serious damage to the enemy seaplane tender *Chitose*. Luckily, heavy cloud cover aided Saratoga to escape detection by enemy aircraft. However, the Japanese strike force did locate, and concentrate, on, the USS Enterprise, which resulted in some damage. American forces fought back damaging the Japanese air group so badly it weakened their air cover capability forcing the Japanese to recall their troop transports before they could reach the Canal.

After landing her returning aircraft at night on 24 August the Sara refueled on the 25th then resumed her patrols east of the Solomon's. A week later a tin can warned of an incoming torpedo in the water. The Saratoga was unable to turn fast enough to avoid the tin fish. The submarines torpedo struck the carriers starboard blister. The torpedo failed to kill anyone and flooded only one fire room. However, the resulting explosion damaged and short circuited the Saratoga's electrical propulsion system and left her dead in the water. The cruiser Minneapolis took her in tow and her aircraft were flown to bases ashore. The ships crew worked rapidly to jury rig the electrical system. By afternoon the Saratoga engineering department had her back under their own power making a speed of 10 knots. She returned back at Pearl Harbor on 21 September to make permanent repairs.

Returning back to sea she was involved in several various operations for almost a year. Of special note, as our troops stormed ashore at Bougainville on 1 November, the Sara Air

Group neutralized Japanese airfields on Buka. Four days later the Air Group made another brilliant strike on heavily defended Rabaul. This disabled the Japanese Cruisers surface threat to Bougainville. Plus they made a follow up strike on Rabaul again on 7 November.

By now Saratoga had been steaming for over a year without being scheduled for repairs. She was ordered to return to the states. The vessel underwent an overhaul at San Francisco for a month where she again received another modification of her anti-aircraft batteries. Her 36 20MM guns were replaced with 60 40MM guns.

The Carrier returned to Pearl on 7 January 1944 and went through a brief training period before returning to sea with light Carriers Langley and Princeton to support the drive into the Marshall's. From 29 to 31 January her aircraft struck Wotje and Taroa and then bombed Engebi the main Eniwetok Island. From then until the 12th of February she concentrated on delivering final blows to enemy defenses prior to the troops 18 February landing. During the operation she flew close air support and CAP over the island until 28 February.

Saratoga then departed the formal Pacific war theaters for almost a year. The first effort was to aid the British initiate their carrier offensive in the Far East. On 4 March, escorted by three destroyers she sailed to Australia to aid the British fleet in the Indian Ocean. On 27 March she joined British forces that included the carrier HMS Illustrious, four battleships and several escorts and arrived with them in Ceylon on 31 March. On 12 April the French battleship Richelieu joined forces adding a real international flavor to the group.

For two days the carriers conducted intensive training with the Sara's flyers. They were teaching experience combat techniques to the eager British pilots. On 16 April the Eastern fleet in company with Saratoga was under way. On the 19th the air groups of the two carriers struck the Port of Sabang off Sumatra. The Japanese were totally surprised by the attack and considerable damage was done to the port area and the oil storages. The attack was so effective the Saratoga delayed her departure to participate in a second attack. On 6 May again sailing from Ceylon, the combined force struck Soerabaja, Java on 17 May with equal success. Saratoga then departed the following day passing down the line of British Vessels as they rendered honor to each other.

On 10 June 1944 the Navy Aircraft Carrier, USS Saratoga CV-3 again arrived in Bremerton, Washington and was placed under extensive repair throughout the summer. Returning to Pearl Harbor 24 September she began her second special assignment. This time it was training night fighter Squadrons. Saratoga had actually started experimenting with night air operations as early as the 1930's. During the war many carriers, in an effort to save both pilots and aircraft had to turn on the lights to land returning strike aircraft. But up till now, no squadrons were specially trained for night landings. As I recall, some effort had been made by Cdr. "Jimmy" Thach, former skipper of Saratoga's Fighter Squadron VF-2, designer of the famous "Thach Weave" had also experimented with night fighting tactics.

The Saratoga and the Ranger CV-4, our two oldest remaining Carriers were assigned the responsibly to train night flying pilots and establish a formal night flying doctrine. This important duty continued for four months. However, in October it was determined that despite the importance of her mission the Sara had demonstrated greater value as a combat vehicle therefore it was to be kept available for combat duty. In January 1945 it was determined to return her to combat duty to form a night fighter Task Group along with the Enterprise for use during the Iwo Jima operation.

Working in the early Iwo Jima operation with the Enterprise and other fleet elements prior to the beginning of landings on Iwo required continuous fighter cover. Saratoga with an escort of three destroyers was detached to join the amphibious forces to carry our night patrols over Iwo Jima. Approaching her operation area on 21 February an enemy air attack by six aircraft penetrated her small escort and scored five hits on Sara in three minutes.

Sara's forward flight deck was destroyed, two hits were holed in her starboard side and fires were started on her hanger deck. She also suffered the loss of 123 of her crewmen. In approximately three hours the fires were under control and her aircraft had been recovered. She was immediately ordered back to the states for repair, arriving in Bremerton 16 March 1945.

By 22 May 1945 she had been fully repaired and again left Puget Sound behind as she steamed back to good old Pearl Harbor. She immediately began to again train pilots in order to prepare them for combat duty. All training ceased as of 6 September following the Japanese surrender.

On 9 September she made her first "Project Magic Carpet" run transporting 3,712 naval veterans home from the Pacific Wars. By the finish of her "Magic Carpet" runs she had returned 29,204 Pacific War Veterans. This was more than any other individual vessel. She also held the record for the greatest number of carrier landings. A 17 year total of 98,549 landings.

As the oldest Aircraft Carrier in the service of this nation the USS Saratoga CV-3 had become surplus to the nations post war requirements. On 15 August 1946 the USS Saratoga CV-3 was struck from the Navy's active duty list.

USS Saratoga CV-3

This famous vessel by destiny had survived the greatest war in history and had earned a total of eight battle stars. It's my personal opinion there should be at least one more star added to her record. Plus as the oldest U. S. Aircraft Carrier afloat she should have been chosen as a historic monument, an old war horse of a time long past. Instead her fate was to die as a Ginny Pig. She was selected as a test of nuclear Power. She was one of the naval vessels selected for Operations Crossroads conducted in the Pacific at the Bikini Atoll. Its purpose was to determine the effect of atomic bomb detonations on certain naval vessels. Test Able was an airburst that the old girl survived with only minor damage. Test Baker was an under water explosion detonated only 500 yards from the oldest U.S. Navy Carrier. This shot broke her back. But she refused to go swiftly. It took almost eight hours for her to slip below the surface

For that 5 year old kid in 1925 the USS Saratoga CV-3 became his Hero vessel that inspired a Naval career that began in October of 1937 and extended until mid-December 1978. A period of over 41 years.

In the interest of keeping the record as straight as possible several historical items were consulted to keep times, dates and events covered in this short rendition as accurate as possible.

THE SAVO ISLAND BATTLE
GUADALCANAL 9 AUGUST 1942

The early morning sea battle fought off the coast of Guadalcanal 9 August 1944 between an attacking Japanese strike force, and the allied protective screening forces was the greatest individual surface defeat ever experienced by fleet elements of the United States Navy and their allied Aussie units. In the opinion of this retired Chief Petty Officer, it pains me to state, that in reality, it appears we had no one to blame except ourselves. For years, the combined Fleets of the United States had failed to update their combat training doctrine to bring it into the twentieth century by including the science of conducting night combat warfare.

From the time of sail and wooden hulls, the basic combat philosophy had seen only a few minor changes. The combat doctrine seemed to be whenever physically possible, fight in the daytime so you can monitor and evaluate the effect of what's going on. In those earlier times attacking battle forces normally chose to close on an enemy singly or in file formation with the intention of overpowering their opponent with massive broadside fire. This conclusion was based on having spent two tours of cruiser duty in the late 30's. Your scribe failed to recall a single training exercise that might have resembled night battle practice. At the same time considerable efforts was consumed in conducting short range battle practice, which was reminiscent of the USS Constitution's battles reported in my high school history books.

A contributing factor to the Savo Island defeat was the loss of their air support and reconnaissance capability. Heavy Japanese air action out of Rabaul on the 7th and 8th forced a protective decision to withdraw the Aircraft Carriers, USS Wasp, Saratoga, and Enterprise, the Battleship North Carolina, six Cruisers and sixteen Destroyers out of the range of possible major damage by possible future Japanese air attacks.

Now you might think, the remaining naval vessels, being short handed with a reduced capability, might have made the remaining Commanders of the Allied screening forces more cautious and extremely alert. However, by all appearances it did not. In fact, most of the Allied ship's Captains were asleep in their Sea Cabins until after the first Japanese torpedoes exploded!

The Cruiser and Destroyer forces that remained in place were divided into three defensive groups to cover the northern, southern and eastern passages around Savo Island. Two radar picket Destroyers, the USS Blue and Ralph Talbot, was screening the area Northwest of Savo Island. The eastern approach was being patrolled by the Light Cruiser USS San Juan, HMAS Hobart, and the Destroyers USS Monssen, and Buchanan who were operating between Guadalcanal and Tulagi. The southern screening group included the HMAS Canberra, the USS Chicago and the destroyers USS Bagley and Patterson. While the Northern group consisted of the Cruisers Vincennes, Quincy, Astoria and the Destroyers USS Helm and Wilson.

In comparison the attacking Japanese force not only had extensive night fighting training, they also had exceptional good luck. As they approached the southern entrance around Savo Island they arrived just after the Destroyers USS Blue and Ralph Talbot were both stern to on their patrol. They were sailing away from the attacking force. Further, the pickets ships limited shore range radar capability was shadowed by the island, which permitted the Japanese to pass the Blue undetected with a separation of approximately 500 yards as they entered the southern passage around Savo. Nor was it really understood why the picket destroyers were cruising together. If they had been patrolling on reverse courses one of them might have picked up on the enemy vessels and sounded an alarm.

In addition, the Allied vessels of the southern force were casting shadowy silhouettes because of a burning vessel in the distance. This permitted the Japanese to prepare and launch a bank of torpedoes prior to having being detected. At the same time their first torpedo exploded, the Japanese cover aircraft lighted the area with flares letting the allied forces realize they were in serious trouble. The Canberra was instantly struck by two of the torpedoes and began to receive heavy enemy shelling. The Allied vessels began to fire star shells and returned fire. By then the USS Chicago was also struck by a torpedo and was severely damaged.

The Japanese immediately formed a double column and swiftly turned to attack the northern force who, for some unbelievable reason, initially assumed the southern force was firing at enemy aircraft. The Japanese columns of vessels passed on either side of the northern force and opened up with torpedoes and heavy gunfire on the USS Astoria, Quincy and Vincennes. Due to the confusion some of the U.S. Captains ordered a "cease fire" because they thought there own vessels were firing on them. This cost the Allied forces dearly. The Vincennes by then had also caught a torpedo as well as sustained intense fire from two sides. The destroyer Ralph Talbot rapidly steamed south to aid the attacked vessels but for their trouble they were first showered with friendly fire then peppered with enemy fire from Japanese vessels escaping to the north.

Both the Vincennes and the Quincy were already doomed in sinking condition and headed for the bottom. The Canberra was also slowly sinking as efforts were in process to offload personnel. She eventually had to be sunk the next day to prevent her possible capture. The USS Astoria had been taken in tow but the effort was a lost cause, she finally slipped below the surface about noon. In addition, the USS Chicago and a destroyer were also so badly shot up, they were out of commission for about five months.

The battle lasted just 32 minutes for the Japanese to destroy four heavy cruisers and do massive damage to one heavy

Cruiser and a Destroyer. There were 1,270 dead recorded and 708 wounded. Actually, the Navy's personnel losses in 32 minutes exceeded the losses of the Marines during in the entire Guadalcanal Campaign (1,207). The enemy sustained only slight damage to three Cruisers. From that day forward that particular stretch of the slot has been known as Iron Bottom Sound.

How was it possible for a powerful naval force that prided itself on its military seamanship, combat readiness and its personnel training programs suffer such a defeat? Having spent almost 22 years in Naval uniform as well as having a major interest in the study of Naval history and having reviewed various writings of former sea battles, this retired navy man arrived at some personal conclusions. What is written here is a personal analysis of the cause for the defeat and may not necessarily agree with the findings stipulated in the official records.

The initial U.S. losses during the Japanese attack on Pearl on 7 December 1941, the loss of the Lexington at Coral Sea, and the Yorktown at Midway plus the possibility of additional aerial attack losses might have influenced the command decision for the withdrawal of the Carriers and other vessels. Also the temporary loss of air cover definitely might have eliminated the possibility of an early warning capability.

As previously stated, there was no formal standing order for conducting night combat training. The formal Court of inquiry confirmed this fact. Communications was also a problem. For example there appeared to be a definite lack of cooperation between the Army and Navy. The contest between his Royal Highness, General MacArthur and Admiral Nimitz as to who was the biggest big shot in the Pacific didn't help communications much either. Plus no communications system existed between the U.S and the Australians. They lacked the short range TBS (Talk Between Ships) system, which made direct communications impossible. In most cases tactical discussions had to be done in face-to-face meetings. Another thing that was never explained, how come not one of the many so-called mid-watch lookout personnel on the various vessels never noticed the approach of any of the enemy ships?

Last but not the least, many of our ranking senior shipboard officers had graduated from the Academy just before or after WW I. By now they were pretty set in their command methods and procedures. I doubt if any of them had been properly indoctrinated in the purpose and use of the new electronics. They were good officers but many were skeptical about those new fangled electronic equipments, like radar, that claimed they could make identifications at great distances. Did those officers really think about or trust those little blips on that screen that they were telling them the truth?

In a manner of speaking, we may have also been lucky that the Japanese sweep in, fired their torpedoes and a few salvoes from their guns and quickly ran back up the slot. If they had stuck around for clean up action they might have really cleaned our clock.

MAJOR JOSEPH JACOB FOSS, USMC
World War II Medal of Honor

Joseph Jacob "Joe" Foss was a leading "ACE" as a Marine Corps fighter pilot during World War II, a recipient of the Medal of Honor, an Air National Guard General and the 20th Governor of the State of South Dakota. This National Hero was born 17 April 1915 on a farm in Sioux Falls, South Dakota. He was raised in a farmhouse without electricity. Had his first aviation experience at the tender age of 12 when he visited a local airfield to see Charles Lindbergh and his aircraft the Spirit of Saint Louis.

At his fathers death in 1933 he attempted to run the farm but it was a lost cause. Two years of dust storms convinced him to seek other employment. He went to work for a service station to raise money for his college tuition, books and pilot training. In 1940 with a degree in Business Administration from the University of South Dakota and a pilots certificate he joined the Marine Reserves to enter the Naval Aviator Cadet Program for the purpose of becoming a Naval Aviator.

After graduation as a Naval Aviator and commissioning as a Marine 2nd Lt. he served as a Pensacola Instructor, and attended the Navy School of Photography. He was then assigned to the Marine photo Squadron 1 at NAS North Island. He qualified in the Grumman F4F Wildcat fighter and was then transferred in October 1942 to Marine fighter squadron VMF-121 as their Executive Officer. The Squadron was transferred to the South Pacific where they became a part of the famous Cactus Air Force during the Battle of Guadalcanal. On combat missions Foss lead a flight of eight Wildcats that became known as Foss's Flying Circus.

On 13 October on their first combat sortie he shot down his first Japanese Zero. However, he didn't come out unscathed. His aircraft had been hit. With a dead engine and 3 zeros on his tail he landed dead stick, no flaps on Guadalcanal's Henderson field. By the time Joe departed the Canal in January 1943, his Flying Circus had destroyed 72 Japanese Aircraft of which 26 were credited to him personally. As America first WW II "Ace of Aces" he was recommended for and awarded the Navy Medal of Honor. President Roosevelt presented the medal to him at a White House Ceremony. A picture of which appeared on the cover of LIFE Magazine.

The Medal of Honor Citation read as follows:

For service as set forth in the following CITATION

For outstanding heroism of and beyond the call of duty as Executive Officer of a Marine Squadron at Guadalcanal, Solomon Islands. Engaged in almost daily combat with the enemy from October 9 to November 19, 1942 Captain Foss shot down 23 Japanese planes and damaged others so severely that their destruction was extremely probable. In addition, during this period he led a large number of escort missions, skillfully covering reconnaissance, bombing, and photographic planes as well as surface craft. On January 15, 1943, he added three more enemy planes to his already brilliant successes for a record of aerial combat achievement unsurpassed in this war. Boldly searching out an approaching enemy force on January 25, Captain Foss lead his eight F4F Marine planes and four Army P-38's into action and, undaunted by tremendously superior numbers, intercepted and struck with such force that four Japanese fighters were shot down and the bombers were turned back without releasing a single bomb. His remarkable flying skill, inspiring leadership and indomitable fighting spirit were distinctive factors in the defense of strategic American positions on Guadalcanal.

Following the war Joe Foss had excellent name recognition. He assisted in the organization of the South Dakota Air National Guard. He served as a Lieutenant Colonel, Commander of the Guard's 175th Fighter Interceptor Squadron. Now a Colonel, during the war in Korea he was recalled to active duty by the U.S. Air Force where he served as the Director of Operations & Training for the Central Air Defense Command.

Foss then entered politics and was elected to two terms in the South Dakota Legislature. In 1955 he then ran for, and was elected as Governor of South Dakota. In 1958 he ran for a seat in the U.S. House of Representatives but was defeated by George McGovern. In 1958 Foss accepted the position of Commissioner of the American Football League and held that office until 1966, two months before the NFL agreed to merge with the AFL. Foss also hosted the "American Sportsman" television show from 1964 to 1967, as well as "The Outdoorsman", from 1967 to 1974. In 1988 Foss was elected President of the National Rifle Association and held that position until 1990. While in that capacity he appeared on the cover of "Time Magazine" wearing a Stetson hat and holding a revolver. Your scribe had the privilege of meeting the famous Marine Ace at the Rifle Association annual gun show in 1989.

At the Phoenix Sky Harbor International Airport on 11 January 2002, Joe Foss, now in his late 80's was on his way to make a speech at the U.S. Military Academy, West Point. Here he experienced new fame. He was stopped by security because he was carrying his Medal of Honor, the star had "sharp" pointed edges, a key chain with a clearly marked dummy cartridge and a small knife having a Medal of Honor Star on it. No one recognized the significance of the Highest ranking National award for combat heroism so his departure was delayed. That delay was later used as an example of widespread abuse of passenger's by airport security.

Foss was either the coauthor or was the subject of or included in at least four books. One of which was written by his wife, Donna Wild Foss titled "A proud American."

Joe Foss, a homegrown American Hero passed on at age 89 to his final reward, three months after a severe stroke on 1 January 2003. He had lived a full life, experienced success in his many efforts especially when he served his nation with honor and distinction. He was laid to rest in our nations final home for hero's, The Arlington National Cemetery 21 January 2003 with full Military Honors.

MAJOR GREGORY "PAPPY" BOYINGTON
C.O. VMF 214, Black Sheep Squadron

Probably one of the best remembered, most notorious, Naval Aviator in U.S. Marine Corps History was born in St. Maries, Idaho on 4 December 1912. His early life was tough, raised in a broken home dominated by an alcoholic stepfather whom he thought was his real father until the day he joined the Marine Corps. It's possible his upbringing may have impacted his future life style and fighting ability.

In High School he trained as a wrestler and continued in the sport after enrolling at the University of Washington in 1930. On graduation in 1934 as an aeronautical engineer he worked for Boeing Aircraft for a year then enlisted in the Marine Corps. Upon completion of training Greg qualified for Flight training and was issued orders to NAS Pensacola in January 1936. During flight training his use of alcohol and fighting gained him a Marine Corps reputation as a well liked, hard drinking, brawling, individual that was slowing his progress toward earning his wings. However, he finally completed the course in March 1937 and he became Naval Aviator #5160.

Stationed with VMF-1 he began flying Boeing F4B-4 biplanes but in March 1938 the squadron pilots were happy when they received delivery of the new pot-bellied Grumman biplane fighters, the F3F-2 which were fast and rugged, and equipped with manually retractable landing gear. During this period he also completed the Corps Basic Training ground-pounder course in Philadelphia.

By this time it seemed that everything he did on the ground disturbed his superiors who issued him poor official performance ratings. As for flying, it was an entirely different story; Greg had become an excellent seasoned pilot.

Concurrently, the U.S. Government was anxious to assist the Chinese government against the Japanese invasion. Through the Central Aircraft Manufacturing Corporation (CAMCO) Pilots and Aircraft were being provided to the Chinese Government for use by the Flying Tigers.

It appeared to everyone that volunteering for service in China would solve most of Greg's personal problems. He signed up and resigned from the Marine Corps with their approval. Normally these agreements included return to active military duty on return to the states. However, in Greg's case they were glad to get rid of both him and his problems. His file recommended he not be recommissioned.

During his tour with the Flying Tigers Boyington claimed he destroyed six Japanese aircraft. This would have made him the first American Ace of the war. However, there was a conflict with the loosely kept Flying Tiger records which stated he had been paid for only two destroyed in the air the rest were destroyed on the ground. He, like he did with many others commanders, clashed with Flying Tigers Commander Claire Chennault. Quitting the AVG in April 1942, Chennault issued him a dishonorable discharge and returned him to the U.S. For his entire life he continued claiming those six kills. The Marine Corps eventually credited him with those victories.

Despite his spotty pre-war reputation the war put him back in the Marine Corps where he was flying the famous F4U Corsair. Boyington, if nothing else, was a fighter. He was relentlessly aggressive which was exactly what was necessary as a fighter pilot. At first, he completed a full tour in the Solomon's without once seeing a single Japanese airplane.

When Major Pace, the C. O. of VMF 214 was killed in action, Greg approached Group Commander Lt.Col. Sanderson and submitted a request to reorganize VMF-214. Sanderson who had taken a liking to Boyington consented. Greg searched out pilot pools, unassigned aviators and a group of older pilots. VMF-214 on 4 September was recommissioned with a total of 45 aviators of which almost half had combat experience. At age 30 Greg was in the middle of his pilot's age bracket but somewhere along the line they began calling their C.O. "Pappy."

Greg's pilots began to be called the "Black Sheep" but it was not for the usual reasons. None of the personnel had been, or were up on charges. The Squadron arrived in Munda in mid September. Their first sortie was a bomber escort mission to Ballale where they ran into about thirty Japanese fighters one of which crossed directly in front of Boyington. He added power, caught up and sent him spinning down in flames toward the water. In the next several minutes he destroyed four more to become an Ace in a day. The remaining Black Sheep pilot's knocked down six more Zekes plus eight probables. Only one 214 pilot failed to return. In the first month of operation the Black Sheep claimed a total of 47 confirmed victories.

The Black Sheep, on returning to Vella Lavella for their third and final tour, they found that massive joint fighter attacks would tend to keep the enemy grounded. They then revised their tactics by the appearance of a smaller group of not more than 48 while their sweep group were holding back at altitude. Two days before Christmas ninety-two Allied fighters attacked Rabaul half of whom were escorting bombers for the purpose of drawing up the Zekes. About 40 Zekes were still airborne when the 48 sweep aircraft arrived. Thirty of the enemy aircraft were claimed destroyed. VMF214 claimed twelve, four of which fell in front of Pappy's guns bringing his wartime victories to 23. On the 27th of December Greg downed his 24th enemy aircraft.

By now Boyington was only one shy of breaking Joe Foss's record of 25 and only two shy of setting a new record. VMF 214's tour would be over in mid January, which meant he had only a few days to accomplish it. Only he was aware of how tired he really was. He was having a tough time staying awake while airborne. On the next day, 3 January Greg lead the sweep to Rabaul. Sixty enemy aircraft were encountered with an altitude advantage. The Corsair's attacked. VMF-214 saw Boyington flame a Zeke to tie Foss's record score but when they returned

Boyington and his wing man were missing. No one knew if he was still alive until after the war.

In reality, Boyington and Ashmun dove on a lower formation pursued by two Zekes. Each pilot shot a Zekes off either's tail. Ashmun's nosed down streaming smoke. Trying to protect Ashmun, Boyington shot down another Zeke just as the smoking Corsair struck the water. Racing away at low altitude Greg's plane was hit again and caught fire. He rolled the aircraft over and dropped from the cockpit. Luckily the chute opened before he hit the water. The enemy aircraft continued to strafe him until they ran out of ammo. Once they flew off he inflated his life raft. Shortly before dark a Japanese submarine picked him up.

The Japanese never reported him as a POW. Three months after his disappearance, he was "Posthumously" awarded the Medal of Honor. After the war he surprised the Corps by emerging from a Prison of War Camp and returned home to collect his rewards. At the time he was allowed to claim his last two victories even though there was no one to confirm them. Boyington was therefore declared the top Marine Fighter Pilot with a total of twenty-eight victories. In 1988 "Pappy" passed over to the other side to again join his former Squadron mates.

CDR. DAVID McCAMPBELL, U.S. NAVY MEDAL OF HONOR

The U.S. Navy's World War II Ace of Ace's was born 1 January 1910 and raised in Bessemer, Alabama. In reality young Dave's Naval career almost ended before it began. Depression funding problems forced the government to issue him an official discharge along with his Naval Academy Graduation Certificate. But the Navy really lucked out in June 1934 when he was recalled back to active duty and finely commissioned him as an Ensign. His first tour of duty assignment was aboard the USS Portland as their Gunnery Officer. After three years of cruiser duty he qualified for flight training and reported to flight training in Pensacola, Florida. In 1937, just one year later, he graduated and was designated a Naval Aviator.

He then received orders to fighter Squadron 4 aboard the USS Ranger CV-4 where he served for two years. He then received orders to report to the USS Wasp, which was his home until she was torpedoed and sunk by a Japanese submarine on 15 September 1942. He was ordered back to the states to assist in establishing a new Squadron for Air Group 15, which was known as the "Fabled Fifteen" aboard the USS Essex CV-8. His Squadron VF-15 was one of the first squadrons to receive the new Grumman fighter the F6F "Hellcat".

From February 1943 through early 1944 the Essex was part of a Task Force steaming westward making combat history as they battled through the Japanese controlled island chain. In February 1944 at the tender age of thirty-four he was promoted from Squadron Leader to "CAG', Commander Air Group 15. He now commanded all the combat squadrons aboard the Essex. His fighter, bomber, and torpedo aircraft in a seven month tour exceeded 20,000 airborne operating hours, shot down 318 aircraft, destroyed 348 on the ground and sank 294,000 tons of enemy vessels, and damaged or sank a possible half million more. The major combat vessels destroyed, included the Japanese Battleship *Musashi*, three aircraft carriers and a heavy Cruiser.

As to Dave McCampbells personal efforts on 11 June flying near Saipan he spotted a lone Zero break out of cloud cover. Executing a fast turn toward the enemy aircrafts flight path and fired three quick bursts from his .50 Caliber wing guns which resulted in the zero spinning in trailing smoke. This was the first of many to fall in front of his guns. Eight days later the Japanese launched two massive raids. Another carrier group took on one group of raiders while the Essex's CAG 15 took on the second group of sixty aircraft. McCampbell was able to flame the first aircraft and then quickly splashed a Judy, then a probable third. In just a matter of minutes he had downed five enemy aircraft and one probable.

In a follow up combat the same afternoon he scored his sixth victory of the day by downing a lone Zero. He was now detached from his own group so he headed back to the carrier. On the way back he observed two zero's at low level attacking a Navy SOC trying to rescue a downed navy pilot from the water. He immediately attacked dropping one of the Zero's at the same time another of the CAG 15 pilots had observed the action and arrived just in time to clobber the other Zero. This action had run McCampbell's seventh victory of the day and his ninth in the past 8 days of combat. By the end of September he was the first Hellcat F6F pilot to have destroyed 20 Japanese aircraft.

On 24 October McCampbell and two of his wingmen were defending attacks against his Task Force. In that particular engagement he added nine victories and two possibles to his overall total. For his effort he was recommended for the Navy Medal of Honor, which was presented to him at a later date by President Roosevelt. By the end of Air Group 15's combat tour he had topped out his total victory score at thirty-four.

In six and a half months the "Fabled Fifteen" had inflicted the highest aircraft and shipping losses against the enemy by any U.S. Navy Carrier Air Group. McCampbell became the only carrier pilot to be awarded the Medal of Honor in the last three years of the war. He was also awarded the Navy Cross, the Silver Star, the Legion of Merit and the Distinguished Flying Cross.

Following the war he continued to serve until his retirement in 1964. He quietly made his final transfer to the great beyond on 30 June 1996 after a long illness. David McCampbell was a great man, a national Hero, a credit to the United States Navy. He will never be forgotten as long as that F6F fighter, sporting 34 victory flags, hangs from the overhead of the Naval Aviation Museum in Pensacola, Florida.

GENERAL DOUGLAS MacARTHUR

(As reviewed by a forty plus year U.S. Navy Veteran)

Our future General was born into the U. S, Army 26 January 1880 at the Tower Building located at the Little Rock Arkansas Arsenal. He was the son of Captain Arthur MacArthur, Medal of Honor recipient and Mary Pinkney Harty MacArthur of Norfolk, Virginia. Douglas himself claimed the first sound he could remember was the sound of the bugle. His youthful years were typical for a child born to a career Army Officer.

During his schooling years he was considered an excellent student who quite naturedly entered West Point in 1898. He was an outstanding Cadet, graduating first in a class of 93. As a result he was awarded the title, "First Captain of the Corps of Cadets." It is assumed that this title possibly generated his taste for distinguished military titles originated

His rise through the pre-World War One era was typical. During that war he served as Chief of Staff of the 42nd Rainbow Division. By then he had been promoted to the level of Brigadier General, commanding the 64th Infantry Brigade. Prior to the wars end he had been promoted to Division Commander. One thing for sure, his bravery and willingness to stick his neck out, especially where it might best be noticed. He received a goodly number on medals including two Purple Hearts. As I understand it he made a special trip to the front to get wounded! General Menoher once claimed that "Doug" was the best fighting man in the Army. That had to be a real ego builder for him!

Skipping rapidly through the slow years to the late 30's, he finished his duty tour as Army Chief of Staff. His criticism of the Roosevelt Administration's policy toward a strong military, pacifism and other military problems led him to the decision to retire to accept Philippine President Quezon's offer to establish and train a Philippine Army, On reviewing the offer he suddenly changed his mind on retirement.

He decided to remain on active duty as a Major General. Then, with President Roosevelt's special approval he accepted the Philippine assignment. In reality, the President actually stated he was happy to get the general out of his hair. As an item of interest, the future General of the Army and eventually, President elect of the U.S, Eisenhower, had been assigned to MacArthur as his Military Assistant. Later, MacArthur stated that Eisenhower was the best clerk he ever had. Wasn't that damn decent of him?

On 7 December 1941 when the Japanese bombed Pearl Harbor, MacArthur was Allied Commander in the Philippines. He had been given an eight hour early warning message that the Japanese might attack. Plus, the Army Chief of Staff General Marshall had issued him a Direct Order to take immediate defensive action. In review, MacArthur had actually misjudging the Japanese capability and chose to ignore this order. His failure to take direct action as commanded permitted the Japanese to snatch air superiority control over the Philippines. This gave the Japanese the opportunity to destroy the Allied air defensive capability before they could even get their aircraft airborne.

Despite this grave error, that bordered on possible Dereliction of Duty, nothing was ever done to review and or investigate his failure to respond to a Direct Order Instead President Roosevelt saved the General and his family from possible capture by ordering him out of the Philippines to Australia. This was accomplished via PT Boat and B-17. There appeared to be no doubt he was thankful that the Philippines surrender didn't show up on his personal military record. What was even more ironic, on 1 April 1942 they finely awarded him the Medal of Honor. The citation read, "for gallantry and intrepidity above and beyond the call of duty in action against invading Japanese forces, and the heroic conduct of defensive and offensive operations on the Bataan Peninsula."

You will note that this scribe makes no personal comment on the presentation of this award because the expression of his thoughts might be considered a violation of some military code related to respect for your seniors!

MacArthur was probably one of our most familiar of all our military figures. That was mainly due to the methods in which he presented himself. He always worked extra hard to make himself conspicuous. He personally designed his own uniforms, which definitely made himself stand out in a uniformed crowd. He was actually very intelligent. I'm sure when a picture was snapped he always seemed to be at least one step closer to the camera than anyone else. Another example, in the photos of the President and Adm, Nimitz talking to each other, guess who is sitting or standing between them?

Further. It seems obvious to me that in his own mind he considered himself superior to any other human being on earth. In fact, he must have also considered himself his own best friend! Who else could qualify? Within the MacArthur alphabet the letter "I" had to be his favorite letter. I'm certain everyone will remember, "I shall return", after all he did repeated it often enough. He was respectfully requested by President Roosevelt to change it to read, "We shall return." However, he chose to ignore the suggestion. The word "I" in his own mind rang much clearer and brighter.

He definitely disliked anyone that considered himself his equal and despised anyone that was, or considered himself, his superior. For example most senior government high-ranking politicians, including President Roosevelt fell into this category. Despite the Presidents efforts in his favor, he really disliked the President but was smart enough to know when to respond to his direction, as well as, know when he could successfully upstage him. At one point he even planned to run against Roosevelt for president. But luckily, he withdrew when he realized he couldn't displace Tom Dewey, the Republican Candidate Dewey never made it to the presidency but still might have done the world a big favor. Please try to visualize, an egotistical person like MacArthur, with his finger on a nuclear missile button?

Now, if you have been paying attention to the previous paragraphs you will understand the reason the Pacific war failed to have a single Combat Commander. Due to the ongoing verbal confrontation between MacArthur and Admiral Earnest King, Chief of Naval Operations, which basically revolved around MacArthur's claim he naturally considered himself the best man to command the Pacific, At the same time Admiral King violently objected for two reasons, his dislike for MacArthur and the fact the Pacific war being mainly a war at sea. Therefore, it should have a Naval Commander.

As a result, the Pacific theater was divided into two sections.

The Navy's Admiral Chester Nimitz was assigned Command of the Central Pacific, which extended out to, but did not include, the Philippine Islands. While General MacArthur was assigned Supreme Commander, (always his favorite title) of the South West Pacific. His well-selected Personal Staff contained the proper number of Yes men plus the necessary number of publicity and photo personnel.

By late 1944 Both Commanders were rapidly closing in on the Japanese home islands. Despite the objection of the Navy Department and the Joint Chiefs of Staff, MacArthur convinces President Roosevelt at a joint meeting on board the USS Baltimore at Pearl Harbor 26 July 1944, MacArthur convinced the President we were morally obligated to free the people of the Philippines from the yoke of Japan. Based there on the Joint Chiefs directed the general to prepare a plan for invading Mindanao by 15 October 1944.

However Admiral Halsey's Task force had done such a fine job of clearing the south western and southern area of elements of Japanese resistance it was determined that the invasion be shifted to the Island of Layte. This effort began 21 October 1944. A day later our noble Supreme Commander boldly wadded ashore stating, "People of the Philippines "I have Returned!". Most of the Senior Military Service Commanders sighed hoping he would say "We have Returned." Now why would he have said that? We all know that really deep down he really did mean "I"!

By choice this article is ended at this point because this evaluation is part of a World War Two effort. Everyone is aware old Doug-out Doug accepted the Japanese surrender aboard the battleship USS Missouri in Tokyo Bay 2 September 1945.

"A SAILOR AND HIS SHIP"

Once upon a time long ago there was a midwestern country farm boy with a burning desire to sail the seven seas. In 1929 he departed the farm to join the U.S. Navy. Finishing boot training he received orders to report to an old four-pipe destroyer, the USS Montgomery DD 121. Now these old flush deck four pipe tin cans were notoriously hard riding vessels. Much to his shame and disgust, every time this old destroyer weighed anchor, our young farm boy immediately got the urge to toss his cookies. Usually, the roll and pitch of a vessel was something one normally got use to. However, the normal reaction didn't apply in this particular young sailors case.

Eventually, his skipper concluded he should be surveyed as unfit for sea duty. The young sailor protested because he had no desire to return to the farm. He felt that maybe a larger vessel might solve his problem. Based thereon he was given permission to search for a swap. Luckily, he was able to negotiate a swap with a sailor on the battleship USS Tennessee BB 43. Once underway he was delighted to find out he was right. All thoughts of survey faded away. Aboard the Tennessee where he gained quite a reputation representing the ship as a wrestler. In 1932 he claimed the Pacific Fleet Middleweight Championship. That year he entered the Olympic tryouts both as a wrestler and as an oarsman for the USA's racing shell. He also tried again as a wrestler in 1936 almost making the semi-finals. By 1941 he now competed as a heavyweight and again attained Fleet Championship status.

However, his sports career was concluded because he was aboard that fatal morning 7 December 1941 when the Japanese bombed Pearl Harbor. Once the ship was repaired she was put to sea going in harms way during several encounters. In 1945 off Okinawa, the Tennessee was struck by a Kamikaze causing considerable damage to the vessel. Our sailor was severely wounded in the encounter and was awarded the Purple Heart. Shortly thereafter, he received orders detaching him from the vessel he loved so well. He had served in that ship fourteen and one half years, which set some sort of endurance record.

This lifetime sailor continued to serve his country for a total of 30 years retiring as a Chief Motor Machinist. He bought a home and settled in the state of Florida. His old battleship Tennessee by now had long passed into history. When the nuclear submarine USS Tennessee USBN 734 was launched in December 1986, the U.S. Navy Department saw fit to invite the long time veteran of the old battlewagon Tennessee to participate in the event. He was both pleased and honored to be in attendance. He returned to live out his life at his Florida Home. At the ripe old age of 88 this veteran hero of two wars followed his beloved ship into history. He had been a member of the Tennessee Assn., President of the Florida Pearl Harbor Survivors Assn., The Fleet Reserve Assn. and the American Legion. He now rides high on a soft warm breeze in a following sea. You had a wonderful life Chief. Your spectacular cruise through life has now been completed.

A "NAVY" MARINE

"Pearl Harbor Bombed!" shouted the newsprint. Well, there was a patriotic marine that I know, that as a 17 year old kid who rushed down to the Marine Corps recruiting office to put his name on the dotted line. It wasn't long thereafter he was introduced to a new type of education on a Pacific tropical isle know in Marine history as Guadalcanal. He then received an additional education on 4 or 5 of those tropical paradises that the Navy Department often dropped Marines off for a few rousing beach parties. His tour lasted 42 months of swimin' and crawlin' ashore to perform such tasks as recon scouting and sniper duties to improve his marksmanship. But, he was also, extra lucky and knew how to keep his head down. When asked why he never got hit, his reply, "I crawled ashore under water because I was able to watch the bullets comin'."

On his return to the states, he was allowed a short leave and issued orders to the Monterey Language School to learn Japanese. Now this sorta training usually indicated a follow up cushy tour at the Navy's Far East Command. Then, how come, his next set of orders was to the Navy's Transportation Quartermaster's School? It may sound silly but here was a top notch combat Marine being trained to load military cargo vessels in fluent Japanese!! Upon graduation the cheese got even more binding. Orders were received to report to the USS Muliphen AKA 61.

On reporting aboard, direction was requested to the Marine quarters. What Marine quarters? What was one stalwart Marine doing in a cargo vessels Ships Company of sailors? Well at least there weren't any foxholes to dig. This was quite an adjustment for this young man. The crew soon accepted him but he ran head long into a lieutenant that made him well aware that he had no use for Marines of any type or caliber. This officer had an extremely bad habit of talking to someone closely face to face and literally spitting out orders. For this the crew had nicknamed him "Slush Pump."

This ship was assigned to an Alaskan flotilla hauling drilling equipment and prefab buildings to Point Barrow. Nothing like recreation in Alaska to recover from almost 4 years of tough tropical combat experiences. At least when he crossed the Arctic Circle he got initiated into the "Order of the Bluenoses." Except for his nemeses, "Slush Pump" the duty and friendships wasn't that bad. Three cruises to Alaska where his toughest battle was with flea infestation. So much for his combat equipment loadmaster training.

Eventually my friends luck improved when he received orders returning him to the Marine Corps duty and his knowledge of Japanese. By golly, if he didn't end up promoted to Sgt Major, and detailed as Governor of the Japanese Island of Truk! This lucky devil finally retired from the U. S Marines as a top grade Sergeant. But, remember the old adage, "Once a Marine always a Marine." This former soft-spoken Sgt Major probably owned a good hunk of the Marine Corps League as well as the Fleet Reserve Assn. He might even have his Sergeant strips sewed on his undershirts.

Of course this may be just an opinion of an ole Navy CPO shipmate. However, the last I heard this youthful war hero's memory has been dulled by the wear and tear of 80 some remarkable years. Any warrior that hit five beaches under fire and lived surely had God by his side. Sgt Major Leroy Edwards, U.S. Marine Corps (Retired) resides in an Assisted Living Quarters in Tampa, Florida. A Good friend and former shipmate!

SALT WATER COURAGE

For a guy that spent his life, with the exception of the last ten or eleven years, within spitting distance of salt water, the Navy sure got me more farm boys and westerners for shipmates that I've been able to keep count of. Again I would like to tell you about a quiet, soft spoken kid who was a self made hero and a credit to his country

It was the Mid 30's and if you were around at the time, this nation was experiencing a deep depression. A young man from the mid-west had been raised in a poor, but loving, family. At the tender age of 18, poorly educated and unable to find work, he joined the Navy. He hoped his departure from home would remove some of the pressure from his Mom and Dad. He wasn't very happy about his decision when he reported to boot training in San Diego but he figured it was the best thing he could do to help support his family. At first his pay was only $21.00 a month but I'm certain that most of that went home because to my knowledge he never went on liberty!

He found the conditions of having to live and work in close proximity with large numbers of individuals both strange and unsettling. Further, having spent his lifetime walking to get wherever he wanted to go, he really hated marching. To his few new friends, he exclaimed, "If I wanted to march and play with guns, I would have joined the Army or Marine Corps." It seems his Navy recruiter assured him that if he didn't want to march or carry a rifle, he should join the Navy. It was explained, "Aboard ship there was little room to march and only the ships carried guns."

Eventually he began to blend in as he became more accustom to the seaman's style of living. Each month a small amount of his monthly pay was sent home to aid his folks. He was determined to learn as much as possible during his service because it would aid him in finding work when mustered out at the end of his four year enlistment. However, that thought faded away as he raced for cover at Pearl on 7 December 1941. The nation was now at war. By early 1944 this man had served bravely advancing to Boatswain's Mate 2nd Class. He was now temporally attached to a troop transport vessel approaching in convoy toward a Japanese held island position.

During the first day of the invasion, he found himself in charge of a landing craft full of marines headed into harms way. Moving in with the first wave of boats he nervously manned a machine gun in the bow of the landing craft. By the end of the day, operating that gun, and rescuing wounded marines from the water and carrying them to safety had earned him a Bronze Star. It was after his return to the states for shore duty that I got to know him.

By wars end he had earned the rating of Chief Petty Officer. After considerable thought, and his desire to marry he determined to remain with the Navy as a career. After two wars and 25 years of outstanding service, he finally chose retirement as a Chief Warrant Officer 2. He and his small family finally settled down in the San Diego area. A few short years later, like many of his comrades in arms, this acknowledged military hero passed quietly into history.

CHRISTMAS IN MARCH?

We had been marooned in the beautiful Newfoundland wasteland for almost a year defending the peat bogs surrounding the Naval Air Station, Argentia. During that period we had assembled enough weapons to put a Hell of a big dent in German armor. However, we had been limited to chasing a few enemy submarines and sinking a couple. The only other joy (?) we had was one 72-hour pass to St. Johns. That was about as much fun as going to the downtown Barber Shop on Saturday night to watch haircuts.

The calendar was beginning to sneak up on what we all use to refer to as Christmas. Everyone was trying to shift to a festive spirit and be in a good mood. Some one even found a pine tree, cut it down and dragged it through the snow to the barracks. We sort of suspected he stole it out of some native "Newfies" yard.

Concurrently our noble President, Mr. Roosevelt, who on one of his many fireside chats, made a bold, broad statement that went something like this,

"MY fellow citizens, all our boys serving overseas this Christmas, whether it be in a foxhole in Europe, the steaming jungles of the South Pacific, or serving in the frozen north, will this year be enjoying a typical Christmas Dinner of Turkey and all the fixin's."

Now everyone in his right mind realized that this was a rather typical, bold, morale-building, good ole boy, U.S.A. promise that might be difficult to accomplish. Why even the German or Japanese high command listening in might even think of mounting an equally bold frontal attack for no other purpose than to screw up that promised dinner. Either that, or share in the goodies.

However, the sterling defenders of Argentia were not the least bit worried. No thought was ever given to the fact that some mean spirited German Sub Skipper out there had other ideas. I guess he felt that his Christmas joy was already in the toilet and that his misery should have lots of company. Based thereon he made a bold attack on the convoy making its way to Argentia with our Turkey and all the fixin's.

That lousy German S.O.B. slipped a pair of torpedoes Hell bent for election passed one of those swift destroyers straight into that supply vessel carrying our turkey an fixin's and Pabst Blue Ribbon Beer. The defending tin cans depth charged all over the north Atlantis trying to sink the no good bastardly submarine. However, the only thing we were certain of, was those damn fishes sure had one heck of a better Christmas dinner than we did.

On Christmas Day we had canned Spam powdered potatoes, dried black-eyed peas, and canned prunes for the President's promised delights. In fact, we ate a lot of Spam, Vienna Sausages, and various kinds of powdered milk, potatoes and various canned junk like Okra before the next supply vessel arrived.

I must admit that the President eventually made it right because Christmas dinner was finally served in late February or early March. Like everyone always said, "Better Late than Never."

FIRE IN THE HOLE!

At war almost 70 years ago, it became necessary that the government build and maintain quite a number of advanced support bases in unusual out of the way places. The reason I enjoy writing about these stink holes is because of the poor unfortunates that were ordered to man these outlandish bases actually thought they deserved some form of special recognition for the services they performed. In their minds, they definitely had something to complain about. Despite the disappointment, and grumbling they faithfully served their country the best way they knew how.

However, deep down they felt as though they were possibly missing out on the good recognition and all of those spiffy hero medals with the pretty colored ribbons. Therefore, you might at least feel a little bit sorry for them as you read, and enjoy, the misery they felt they had to live through. Also, the military, if nothing else might have issued some form of a thank you medal for faithful service in a lousy back breaking supply dump! They did acknowledge their only salvation was that nobody was taking pot shots at them!

In this particular place, which for good reason shall go nameless, while going along with their usual every day problems, one day they had the misfortune of having an Army B-17 make an emergency belly landing on their only runway. Those Army flyboys did an excellent job of tearing up their aircraft's belly, bomb bay doors, as well as, damaging the outer shell of several pieces of live ordnance they were carrying on board. Those chicken army fly boys stated those depth charges were really Navy property and therefore as Army throttle pushers they had no idea how to handle the situation. Honestly, they did considered themselves extra lucky to have come out of the crash safely

Luckily, this facility had just one 1st Class Aviation ordnanceman on board. With the help of a couple of civilian contractors, and their power hoist we were able to rig up an "A" frame so the contractors hoist was able to raise the aircraft to access the damage. On observation things looked pretty badly torn up. The belly flopper destroyed the bomb bay doors and tore holes in a couple of the depth charges in the bomb bay. They were damn lucky they didn't have a fire or an explosion during the exceptionally bad landing.

The navy bomb jockey safely removed the pistols and extenders from the depth charges. This made the damaged weapons safer to handle and allowed the release of the bomb shackles to permit dropping the charges on to skids. They were then safely removed from under the aircraft. Because of the damage to a couple the charges, the follow up discussion he had with a couple of Army demolition guys, who had been contacted for safety sake, three ordnance specialists agreed we should temporarily bury the charges. One of the contractor's personnel bulldozed a deep trench in a safe area well outside of the runway and all traffic areas. With the help of the contractors crane the damaged charges were lowered side by side in the deep hole.

The recommendation of our ordnance man and the Army demo guys, three actual weapons professionals, they considered it prudent to temporarily bury the charges in that hole, report same and request aid from higher authority. They explained to the officers that the charges were loaded with Torpex, which was similar to TNT but more powerful. Our Recommendation was ignored by our local "higher authority" who overruled them. In a discussion between the senior officer present and a couple of other officers, they concluded it was safer, and would close out the problem, by destroying the damaged weapons.

Again the army demolition personnel and our own Gun Cocker indicated they didn't agree that this decision was the proper solution, however, when requested, the army guys reluctantly provided the necessary material to perform the task. The plastic explosive material was rigged to the damaged weapons and the wiring strung out a considerable distance to a detonator. Again the Gun Cocker tried to explain that we were not dealing with ordinary TNT, it was Torpex, a new type of explosive. But, that fell on deaf ears. It was obvious that nobody but the armament people had ever heard of Torpex before.

The entire surrounding area was evacuated, checked, and double and triple checked, to make sure everyone was clear. Plus our ordnance expert had dug himself something similar to a GI foxhole to make the shot from. The Senior Officer, who was standing up in his jeep, asked if everything was ready. "As soon as the wires are hooked up to the detonator Sir" was the response. "OK, let's do it," the officer ordered." As a final cautious, the Petty Officer said, "Sir, Don't you think you should get down here with me?" "No, he stated, I want to watch."

"Fire in the Hole!" he yelled. Immediately the handle on the detonator was twisted. There was a slight silent pause, followed by the most ungodly roar of ripple fire ever heard before, or since! It was immediately followed by a concussion shock wave that blew the Senior Officer out of his jeep! The shock wave also busted some windows in the barracks area a good distance away. Other Military personnel totally unaware of what was in process were scared silly, (really a better word), wondering what the hell happened. We also heard later that people in the little town off the base were also scared thinking we had been attacked.

Our "detonator" was rolling around in his foxhole laughing his fool head off. Despite the fact his ears rang like church bells for over a week, he and the two Army guys shook hands with big smiles on their faces. This event was probably the most memorable day of his tour in this God forsaken hellhole. For years it has been remembered as a laughable memory of the distant past. There has been serious doubt if this event was ever officially reported. But if it was, the odds are in favor of the official story submitted being slightly different than the one reported herein.

"A NEAR MISS!"

An individual with whom I'm quite familiar had just been assigned a half set of Flight Orders for the month. He was exceptionally happy because as a Combat Aircrew Man, a half set of flight skins was worth about 20 bucks extra on payday. Not much in the order of a fortune, but certainly more acceptable than straight pay.

This young mans work station was in the weapons assembly area where aerial bombs and other weapons assembly was conducted under the direction of a newly assigned "pin stripped" Warrant Gunner. It was the Warrant Officers first duty assignment since his promotion from Chief to Warrant. Since reporting aboard, he and our young friend, a 2nd class Petty Officer had developed a pretty good working relationship since his arrival.

To insure he would be assigned a flight to qualify for payment, he dropped by the Operations Office in the hanger to insure his name was placed on the flight schedule. His information and phone number was recorded so he could be contacted and informed the flight assignment and when to arrive for aircraft pre-flight prior to take off. Just a few days later the call was received telling him to report to the hanger with flight gear. The Warrant Gunner hadn't arrived at the shop as yet, so the Petty Officer left him a note telling him where he was going.

Arriving at the hanger, our friend assisted the aircrew loading the depth charges and gun ammunition. The crew was preparing for about a 4 to 5 hour anti-submarine sweep. These flights were pretty much considered milk runs due to the lack of formal contacts. Once loaded they boarded the aircraft and conducted the normal pre-flight check and determined the mission aircraft was a go. The pilot ordered the chocks pulled and our aircraft began to taxi out toward the runway. Suddenly, the pilot throttled back the engines to idle and brought the plane to a halt. On opening the hatch the Warrant Gunner stated he would have to remove his Petty Officer due to an urgent work assignment.

The Petty Officer was a little disappointed that he missed the chance of getting in his required flight time. However, the Gunner had an excellent excuse for removing him from the flight. As a collateral duty we were responsible for providing ordnance requirements such as depth charges, 5-inch projectiles, torpedoes, etc. for incoming vessels. One of our destroyers had returned from a short run at sea where they had accidentally expended one of their torpedoes and were returning for a replacement.

A couple of hours later they were finishing up work on the tin fish and preparing it for delivery to the destroyer when they received a phone call. It seems the Gunner was requested to report to the hanger. In a short while he returned to the Ordnance Shop. He was really excited. "You are not going to believe this. It seems Operations assumed you were still on the plane I removed you from. They wanted to advise me of the possibility you might be missing." It seems the aircraft had transmitted a message they were about to make an attack run on a partially surfaced submarine when their radio went dead.

A search aircraft had just departed to make a visual look see and a destroyer in the area was also making a surface search. Whatever, might have happened was a mystery. No remains from the lost aircraft nor were any of the crew members ever found! You can be assured that the young Petty Officer was forever ready to kiss the ground that the "pin Striped" Gunner walked on.

This is a perfect example of several near misses reported during World War II.

"THE LONG, LONG, ROAD"

Often while daydreaming, I let my thoughts drift back to the "OLD" days thinking about a method of providing a totally different type of World War II war story. The following came to mind!

Occasionally, these memory's, drift back a set of Navy travel orders dated March 1943 almost 69 years ago. That document directed my return to the United States and to a new Duty station, the Naval Air Technical Training Center (NATTC) Pensacola, FL. Having just completed six years of sea duty and almost continuous overseas deployment, we, (The wife and I) were extremely happy of being ordered to shore duty and finally being reunited together. The basic orders authorized travel by personal vehicle. By the time I arrived "home," the wife had our 42' Buick serviced and we were almost ready to roll.

Now if you're old enough, I want you to think back to war time USA in the spring of '43. To begin this story, remember the guy that designed the interstate highway system had not been born yet. In those days the highways consisted mainly of two lane black top roads that wandered back and forth from town, to city, and village across the countryside. They also sported unbelievable high speed limits in towns of 15 to 25 MPH and 35 to 55 MPH World War II long distance speed limit on the open highway.

You were also guaranteed a trip straight through the downtown main street of each city and town with red lights or stop signs and 15 to 25 MPH signs on every corner. I assure you, it was time to pay attention. This was how each community attempted to siphon off a little outside revenue from every stranger passing through. Despite the fact we had been in a state of war for well over two years, crippled by rationing and living with poor road conditions, it was really amazing that in just a few days anyone could still travel from Newport, R.I. to Pensacola, Fla. by an almost direct route. However, a long trip was measured in days rather than in hours of driving time.

I reported to the Naval Base at Melville, R.I. to arrange for packaging and transfer of our personal effects and to pick up government gasoline authorizations required to make the trip. We were issued 10 government gasoline purchase certificates worth 10 gallons each. A few days later our furniture was on its way and so were we. Good old route US 1 would take us to Washington, D.C. where we would make a connection with US 29 that, believe it or not, ran all the way to Pensacola, Florida.

At least the drive would provide us a bird's eye view of the good old U S of A. For example, we battled the 100 plus traffic lights, all red, between Connecticut and Manhattan's famous Holland Tunnel into New Jersey. On reaching the New Jersey Pulaski Skyway, we enjoyed the only 2-lane one-way concrete section we recalled on the entire trip. We struggled our way south on what one day would be the famous Jersey Turnpike finally hitting our nations capital. However, all we saw of the National Capital was the decrepit back streets whose road signs lead us directly to US 29 and out of the District. We saw absolutely none of the wonders of government that made Washington D.C. famous.

Another thing that hadn't been designed yet, was the national hotel, motel and restaurant system. Most motels were little cracker boxes on the outside of the town. Furthermore, you had to be extra careful when you pulled in to register because many of these units were "hot pillow joints" that rented by the hour, not the night.

On the open road places to chow down were non-existent. In defense of hunger it was best if you had emergency rations. But even here you had to be careful because another thing that had not yet been invented was the insulated cooler. Our best bet for eating was programed ahead to stop for food in one of the smaller towns. These small family-run eating-places actually served outstanding inexpensive meals.

In South Carolina one morning I had my first run in with southern Grits. When the young lady served my breakfast a white mess that looked like cream of wheat, (which for me held the lowest spot on my food chain), was nestled between my eggs and the bacon. I asked, "What is this?" The waitress responded, proudly, "Young fellow, that there is grits, it comes free with the meal." Politely, I asked, "Could you please remove it? I don't particularly care for the looks of it." She picked up the plate with a very pretty smile stating, "I guess you must be one of those Damn Yankees I heard about." Actually, we both had a good laugh.

The Buick's gas tank held 18 gallons of fuel so we had to keep track of our mileage to estimate when we could procure gas in 10-gallon increments. Everything ran rather smoothly until we got deep in rural areas where people had never seen nor heard of these fairly large U.S. government gasoline chits before. Some stations made calls to determine if they were legal. One man actually refused to take the chit but was willing to sell us the gas if I forked over double the gallon sale price. I paid him the four dollars he demanded and he pumped the gas. Plus it left me an extra ticket for another 10 gallons of gas. A little later we got a real kick out of one skeptical older station owner. He was reluctant to take the chit, but only accepted it because he couldn't figure how to get the gas back out of my tank. As we drove away, he stated, "If I can't cash this, I'm going to frame it and hang it on my wall. It will remind me that during WW II a young sailor, hundreds of miles from the water, cheated me out of 10 gallons of gas."

Except from realizing we still lived in a very primitive nation the trip was rather uneventful except for passing through a city in South Carolina who will remain nameless. As I entered the city limits on the main road a real jerk came flying out of a side street directly in front of me. I slammed on the brakes but still put a ding in his left rear fender the size of a baseball. He immediately pulled over to the side, jumped out and started yelling for the cops.

In nothing flat, we were in front of a judge. I knew I had it when the judge turned to the jerk and stated, "Morning George just explained what happened." He listened to George's story then turned to me, "Well, sailor I know George here but I don't know you. When strangers come racein' through our little town, and do damage, your just gonna' have to pay the piper." When I tried to explain, I was politely told he wasn't interested.

Thinking fast, I told the Judge, "Your Honor, I'm traveling on confidential government orders with a minimum of funds. If it's your intention to fine or hold me, I wish to immediately telephone the Navy Department, Bureau of Navigation in Washington. D.C." That old Judge just sat there and continued to stare at me in total silence. After a specially long pause, and some obvious thought, he stated, "That wont be necessary sailor. Advice us where you will be stationed and we will send you a bill." When released it took us less than 10 minutes to get the hell out of that town.

On my arrival in Pensacola I reported the incident to the stations Legal Office. When the bill arrived I turned it over to them. Nothing was ever heard about it.

My, how "long distance travel" has changed in the past 69 plus years!!!!

"SCHOOL TEACHER"

Finally after a total of six years at sea and on overseas deployment this Aviation Ordnanceman 1st Class had received orders returning him to the states for duty. Upon reporting aboard NAS Pensacola, Fl, the assignment was to the Naval Air Technical Training Center (NATTC). As a qualified Combat Aircrewman, plus working up to a qualified 1st Class Petty Officer in the Ordnance field, my position, with luck would normally have been an intermediate supervisor. However, your writer was selected for a position with the Aerial Gunnery Ground School as an instructor. This was certainly a switch. Converting an aerial gunner to a schoolteacher? Well, I was well trained in ordnance and gunnery but being suddenly surrounded with aerial turrets made me wonder because at the moment my knowledge was limited to only one.

My assignment was in the Aerial Gun Turret Division. As previously mentioned the only aerial gun turret I had ever seen or had any contact with was the British turret mounted in the PBO-1 Lockheed Hudson's, that had been built for the Limeys and swapped from them to equip VP-82 the north Atlantic Anti-Sub Squadron. None of which, by the way, would be covered in our navy curriculum.

The good part of this, the division was top heavy with five 1st Class Petty Officers and all the remaining personnel were 2nd Class and below. The objective of the program was to train the students to be expert turret gunners, or the added qualification of Combat Air Crewman, not necessarily turret mechanics. This would give our personnel, (I wasn't the only novice in this business), time to learn more about the turret electrical and hydraulic drive systems. These mobile gun platforms were new to the air gunnery business and most of us were in the process of learning while we were teaching; it was obvious from the programs size and the expected number of students. We were well aware that these turrets would be getting more extensive use in the training cycle than in operational squadrons. Therefore, we had to be ready to repair, as well as, just operate and maintain this equipment.

The turrets were mobile, specially mounted on trucks and trailers for easy transport to and from the ranges. A Briggs & Stratton auxiliary generator provided each individual turret operational power. Two firing ranges had been constructed at the Navy's Gulf Beach gunnery range. Triangular shaped narrow gauge railroad tracks had been laid for remote target tow cars powered by a V-8 Ford engine. This car could tow sleeve targets at speeds in excess of 60 miles per hour.

Students would man their turrets, load their guns and prepare for firing under the sharp eye of their instructor. Their ammo tips had been dipped in colored paint to identify the number of hits on the sleeve by each student. Records indicated that each turret gun fired well over a 1000 rounds each day! Between the heat generated by the guns and the sun, barrel life of those 50's was rather short.

Because of the high usage we began to keep written records of turret hours and gun usage and parts failures. Unknowingly we had begun the first studies of mean time between failures on ordnance equipment. It left no doubt that old man Browning had designed very reliable 30 and 50 caliber automatic weapons. The high usage also showed that our turrets equipment far exceeded its original design specifications.

We were proud to state that some of our top pilots and aircrew gunners passed through our aerial gunnery school before the end of WW II. As a final statement, many of our top gunnery instructors were well qualified to open power mower businesses after the war because of their experience with Briggs & Stratton engine repair!

NAVY BLUE JOINS THE
ARMY AIR CORPS

October 1943, it was a happy day when advised I had been selected for advancement to Chief Petty Officer and at first, it was assumed I would be frocked in January. Everyone, including myself, was amazed that the advancement to top enlisted man was accomplished in just six years. Normally, it took about sixteen years but World War II, Tojo, Yamamoto and the rapid advancements in combat air power shortened the timetable. At the tender age of 25 was it possible for me to be the youngest, or one of the youngest Chiefs in the US Navy?

However, a few days later, a phone call was received to report to the Administrative Office. On arrival, there was another surprise. I was told of being selected to attend the U.S, Army Air Corps Aircraft Turret School at the Briggs Manufacturing Corp. in Detroit, Michigan. Still another surprise, they stated the billet was for an E-7, therefore, the following day I was to be sworn in as a CPO. Surprise #4, was direction to report to disbursing, draw the $200.00 clothing allowance and take the rest of the day off and procure enough proper clothing to last for the next three months.

Coincidently, this was all happening on our third wedding anniversary, which made the promotion date of 23 October 1943 to Chief Petty Officer, one unbelievable fine anniversary present. In a few short days the small draft to Briggs boarded the train in Pensacola for an overnight trip to Detroit, Michigan.

Upon the Detroit arrival we reported to the senior Army Officer in charge, a Major. His first comment on meeting us uncovered was "Didn't any of you Navy people ever learn to salute senior officers?" He never got use to us not saluting him as we passed in a corridor. He finally did comment one day, "The least you sailors could do was follow our rules while you are under our roof. Actually, the Major was a nice guy, so we made a pact. One day as he was passing in the corridor, a group of us saluted him and said "Good Morning Sir." He damn near broke his neck trying to respond to the unexpected salute. The joke was taken real well and he really appreciated our gesture.

Another neat deal was for berthing. Instead of moving us in with the Army personnel, The Navy Department had contracted for the whole first floor, less the lobby, of a small hotel diagonally across the city park from Briggs. Another Chief and I were billeted into a large double room with a bath. We both had to admit this was the best quarters either of us had since we first enlisted.

This was a wildly popular school. People from all the aviation services were fighting to get selected to attend. Naturally, you would think it was because of the schools outstanding educational quality but that had nothing to do with it at all. The real reason was because of the fantastic chow! The food here was, outstanding even gourmet. When Briggs received the government school contract they hired the top chef in Detroit to manage feeding the troops. If the memory is still good, I believe he was originally from the famous Book Cadillac Hotel. Every meal he served was outstanding.

However, the instruction courses were really tough. In the opening first two weeks of study, the instructor advised we had only ten days to digest a two year course in Electricity and Hydraulics. This was rapidly followed by a self computing sights study and a comprehensive rundown of all of the in service nose, tail, upper deck, lower ball and waist turrets as well as powered waist gun systems both electric and hydraulic. How we were doing was checked by written tests every morning.

However, each day the chow rated double thumbs up rating! Plus it was whispered about that some of the guys that were dating would leave their young lady at the corner cocktail lounge and would return to eat for fear of missing a good meal. Please tell me how you possibly explain that to a date? There were a lot of good perks besides good meals when every day was like Thanksgiving. The city of Detroit was an open City for the man in uniform. All public transportation was free and you could ride in a cab for half fair. Briggs owned the football Stadium where there were a group of free seats in the stadium for guys going to the school. Buying a drink at a bar was an impossibility. Before you could sit down there would be at least a half dozen or more in front of you.

This school was also the place where I first met former CPO John Finn, Pearl Harbor Medal of Honor recipient. He had since been promoted to LT. and had arrived in town to visit the B-24 plant as well as attending a War Bond reception, or both. He was a great guy, a typical Navy Chief who had responded automatically in a combat situation, as any trained military person should. He was very modest for a decorated combat veteran with a Medal of Honor that even the highest-ranking Admiral or General would salute.

It's difficult to explain but prior to graduation a special trip was made to the plant where they were building the B-24's to view the installation and testing of the turrets. Shortly thereafter, in a matter of weeks, we found ourselves back on the train headed south for Pensacola; I was lucky to be going back with an honor graduation card in hand. My tour with the U.S. Army Air Force was complete. The only thing I ever missed was the gourmet chow. The one missed the most was the wife that had to remain in Florida for the weeks spent in Detroit.

The only thing that ever bothered me as well as the 20 some other ACOM's was to have their rating changed to ACOMT meaning Aviation Chief Ordnanceman, Turrets. Almost everyone else in the Navy and the entire world thought the T stood for Temporary. Other people, especially other Chiefs, bugged us about it. It was the happiest day of my life when that damn T was eventually removed from our rating designator because of its being misinterpreted.

PROTECTING THE CHICKENS FROM THE WOLVES

By the middle of 1943 our Pensacola, FL naval aerial gunnery school had becoming an outstanding training ground for development of future Combat Aircrew gunners for our fighting aircraft. The depth of training ran all the way from teaching the .30 and .50 Caliber Browning machine guns to the depth of efforts required for the aerial turret protection of the four engine Navy PB4Y-2 knock-off of the Army Air Forces B-24.

Our original homemade training devices were rapidly disappearing from the classrooms. They were being rapidly replaced by operational turret systems mounted in mobile stands and commercially designed fully operational electrical and hydraulic flat board training aids. Many of these contractor designed training aids were replacements for many of our homegrown efforts but were more professional looking to the students. One of those special interest training aids was an item that would have thrilled our later day kids in their electronic shooting galleries. If the old memory is working effectively, it had an odd name something like a Gun-Air-Structor. It was a round imitation aircraft turret which mounted two wooden .50 Caliber machine guns. Between the guns were a standard electric gun sight, turret control handles and gun firing buttons.

What did they shoot at? There was a large movie screen complete with sound effects. The student entered this land-based turret. When turned on the sound was complete with aircraft engines, the roar of attacking aircraft coming in from various angles. The shooter tracked the screen image and opened fire, complete with the sound of incoming and outgoing gunfire! It even scored the percentage of the student's hits!

With all this new equipment arriving we definitely required more instruction capability. Most of our available personnel were tied up in the out-door firing gunnery range efforts. However, we had a shortage of Classroom instructors. On discussion with the senior Gunnery Officer he advise, "Don't worry about it Chief, additional trained instructor personnel will be arriving shortly."

A couple of weeks later a navy bus pulled up in front of the building. What got off that bus was a far cry from what had been expected. Everyone was shocked to see a stream of Navy blue jackets, white blouses, skirts and silk stockings emerging from the navy bus! These were a new kind of Sailors. A bunch of about forty Waves but not a single drop of water! Some of us knew the Navy was experimenting with the idea of using women for specific shore jobs like Yeoman, storekeeper's galley personnel and school teachers. It was obvious our detachment of ladies was the latter.

We never found out for sure but we assumed they were all qualified instructors. Remember the old Navy expression, "Never volunteer for anything and always muster last." When the word went out for volunteers as qualified teachers with classroom management experience, many of these ladies saw the opportunity to serve their country in time of war. We actually had volunteers coming out of the woodwork.

For those that are old enough to remember a goodly number of our male working personnel dressed in dungarees. However, in the 40's the ladies definitely didn't approve. After all, dungarees were baggy and didn't reflect the form-fitting feature that developed 10 or maybe, 20 years later? In those busy times who bothered keeping track? However, in the interest of resolving ladies comfort something had to be done to improve their working dress by getting them out of these skirts and silk stockings. Let's rephrase that, it was almost impossible for a Wave to climb in and out of a gun turret wearing a skirt.

One day a couple of the lady teachers fell in at muster wearing pants. This Chief walked to one of these pants ladies and quietly stated those pants look like your problems are solved. The ladies response, "Chief, these are not pants they are slacks." Slacks? What the devil makes them different than pants? Thinking back, it had something to do with the type and placement of the closure. To us they still looked like pants, but why argue with the ladies as long as those "slacks" solved the work-a-day problems.

Once the Wave's became proficient with their subject material they became a real asset to the program. A basic analysis considered them far more serious about what they were doing than the average male instructor. We felt this was due to their teacher training background, which almost all of our male instructors lacked. Everyone had to admit, once oriented to the job these gals were not only serious about what they were doing, they were good at it as well. Another thing that was interesting, it didn't take long for them to pick up on the sailor lingo. They may not look like regular sailors but they sure began to talk the talk!

Just the same we found out that they definitely had to be handled differently. For example, their understanding and definition of time was slightly different. When a male sailor was told to be on hand at 10:00 hours, he in most cases would be there a couple of minutes earlier. Not these ladies! Further, for the months these 42 Waves worked for my department, I can't ever remember having all 42 of them on time for 08:00 muster in the morning! Another thing, when you raise your voice to a male they would jump to. It did not work with a Wave. It just made you feel stupid when you saw those two little puddles of water develop in her eyes.

Another amusing thing also comes to mind. Within our office spaces the ladies desks and tables were all on one side of the room. Now it became very obvious that during the day our male personnel seemed to be drifting over to the ladies side of the room. However, that was easy to solve. One morning when everyone came to work they found a chicken wire fence had divided the room. There was some mumbling, but as CPO in Charge I considered it my duty to protect the chickens from the wolves!

Dedicated to our own Legion Post 76 former World War II WAVES:

Evie Hallas & Rita Brengel

THE BATTLE OF TARAWA
20-23 Nov. 1943

PRELUDE—Prior to the war in the Pacific, little was known around the world about the west central Pacific and the coral islands that existed there in. There was several small groups know mostly to the Captains of the small trading vessels. One such Captain came upon this small group of Island atolls in 1788 and decided to name them after himself. Since that time they were known as the Gilbert Islands.

Within that group, one of the atolls was the island called Tarawa, which in reality was a series of small coral islands located 80 miles north of the equator. The largest Island of the group is called Betio, (Pronounced Bay-shu), which was crescent in shape. It consists of approximately one square mile of surface, about two and a half miles long and only about 800 yards wide at the widest point. This island extends not more than 12 feet above Sea level.

A couple of days following the attack on Pearl a token Japanese unit landed at Tarawa surveyed the area and declared it "occupied". Following the early Carlson Raiders attack on Makin Island the Japanese selected to station a force on Betio because it appeared to be the best site available for building a usable airfield. In September '42 a force of 1,100 from the Imperial Japanese Naval Landing Force were garrisoned there on. They were shortly supported by a team of 1,250 members of the 111th Construction Unit for the purpose of constructing the airfield and establishing the military defensive positions. In March 1943 an additional 1,000 members of the Fleet Construction Department arrived to complete the airfields construction as well as the various defensive positions.

The construction of the defensive plan was rather simple. Their efforts were strictly based on preventing any possible attack force from overrunning the island without dieing in the attempt. The off shore geography of Betio had surrounded it by an under water shelf like coral reef that extending about 800 to approximately 1200 yards from the beach shoreline. At certain low tidal times the reef becomes a natural barrier to normal boat operations.

The continued manufacture and placement of additional submerged concrete and palm tree log barriers made invasion tactics even more catastrophic for eager attackers trying to make it ashore. Hundreds of Coconut trees were cut down for the purpose of making more barriers, to form rifle and machine gun positions and to build log, concrete, coral and sand pill boxes just above the shore line. Anti-tank traps were dug wide but were limited in depth due to island water tables. Fourteen heavy coastal defense guns ranging in caliber from 8 inch down to 80mm was installed at strategic points. Some of these weapons were British made that had been originally installed at Singapore aimed at keeping out the Japanese.

Work had begun almost immediately on the airfield, which covered the main center portion of Betio Island. The main runway was 4000 ft in length. The central Command Post was located at the center of the island just off the north side of the taxi strip leading from the main runway. It was a reinforced concrete structure protected by mixed sand and coral heaped high thereon. From this command point contact with minor command areas was maintained by radio control.

In reality, this operation being the first amphibious island assault under fire, Adm. Nimitz chose old steady Vice Adm. Ray Spruance to organize the assault named, "Operation Galvanic." He was considered one of the most level headed men when it came to analyzing and resolving anticipated problems facing both the Navy and Marines factions entering their first assault.

The Marshall Islands had been the Navy's original choice to advance in the Central Pacific. However, Spruance convinced everyone that the Marshall's was an unknown factor because the Japanese had closed those Islands to the outside world when they took them over in 1919. What intelligence they had on those islands was rather vague. Plus, they were in closer proximity of the major Japanese complex at Truk in the Caroline's. The final choice for Operation Galvanic fell on the Gilberts Islands, Tarawa, Makin and Apamama, a small island southeast of Tarawa.

In May of '43 six months prior to the assault on Tarawa Maj. Gen. Julian C. Smith was assigned command of the 2nd Marine Division. Gen. Smith had an outstanding career record. However, the frontal assault and the battle of Tarawa would become the peak item of his military career.

THE BATTLE—It was now 05:05 hours 20 November '43, the attack on Betio Island which was probability the heaviest fortified position ever encountered, was about to begin. The U. S. Navy opened with a sea-borne Battleship, Cruiser salvo bombardment. Monstrous projectiles weighing in at 100 pounds to over a ton went whistling in toward Betio. As they burst on the small island the early morning sky above was brightly lighted by the orange flame from the bursting shells. The bombardment continued by volley fire for quite some time. When the big guns went silent the navy would learn from the aerial survey, the damage indicated the bombardment failed to serve its primary purpose of destroying the north shore strong points. Nor did it kill many of island defenders in their block-houses.

Next the air was filled with the roar of hundreds of aircraft engines. The sky was filled with approaching carrier aircraft and incoming Army B-24's. First came the Navy torpedo planes unloading their weapons, and the SBD and Helldiver SB2C dive-bomber popped their dive breaks and pushed their noses over into a deep dive to deliver their weapons. The F6F Hellcat fighters provided the grand finale as they strafed the enemy ground firing positions. Here again the aircraft efforts were of little value due to the lack of close air support experience against land based defense installations. It was a proven fact that fighter strafing was a waste of ammunition because it had little effect on personnel with well-protected overhead cover. This invasion would be the first severe test of the navy's amphibious philosophy for attacking a heavily defended position.

To complicate the invasion problems even more, it was discovered early the troop and support ships had anchored in too close and would now be subject to dangerous shelling while trying to offload there Marines. Which unfortunately had already begun. They were immediately ordered to shift anchorage. The troop ships had already started loading troops into their vehicles for transportation to the beach. These vehicles provided little protection to their occupants, and were incapable of being able to clear the reef. In the present low tidal conditions this situation concerning delivery of personnel to the enemy's beach was pretty much a learn as you go proposition.

Except for the amtrack's most of these so called "assault" boats were slow unarmored, weaponless vehicles that failed to protect the Marines or even have a drop down frontal bow area for rapid discharge of personnel. Plus there was massive confusion, as well as delays in getting the boats together at the point of departure which was also complicated by continuous changes of departure times to head for the shore. The situation was confusion personified.

To make matters even worse, as previously stated, the effort was being made at low tide when the water depth at the reef was approximately two feet. When the first wave received the signal to leave the departure point only a few of the assault vehicles, mostly amtrack's, were able to make it over the coral reef. Many of the following vehicles were hung up on the reef. The Marines carrying heavy assault equipment found that they had no choice but to climb over the side with their heavy gear. Once in the water they found themselves anywhere from waist deep to totally under water. Now it became necessary to wade approximately 700 to a 1000 yards or more to the shore while under heavy automatic gun fire. Many of them never make the beach. Your narrator had a Marine friend who made that wading trip to the shore without getting wounded by any of the intense fire. Being a typical Marine trying to explain the situation to a Sailor, he said. "I waded in under-water where I could see and dodge the bullets comin" at me."

The incoming waves of marines that followed that morning suffered from many identical problems. The Marines that reached the beach all in one piece found that just trying to stay alive was causing considerable confusion. Of the many things the might have left their boat with, the most important thing they still had was their M-1 rifle and bandoleers of ammo. They may not even operate with their own company or squad. It was damn near liking being all alone. What the Hell, they were all wearing the same uniform and were willing to respond to the ranking individual in the group.

My Marine friend had his first baptism of fire as a private on Guadalcanal and departed about 5 months later as a Sergeant. My assumption was, obviously he knew what he was doing. He immediately took charge of a group of marines crawling around on the shore, not one of them did he know. If I recall what he claims he said to them, it went something like this, "Saddle up, lets get under way. The idea of this game is to get on to the other side of this friggin' island. The game is kill your enemy before he has a chance to kill you. If a body on in the ground so much as twitches a muscle, shoot! And for God's sake don't keep score. Keep your mind on what we are trying to do, not what's been done. Move out."

Radios had been issued to the Commanders all the way down to some Privates for the purpose of maintaining close contact, issue orders, and even recommend action changes between combat groups. For example, men were badly needed in some sections ashore while other Marines had spent as much as a day and one half, or more, floating around the Departure Point awaiting radio orders that was failing to be received.

The type of fighting being conducted on Tarawa seemed like a bunch of small battles all rolled up in one very deadly major battle, which continued for three very bloody days. It finally ended when the Japanese were down to 17 men that surrendered. All the others had died in the heat of battle or had committed suicide.

After the last round was fired the island looked like a massive pile of deliberately destroyed junk. Now 65 years later many of these junk piles still rest in the same place they were destroyed so many years ago.

The U. S, Marine casualties of killed and missing totaled 980. Plus, 2,290 wounded, total Casualties were 3,301. Japanese total killed or suicide 4,690, Surrendered 17. Overall casualties numbered 7,991. Bloody is not the proper word for 7,991 killed and wounded in a three-day period. Seems like one heavy payment for one square mile of sandy coral in the middle of nowhere!

Medal of honor recipients

Staff Sergeant William J. Bordeion—Posthumously
1st Lt. William Deare Hawkins, Scout Sniper Posthumously
1st Lt. Alexander Bonnyman—Fng. Officer—Posthumously
Col. David M. Shoup Operations Officer, 2nd Marine division

Presidential Unit Citation—2nd Marine Division

"KAMIKAZE"
The Divine Wind

"Kamikaze" is a word of Japanese origin. In English it referred to the suicide attacks conducted against Allied military vessels during World War II. Dedicated Army and Navy Japanese, mostly student aviators, who agreed to perform these deadly missions for the purpose of destroying as many combat and support vessels and their associated crews and cargos as possible. The official Japanese term for such attack groups was *tokubetsu kogrki tai*, "Special Attack Units." However, the word, *shinpii* meaning the "divine wind" was also used to identify suicide units.

These trained Kamikaze pilots would get airborne for the specific purpose of intentionally crashing their explosive laden aircraft into an Allied combat or service vessel. By employing qualified aviators it just became a matter of converting the conventional airplane into a man controlled missile for the sole purpose of attaining greater accuracy than that obtained with the use of a free falling bomb.

Before the formation of this formal program there had been cases on both sides, where deliberate crashes had been used as a final effort when a pilot's plane was severely damaged and it appeared his luck had run out. Both Allied as well as Japanese forces had reported this type situation. It was sort of understood as an instantaneous decision made by men who had become mentally prepared to die. There is no real evidence to prove otherwise.

As the war progressed the Allies began closing in on the circle of Pacific islands leading toward the Home Islands of Japan. At the same time the available resources of Japan had been reduced considerably. The Imperial Japanese Navy had suffered some serious defeats, which had drastically reduced the capability of both their surface as well as their airborne units. Captain Masafumi Arima, Commander of the 26 Air Flotilla of the 11th Air Fleet had been credited with the invention of the Kamikaze type attack. He had personally led a mass flight of "Judy" dive-bombers against the USS Franklin. When he died his aircraft crashed into the enemy ship flight deck. There was no evidence that proved his act had been deliberate. Yet the Admiral honored him by crediting him for conducting the very first Kamikaze mission. The Naval High Command saw an opportunity to take advantage of this act by promoting him posthumously to Admiral and awarding him high honors for committing the act.

The result was the formation of an official volunteer group of 23 student aviators assembled and trained by Commander Asaiki Tamai. The Commander also offered Lt. Yukio Seki command of this small special attack unit. He actually turned the position down and thereby became the 24th member of the new volunteer group. He later commented "It is better to die than live as a coward."

There were several early Kamikaze air attacks during the battle of Leyte Gulf. The first vessel to be officially sunk by a Kamikaze was on the 24 October 1945, the USS Sonoma, an ocean going tug boat. The Escort Carrier USS St. Lo, was also sunk. The next day a total of 55 Kamikaze attacks damaged 3 large and 3 small escort carriers for a total of 7 having been struck. Another 40 ships were struck, which included 5 sunk, 3 receiving heavy damage and 12 with slight damaged.

Aircraft constructed specifically for Kamikaze missions were being designed and manufactured to avoid the conversion of useable fighter and bomber aircraft. It was also recommended that piloted glider bombs be developed and manufactured to be carried by a mother plane to the attack point of release. The First Japanese Naval Air Technical Bureau designed such an item. These were first deployed in March 1945. U.S. forces named these items as "Baka Bombs." In Japanese the term Baka meant "idiot" or "Stupid."

The most prolific use of the Kamikaze as a fighting force was during the Battle of Okinawa. On 6 April 1945 hundreds of planes made attacks during Operation Kikusui. These strikes at first concentrated on the destroyer picket warning formations, followed by serious attacks on the aircraft carriers at the center of the fleet. These final action attacks at Okinawa either sank or put out of action at least 30 warships. Plus at least 3 additional merchant ships along with several allied vessels. The attacks resulted in the Japanese loss of 1,465 airplanes and their pilots. Many warships were damaged. However, the process turned out to be least effect on the most desirable targets, large surface warships and aircraft carriers. None of which were ever sunk by a Kamikaze. Most of the ships destroyed fell into the destroyer classes and below.

U.S. Aircraft Carriers, with wooden flight decks were more susceptible to damaged than British carriers and their steel armored decks. On 4 May the advantage of the steel deck was well demonstrated. The HMS Formidable was under attack. A Japanese plane from a high altitude nosed his aircraft over and aimed for the Flight deck. He was struck by AA fire but crashed into the steel flight deck. He put one hell of a dent ten feet long, two feet wide, and two feet deep in the armored flight deck. The deck crater was repaired with concrete and steel plate. In just a short while the aircraft were again landing on deck. The 3 U.S. Midway class ships, under construction in 1945 were also fitted with our first set of armored steel flight decks.

By the time World War II ended the Japanese Navy had used 2,525 while their Army used 1,387 Kamikaze pilots or a grand total of 3,913 to meet with their ancestors. The calculated success totals were much less than that stated by the Japanese. The Japanese claimed that 81 ships sunk and 195 damaged in comparison with the U. S. calculations of 34 ships sunk and 368 damaged. We also claimed the loss of 4,900 men killed and over 4,800 wounded.

THE DEATH WISH:—Many people wonder how a youth in his early 20 or even older might be easily convinced to cut his life short by an unbelievable desire to die for his country rather than stay alive and devote his life to raise a nice family and still be able to serve his country. Unlike Americans, the Japanese beliefs seem to extend back to that of their ancient ancestors. They were influenced by the Shinto beliefs. Once Shinto had been established as a state religion, Emperor worship became general practice. To believe it was an honor to die for Japan and your Emperor. However, by the time almost 4,000 young men died in this manner, the reaction changed as the people began to wonder if the results were really worth the lives of these healthy young men.

In the U.S., Kamikaze was the most recognized name for the Japanese practice of deliberately ordering personnel to committing suicide by flying an explosive laden aircraft into a target such as a surface warship or similar military target.

TEN-GO SAKUAEN—7 April 1945

The final Sea Operation of the Imperial Japanese Navy

"Operation Heaven One" also known as **Ten-ichi-go** was the final major Japanese naval operation in the Pacific Theater during World War II. By early 1945 following the Battle of the Philippine Sea and the Battle of Leyte Gulf, the once powerful imperial Japanese Navy's Combined Fleet had been reduced to just a few remaining operational war ships plus a few combat aircraft and flying personnel. Most of the war ships still operational were stationed at home ports in Japan. The large vessels were stored at Kure, Hiroshima.

Following the invasion of Saipan and Iwo Jima Allied forces began their campaign against the Home Islands. As the next step toward the future invasion of Japan, on 1 October they began the invasion of Okinawa. Recent conflicts had demonstrated that aerial superiority was very effective against surface vessels lacking defensive air cover.

On 1 April 1945 the U.S. 10th Army conducted the final Amphibious invasion of World War II. This invasion indicated that the people of Japan, especially those that controlled the military, were willing to sacrifice a good number of their young people by using desperate Kamikaze attacks against the Allied military and service support vessels participating in the invasion. They were willing to take any form of desperate measure to slow the Allied advances toward the Home Islands.

In March the Army commanders were briefing Emperor Hirohito on Japan's proposed response to the invasion of Okinawa. The Japanese Army was planning air attacks, which would also include the kamikaze one-way flights. It was stated the Emperor questioned the use of the Navy. In response to the question, Navy personnel stated they were considering a possible final battle mission for their remaining combat vessels, which would include the battleship *YAMOTO*.

The proposed plan drawn by Commander in Chief of the Combined Fleet, Admiral Toyoda called for the *YAMOTO* and her escort vessels to attack the U.S. Fleet supporting the Okinawa landing. The vessels were to fight their way to Okinawa and then beach themselves between Higashi and Yomitan and fight as shore batteries until they were destroyed. The crews were then supposed to abandon their vessels, go ashore and fight the U.S. units on land. The Imperial Japanese Navy had no air cover available for these vessels, which would leave them open to concentrated allied air attacks. Admiral Ito Seiichi according to orders prepared for the mission, but did not agree. He considered it both futile as well as wasteful. None of his ship Commanders agreed with the proposed mission but was finally convinced by higher command that it was best for the Navy's reputation.

Once committed everyone began combat drills in preparation for the coming battle. All were given the choice of departing ship but none agreed. However, new, sick and infirmed personnel were moved ashore. After midnight on the departure date, 6 April 1945, the vessels were refueled. The order had been given to take on just enough fuel to reach Okinawa. In secret defiance to orders the ships were fueled with almost all the remaining oil in the tanks. Which in any case would not have been sufficient to return home.

THE LAST NAVAL BATTLE—At 16:00 hours the Japanese forces were under way for Okinawa with Admiral Ito on board the *YAMATO*. The light cruiser *YAHAGI* and 8 destroyers departed Tokuyama. Two U.S. submarines noted the departure but were unable to align for a torpedo shot. But they did notify the U.S. Fleet that the Japanese vessels were underway. At dawn 7 April, they passed the Osumi Peninsula and hit the open sea on a southerly heading for Okinawa. Some time later they shifted into a defensive formation. The light cruiser took the lead followed by the *YAMATO* while the 8 destroyers formed a defensive circle around the 2 larger vessels.

One of the destroyers, *ASASHIMO* began having engine trouble thus dropping out of formation and headed back to port. By now U.S. reconnaissance aircraft began tracking the Japanese vessels. The surface ships began shifting courses in an attempt to confuse the trackers. By 10:00 Vice Admiral Mitschier started to launch almost 400 aircraft in waves from 11 carriers located east of Okinawa. Included were carrier aircraft of several types, F6F fighters, SB2C Hellcat bombers, and TBF Avenger torpedo bombers. A surface fleet of 6 battleships complete with supporting cruisers and destroyers also got underway to meet the advancing Japanese vessels.

Since the Japanese lacked air cover the U. S. aircraft approached without any fear of contact with enemy aircraft. It took approximately two hours before they made contact with the Japanese vessels. They flew just outside the range of enemy anti-aircraft weapons as they set up their attack procedures. The first wave attacked as the ships below increased speed to 25 knots. They initiated evasive action and opened up with anti-aircraft fire as the U. S. aircraft began their runs. The torpedo planes attacked from the port side with one torpedo striking the *YAHOGI*. The tin fish hit directly at her engine room. The explosion killed the entire engine room crew and brought the ship to a stop. It was struck by 6 more torpedoes and 12 bombs. The destroyer, *ISOKAZE,* rushing to the cruisers aid was instantly attacked, hit and sunk. The cruiser finally capsized and it also slid under the waves.

In the face of intensive air attack, the *YAMATO* by evasive movement dodged considerable incoming ordnance but eventually she absorbed two armor-piercing bombs and a torpedo. Her speed was not slowed but one of the bombs started an intense fire aft of the superstructure that they could not control. Concurrently two of her destroyer escorts were heavily damaged and taken out of action. One of which later sank. The 2nd and 3rd wave of aircraft were concentrating on the worlds largest combat vessel. During these attacks she absorbed about 8 torpedo hits and approximately 15 bombs. The bombs did extensive top side damaged and destroyed power to their gun control directors which shifted their anti-aircraft batteries to manual control. This seriously reduced their effectiveness.

The many port side torpedo hits caused the ship to list sufficiently to make capsizing a reality. A bomb hit, had destroyed the water damage control system, which prohibited an attempt to do certain counter-flooding. Therefore in a desperate attempt to avoid capsizing, they flooded the starboard boiler and engine rooms. This might of stopped the ship from rolling over but it drowned several hundred crewmen at their workstations. The loss of the starboard engine and the weight of the internal water slowed progress down to 10 knots.

With the giant battleship progressing more slowly she now became an easier target for the attacking torpedo aircraft. They began concentrating on disabling or destroying her rudder. Once completed, she was no longer capable of being controlled. Admiral Ito ordered the mission cancelled and the crew to abandon ship and that any remaining vessels were to pick up survivors. The biggest battleship in the world, now dead in the water and beginning to capsize, had made her last cruise. As she began to roll over and sink there suddenly was a terrific explosion and she started to be torn apart as she sank below the water. It was assumed that the internal fire started earlier by a bomb hit had finally reached the main magazines.

The U.S. Aircraft ceased attacking and watched as the 3 remaining destroyers were able to save over 1,600 hundred survivors from a watery grave. The total Japanese losses from the battle had been estimated at 3,700. U.S. losses totaled 12 dead and 10 Aircraft shot down.

COMMENT—This operation was the final Japanese Naval effort of World War II in the Pacific. Both sides were critical of the Operation. It has been criticized as being a total unnecessary waist of human life and the forced destruction of national "antique" symbols that Japanese children might have been proud to visit today. While many have often criticized some of the Japanese tactics and beliefs, no one could ever criticize their bravery or their love of country.

INTEGRATED LOGISTIC SUPPORT
Keep 'em Flying & Sailing!

For almost 200 plus years ago the American Navy was not really a fleet. It consisted of a series of clearly independent, self-supported, sailing vessels. The crews not only manned and fought their vessel they also repaired and overhauled it pretty much by themselves. Even when they began to convert to steel it remained very much the same with the exception of repairs that required engineering assistance and the use of more talented labor or specialized tools.

It may be hard to believe, but this support philosophy existed almost into the1940's. The Japanese surprise attack on Pearl Harbor in December 1941 suddenly demanded a complete change in Navy repair and overhaul procedures. The day of the leisurely three or four months overhaul periods disappeared into the distant past. The combat availability of damaged weapon systems was measured on station by damage control repair analysis, which out of necessity had directly impacted on combat need turnaround time. Whenever, and wherever physically possible, repair was performed on site with the aid of a special repair vessel vice returning it to a Navy Yard in the states

Weapons engineering technology of both ships and aircraft had began to become more sophisticated after the end of first World War, but increased costs and the fallacy of the so called "War to end all wars" modern improvements were slow in being incorporated because of new treaty limited control of vessel construction and existing weapon systems. However, the Japanese ignored the treaty restrictions and secretly built a modern fleet.

When war broke out in the Pacific, we found ourselves defensively behind the eight ball. After the damage inflicted at Pearl, the only thing between the Japanese Fleet and our western coastline was our Pacific submarine force, three aircraft carriers and a few light and heavy cruisers and some over aged destroyers.

Most of the vessels sunk at Pearl had to be immediately subjected to the three R's, resurrection, refitting, and rearmed! Those currently under construction had to be redesigned to a 24 hour a day construction schedule to ensure early delivery within months vice years. Never in naval history, had anyone experienced an effort of this magnitude before. A similar situation applied to the quality and the quantities of aircraft under construction. Luckily, we were then a solid industrial nation that began working around the clock with an angry, get even, determination. Industry remained converted to this philosophy for over four years where the work lights never went out except long enough to change a light bulb. What would normally have taken years to design and build turned into months and in some cases months into weeks!

Weapon system analysis was already indicating that basis systems and their test, training and repair parts and support equipment should all begin while the system was still in the design stage. Each system element, spare parts and support equipment had to be manufactured and delivered concurrently with trained personnel available to support the end product. However, combat needs may have forced the emphasis on end product delivery and its spare parts.

By 1944 there was a definite move afoot to begin fleet testing of parts and systems under the new so-called Integrated Logistic Support System concept. A study group called ABATU (Advanced Base Aviation Training Unit) had been assembled by the Training Command to test the possibility of establishing, the assembly and positioning of Mobile Training Detachments in direct contact on station with aviation squadrons and their FASRONS (Fleet Air Service Squadrons).

Its purpose was not to eliminate basic schools. They would still be needed for initial training. However, the plan would save time by stationing trained instructors at the organizational and intermediate maintenance levels. Such services could be school equivalent training performed during on station in days, or hours vice separating personnel from their command for one or more months at a fixed position Training Command School.

It was determined that the detachments would be assembled and manned as two separate elements, Airframes and Ordnance. Assembling hardware to be used by instructors and the means to transport them was the easy part. The hard part was finding proper personnel to man these detachments. First, the aviation activities were sectionalized nationally with an officer in charge of each section. It was further determined that each detachment would be managed by a Chief Petty Officer in charge, with the number of additional personnel determined by the number and types aircraft systems to be supported. Naturally their search for specially qualified personnel began with instructors already attached to the Training Command.

That's where your scribe was found. He had been rotated from a 6 year sea service deployment and stationed with the Training Command's Pensacola's Aerial Gunnery school. His task assignment was teaching young aviation personnel to be Combat Aircrewman. As a CPO, and a recent graduate of the Aircraft Turret maintenance and Gunnery School it was obvious who they were going to be selecting to take charge of one of their ordnance detachments.

Personally, this Chief would have preferred returning to sea-duty with an operating Squadron. However, orders are orders. When received he was directed to report to the Schools area at NAS Jacksonville, FL for special duty with NAMTD (Naval Air Mobile Training Detachment). The details of getting acquainted with the personnel, while selecting, assembling, packaging selected ordnance equipment, tools, test materials and preparing it for transportation was rather boring so these details will be bypassed.

Just how we were supposed to operate in the field was kind of left up in the air. The reason being nothing related to this approach had ever been attempted before. We did sit through several sessions that recommended various methods and procedures to sell the product to fleet personnel. Which, by the way, you can be assured none of the methods suggested ever got a single student into a classroom.

It was assumed the operating details would have to be determined by negation with the on site Squadron and FASRON personnel. Eventually, everything was packed in our tractor-trailer and we were ready to move out. Once the orders were issued detachment NAMTD VPB-7 was ordered to the Naval Air Station, Key West, FL. The personnel would travel by train but the van driver and the CPO in charge would drive the tractor-trailer to Key West. The individual detachment orders, pay records and a generous travel allowance of $10.00 for a 2-day food and room travel allowance were issued prior to departure.

Think back to 1944. Even in those early days, where in Florida could you get 3 meals and a room for five bucks? Thanks again went to whoever selected our Tractor driver. He had been a professional trucker before the war. He advised that in order to avoid traffic and to make the best time we should do our driving at night. He also must have been a Boy Scout because he was definitely prepared for traveling, which included folding cots and most of the general necessities of life on the road stored in the trucks cab.

So we parked in a cool shady spot and broke out the cots and rested. By dark we hit the road making excellent time and pulled into the Miami area by morning. Having done this before, the driver took us to a hotel that had been taken over by the Navy. Displaying our orders we were assigned a double room, had a shave and shower and slept most of the day. While having a meal in the evening before departing, we got picked up by the Shore Patrol for illegally parking the Navy tractor on the street but they turned us loose once we showed our orders.

By early the next morning our vehicle rolled slowly through the gates of NAS Key West, FL. Reporting to the Station Administration Building we immediately hit a clinker. Surprise! Everybody in ABATU was so busy putting these detachment on station, nobody bothered to inform the Air Station, the Squadrons or the FASRON's (Fleet Air Service Squadrons) we were coming or what we were supposed to do when we got there!!! Even better, they had no knowledge what so ever that our NAMTD Command even existed!!!

They also questioned when our Officer in Charge would arrive. When we told them the CPO standing in front of them was it, they had a side discussion between themselves. Thankfully, the orders read that the Chief was in charge and that attached personnel would take their orders directly from him. These officers questioned if we understood the responsibility stipulated in the orders. What was stated in return sort of made them cringe. For example, it was stated that if I decided to go on leave it would be written From me, To me, For me, and By me. I may of missed breakfast, but I sure was enjoying the utter confusion caused by that one.

Naturally, establishing berthing and messing assignments was the first effort in getting squared away. We were billeted with the station Ordnance personnel. As a CPO I had a private room at the end of a barracks shared with another Chief. As to operating space, the Station Ordnance Officer, a former CPO, was real cooperative. He agreed to provide space to set up our 3 Gun Turret mounts and other armament equipment. Once the ordnance equipment was set up and operational, it was time to visit Squadron and FASRON Commanders.

Naturally, no one had ever heard of our Command. Just who do you represent and why are you trying to sell us a program that no one had ever heard of before? Why was one young Chief trying to explain the detachments purpose and its proposed service? One C.O. could not understand why the detachment lacked an Officer. One of the other skippers stated wisely, "I know why. A Chief is about the only person in the

Training Command with guts enough to walk through our front door and try to sell this program." However, they did have the courtesy of sending Officers and Chiefs over to the Ordnance building to inspect our set up. That was about the limits of our operation for the first couple of weeks.

There was an old cliché, "Curiosity killed the cat." Having never seen a turret installed outside an aircraft we did have some sailors come by to take a look. We questioned if they had ever operated a gun turret before. Once getting the equipment turned on and the turret operational the man at the controls began having a great time spinning the turret in azimuth while raising and lowering the guns.

The station Ordnance officer laughed and suggested we sell tickets like in an amusement park. He had a point; giving these young sailors a ride was getting people in the door, so at the same time we began explaining the details of operation.

This was followed by a lucky break. One of the squadrons PBM's nose turret's hydraulic system had a problem. They contacted us for help. We went over to their aircraft and helped them solve the problem. Their C.O. was immediately contacted again and it was stated that we were happy to help but our duty really didn't cover helping with their repairs. Our real purpose was to teach their personnel to be able to make their own repairs. As a result he then agreed to schedule some of his younger maintenance personnel for some basic training. We finally had made a breakthrough, assembling a satisfactory training program took a couple of months to perfect, which also included some airborne check rides, things began to work smoothly between the fleet personnel and ourselves.

With lots of time on our hands in the beginning, we began reviewing the publications we had been issued. Our purpose was to put together outlines for lesson plans to pass on information to the field. In those early years, the design engineers had written the Technical Manuals. Naturally, having designed and built the item, they seemed to be especially proud of their finished product. They sort of intimated it was so good it was something similar to perpetual motion and would never break down. Naturally this was definitely an error in judgment. These manuals said little to nothing about general maintenance, upkeep, required tools, spare parts or test equipment. Absolutely nothing referred to shipboard or squadron environment working condition. That was easy to understand because most of the designers worked from basic drawings and had never been aboard a ship or station to learn what front line working conditions was really like.

The basic problem was the fact the poor sailor trying to fix a disabled piece of equipment was the only one that really knew there was a problem! The government inspector at the plant could see it was a manual. It had the proper title and book number and all the pages were properly numbered 1 through 45 without missing a number. He stamped it OK, which allowed the purchasing agent to pay the contractor!

A small amount of checking proved the problem went even deeper. The guy that wrote the specification for the manual had never seen the inside of a ship either. He clearly defined where the Contractor had put the books title, manual number, made each page exactly like the illustration in the Spec and page numbers exactly as shown. The only problem the necessary information on how to actually perform maintenance was sadly lacking!

Honestly, this was the beginning of a flood of requests to Bureau of Aeronautics and Bureau of Ordnance for major correction to publication specifications to provide detailed maintenance level instructions in ordnance manuals. To temporarily solve the problem our detachment personnel in some cases began developing their own instructions and reproducing them to issue them as handouts. Copies of these handouts were also forwarded to the Bureau with a request the information be entered in the manual. A few years later a publication validation program was finally adopted. This contractually required Technical Publications be reviewed and validated by fleet personnel to determine its usability prior to final fleet distribution.

By the end of over a year of efforts at Key West things began to taper off. As a result HQ had us transferred to NATTC, Jacksonville to be trained to support the PB4Y-2 Privateer's operating out of Masters Field in Opa-Locka, FL. By now the information being presented was having a definite impact on aircraft maintenance programs. We the instructors also benefited. We originally began as knowledgeable technicians, but in reality were not trained as classroom teachers. However, by hit and miss, we discovered methods for developing presentation approaches that retaining student attention and the smooth transmission of maintainability data to the students.

For those unfamiliar with Naval aircraft types the Privateer was an offshoot of the B-24D or PB4Y-1. These aircraft were heavy duty patrol bombers powered by 4 Pratt & Whitney R-1830 1350 horsepower engines. At altitude they could attain a maximum speed of 300 mile per hour. It had a 110 ft Davis wingspan and a single vertical stabilizer vice the dual tail surfaces of the B-24. Its bomb load capacity was 13,000 lbs and was armed with 12 .50 Caliber Browning machine guns in six turrets, a bow, a stern, 2 upper deck and 2 waist teardrops.

Masters Field was actually an extension of the Naval Air Station Opa-Locka, FL. It was a major improvement over our facilities at Key West. It had a ground school area, which were temporary wooden structures. It had fully equipped classrooms, one for each ordnance system including our full size bomb bay layout. Contractor training aids, which were fancy copies of our old hand made units. However, we also had a new class of students. We were also instructing flight officers to improve their overall knowledge of their installed aircraft equipment and systems.

The Japanese finally surrendered after the two atomic bombs were dropped but there was no slowdown in our efforts. These simple mobile teaching detachments were pioneers in the development of an improved Integrated Logistic Support doctrine. From that small effort beginning in 1944, grew a monumental maintainability system that is now so sophisticated that I couldn't begin to explain it. As I understand it, the technician doesn't have to search for the problem anymore. They just plug in the test equipment and the airplane sensors tell them what it wants fixed!!

Just born too soon!!

The Navy version of the modified B-24 series aircraft
The PB4Y-1 and the PB4Y-2 aircraft
The photo is the Navy's PB4Y-2 aircraft

VETERAN'S DAY REMEMBERED

In 1921 an unknown American soldier from WW I was disinterred from an American Cemetery in France to be laid to rest in Arlington on a hillside overlooking the Potomac River. Over the years this site has become a point of reverence for our nations veterans. The 11 November date has been widely recognized as the end of the so called "War to end all wars." The final shot was fired at the 11th hour, of the 11th day, of the 11th month. For years this date was originally know as "Armistice Day."

In 1926 the Congress officially voted by Congressional Resolution to recognize that date as Armistice day. Twelve years later in 1938, Congress passed additional legislation declaring, Armistice Day, 11 November a national holiday. Shortly after the holiday was proclaimed, WW II exploded in Europe when the German army overran Poland in September 1939. On 7 December 1941; this Nation was forcefully drawn into that conflict by the Imperial Japanese Navy's successful sneak attack on our Pearl Harbor military facilities. By war's end over sixteen and a half million Americans served under arms. More than 400,000 of our service personnel died in service. Almost 300,000 of those casualties died of battle inflicted wounds.

Congressional discussions on how to best honor those who served during WW II resulted in a proposal by Representative Edwin Rees of Kansas to change the name of Armistice Day to "Veteran's Day". It only took Congress nine years to officially declare this day to annually honor all brave individuals that had served this nation in an armed conflict. In 1954 President Eiserhower signed the bill proclaiming 11 November as "Veteran's Day".

On Memorial Day 1958 two more unknown dead from WW II and the Korean War were returned from overseas and laid to rest in the company with the WW I unknown. In 1973, a law was passed to provide for interment of an unknown American from the Vietnam War. However, it wasn't until 1984 that a serviceman of that conflict was laid to rest alongside his three comrades in arms. However, his period of rest was shortlived. Modern DNA technology eventually identified this unknown. Therefore, he was disinterred and returned to a greatful family for final burial.

The graves of the remaining three men, known only to God, stands as a national symbol for the many men at arms who made the supreme sacrifice at war to protect this nation's freedom's down through the century's. These lonely three rest in eternal peace. Honored, and protected by a 24 hour vigil by the Army's "Old Guard" 3rd U.S. Infantry.

THE FIRST "BIG" AIRCRAFT CARRIERS THE MIDWAY CLASS

The success of our Fast Carrier Task Force's during World War II contributed to the basic design of our first class of the Navy's "big" carriers. Plus the British proved conclusively that armored steel flight decks stood up better than those made of wood. Historically, our first "Big" armored steel deck carriers were known as the Midway Class.

In fact they have become a long time memorial because the USS Midway CVA 41, now rests majestically on display on the San Diego waterfront as a monument to the transition between the "older" wartime carriers and today's super giant nuclear powered vessels. For her daily visitors she keeps alive the memory of our Navy's power during the early stages of the "Cold War" and the Vietnam era. The Midway had two sister ships The USS Franklin D. Roosevelt, CVA 42 and the USS Coral Sea CVA 43. The latter of which I have the honor to state was my home away from home in the 1950's. Two plus years, 1951 to 1953, of a profitable Naval career was spent aboard the mighty USS Coral Sea.

It had been planned that these three vessels would carry the names of famous World War II battles. However, the CVB 42 was renamed for President Roosevelt following his death in office, in honor of his service to the nation. Most of what will be said herein will refer to the Coral Sea. In my personal opinion, the sea-duty performed on this vessel laid the basic groundwork for extending my lifetime naval career to a total in excess of forty years.

The construction of these vessels began prior to the end of WW II but not one of the three had been completed in time to see action during that war. In fact the Coral Sea wasn't commissioned until October 1947.

The overall length of these vessels was 968 feet, equipped with a straight flight deck of 932 feet. The beam at the widest point was 136 feet and had a basic displacement of 45,000 tons. Fully loaded their displacement went in excess of 60,000 tons. The Coral Sea was constructed at the Newport News Shipbuilding & Dry-dock Co. in Virginia and was launched 2 April 1946. At their day in the sun these three ships were the largest, strongest and fastest military vessels in the world. Some of the major differences between all prior U. S. Carriers was the armored steel flight deck and the steam catapults. They vessels could really have been classified as floating cities with almost 2000 telephone's and sufficient horsepower to supply electricity to a city of over a million people. They were capable of supporting an air group of over 100 aircraft of various types and a crew in excess of 4,000 men.

In the fall of 1951, a shore duty tour at Naval Air Station Norfolk O & R (Overhaul & Repair)) Department, my duty tour as Chief Petty Officer in Charge of O & R's multi-engine Flight Test Unit was coming to a close. To draw a squadron assignment would have made it necessity to sell our home and move the family from Norfolk to Jacksonville. Therefore, a deal was brokered with the assignment Chief at the Commander Naval Air Forces U.S. Atlantic Fleet to accept a two-year tour on the USS Coral Sea CVB-43 to avoid the move. This decision also gave me another couple of months at home because the Coral Sea at the time was in the Norfolk Navy Yard, Portsmouth, VA being modified and overhauled. Plus, it provided this Chief ample time to totally familiarize myself with the ship and the 180 men I had inherited in the Air Departments V-3-O Ordnance Division.

In review of the 80 plus spaces assigned to the division's care, it was discovered there were spaces below the water line that appeared to really need a dedicated cleaning crew! Having been raised as a young Bluejacket on a light cruiser, where most spaces were cleaned 5 times a day, whether they needed it or not I was able to find plenty of work for the 180 sailors in my division. With the aid of an assistant chief, several suggestions and recommendations were made with our V-3-0 1st Class Petty Officers for corrective action. Within a few weeks after reporting aboard it became very obvious when you entered and departed V-3-0 spaces. The Warrant Gunner in charge was more than satisfied, as were the senior Petty Officers themselves. We never had to do anything like that again during my entire tour aboard.

The Roosevelt and the Coral Sea in the 50's operated under the Commander Naval Air Forces U. S, Atlantic Fleet and primarily operated in the Atlantic Ocean and deployed annually to the Mediterranean to serve as a part of the Sixth Fleet. Little to nothing was publicized at the time but these three ships were the first vessels equipped with the capability of launching airborne nuclear weapons missions. The F2H McDonnell Banshee, the Grumman F9F Panther, and the Douglas AD Skyraider's were all equipped with the delivery capability. During these cruises the crew received a present from the government, the WW II Occupation Medal with Europe Bar. Big Deal.

By February 1952 the Coral Sea's repairs and alterations were completed and she was ready for sea and the standard Post Repair Trials. On 26 February Carrier Air Group Four personnel reported aboard and a few days later their aircraft flew aboard. During the flight qualifications along the east coast we encountered a hurricane that put us back in the Yard for some minor repairs.

Shortly there after we had been scheduled for a six-week refresher Training Cruise to Guantanamo Bay, Cuba. At the completion we returned to Hampton Roads to prepare for the departure to Europe. There we would operate with the sixth Fleet from late April to October. During that 1952 cruise the ship visited Yugoslavia and entertained Marshal Josip Broz Tito on a special one day Cruise of Carrier operations. The following year in the Med, 1953, members of the 6th Fleet were invited to make the first visit to Barcelona and Valencia, Spain since the Spanish revolution.

In 1957 the Coral Sea was ordered to Puget Sound Naval Shipyard to receive a major conversion, which included a design change to the angled flight deck, a port side relocation of elevators, and more powerful steam catapults. The modifications also included an enclosed hurricane bow, a greater beam and other minor updates. She was recommissioned for duty in January 1960. The same modifications had been made to the USS Midway CVA 41 at Puget Sound in June 1955 through Sept 1957. The USS Roosevelt CVA 42 also received these modifications, which were completed between April 1954 through February 1957.

Atlantic operations continued for the Coral Sea into the early 60's. In late 1961 she was the first carrier to install the Pilot Landing and Television (PLAT) System, which was designed to videotape every shipboard landing. The system was very valuable for pilot performance review and analysis. By 1963 all attack carriers had the PLAT system installed.

Following the Tonkin Incident the Coral Seal finally departed in December 1964 for the Pacific to operate with the Seventh Fleet. In the late 60's and 70's these vessels were periodically deployed in western Pacific during the Vietnamese war effort. By 1977 The Roosevelt was found to be in rather poor operational condition. She had been experiencing power problems and reduced speed for years from a defective system which was different than that of the other two vessels. Also, her hanger deck overhead distance was shorter which limited wing folded storage for certain aircraft. It was determined that the correction cost might have an impact on the ongoing Nimitz Class construction program. Therefore, in September of 1977 it was agreed that the Roosevelt be decommissioned. In 1978 she was sold for scrap.

The Coral Sea relieved the Midway in the Arabian Sea in 1980 in connection with the Iranian hostage Crisis. The crisis ended in 1981 when Ronald Reagan succeeded Jimmy Carter as President. Later the Coral Sea returned to the Atlantic. In 1985 she made her first Sixth Fleet deployment to the Mediterranean since 1957, a separation of nineteen years.

Aboard was CVW 13 which included the first deployment of the new F/A-18 Hornet the last aircraft logistics' program your writer worked on prior to my retirement from the Navy Department in December 1978.

One of the Coral Sea's last major events happened on 19 April 1989 when in the Caribbean she responded to an assistance call from the USS Iowa (BB 61) due to an explosion in #2 Gun Turret in which 47 Crew Members was killed. The Coral Sea explosive ordnance disposal team flooded magazines and removed powder charges from the 16 inch guns. Medical assistance and supplies was also provided.

The Coral Sea was finely decommissioned on 25 April 1990. She was sold for scrapping in May 1993. At nearly 70,000 ton at the time of sale, she was the largest Aircraft Carrier ever to be scrapped. New laws made it less than profitable to scrap carriers within the states and it was illegal to sell capital ships for scrapping abroad. Legal actions dragged the scrapping out for years until it was finally completed in September 2000.

The Midway the only remaining vessel of the "BIG" three now rests in peace moored in San Diego entertaining curious people and happy children who wonder about how it use to be. May she happily go on forever as a living example of the post World War II reminder of the Cold War Period!

The USS Coral Sea CVB-43 1952

VICE ADMIRAL ROBERT B. PIRIE, U.S. NAVY (RET.)

Ensign Pirie graduated from the Naval Academy in 1926 and was designated a Naval Aviator in 1929. Between that date and 1941,he served as an effective officer in various aviation billets both at sea and ashore. At the beginning of WW II he was superintendent Of Aviation Training at Miami. In 1942-1943 he served on the staff, Commander Air Forces Pacific Fleet. In 1943 he commissioned the escort carrier USS Mission Bay CVE-59 as Executive Officer. In 1944 he was assigned, Chief of Staff of Carrier Division Four, Task Force 38. By 1945 he was designated Air Operations Officer on the staff of Fleet Admiral Ernest J. King.

By wars end he had been promoted to Captain with the assignment as the first Head of the newly formed Aviation Department at the U.S. Naval Academy. During 1948-1949 he commanded the escort Carrier, USS Sicily CVE-118. In 1950-1952 he served as Commandant of Midshipman at the U.S. Naval Academy.

It was shortly thereafter our Chiefs mess was advised he would soon Command the USS Coral Sea CVB-43. In those days it took an exceptional ring knockin' canoe college officer to impress a bunch of serving senior Chief Petty Officers. The Coral Sea Chiefs had received the early skinny on this officer. They knew he had held a lot of extra special billets, which indicated to them that our Carrier would be a tightly run spit and polished vessel.

When he assumed command in February 1952, tightly run it surely became, but not exactly like they had expected. The Captain was no doubt the officer in charge, but he was well liked by the Chiefs Mess, because he always responded to his personnel as a member of the crew. On reporting on board he immediately grew a beard because he had a rare skin condition. From then on he was known as "Old Red Beard" vice the normal term "Skipper." But not if he was within hearing distance! He always seemed to know exactly what he wanted accomplished, as well as the best possible way to get the job done. He was exceptionally knowledgeable, with an approach that was loud, often profane, and very direct. He was a Commander that expected his Chiefs to effectively supervise the ships workload. Once in a while they got their butts chewed but it didn't bother much because we respected each other's opinions.

In July 1952 Captain Pirie was selected for Rear Admiral, which reduced his tour aboard to just one year. During that period as Flight Deck Ordnance Safety Chief I had numerous face-to-face contacts with the Captain. I felt like I had gotten to know and understand him pretty well. He was more than just the boss; he was part of the team. In fact, the Coral Sea Chiefs Mess as a whole hated to bid him goodbye.

In later years while I served on the staff of Commander, Naval Air Forces U.S. Atlantic Fleet, I saw him on and off briefly while he Commanded the 2nd Fleet. It always amazed me when visiting Air Atlantic Fleet Headquarters he would drop by to say, "How's things going, Chief?" He never seemed to forget that I once worked for him. When he assumed the duties, as Deputy Chief of Naval Operations for Air it was his personal recommendation that I retire from active duty and accept the offer of a position at the Bureau of Aeronautics. His advice led to my successful career as a Navy civil servant.

After my retirement from the Naval Air Systems Command in December of 1978, I occasionally kept in touch with my old job through consultant work. In 1990 I learned that Vice Admiral Pirie, pioneer Naval Aviator, had passed away. He never will be forgotten. He will still be able to live on into eternity. A bronze plaque on the wall of the Pensacola Naval Air Museum quarters includes Vice Admiral Pirie with the rest of our early

Naval Aviation Hero's. During my final visit to the museum I photographed and saluted this plaque. To myself I said,

"You crabby old bastard. You finally got it made. Visitors will stare and wonder about you. But this old Chief doesn't have to wonder. I was one of the lucky one's to have known and served you personally. Some day in the future we might be able to sail together again."

NIGHT FLIGHT OPERATIONS

To keep the American sailor up to speed, and on their toes, while cruising the Mediterranean, it was part of a good Chief's responsibility to concurrently insure the sailors minds remained on their military responsibilities, rather than on the bathing beauties sunning themselves while vacationing on the sunny beaches of southern France and Italy. Also, in order to keep our sailors from feeling like they were on a pleasure trip vacation, we often played joint international navy war games. This particular night in question we were preparing for one of these enjoyable events.

The United States Aircraft Carrier, USS Coral Sea CVA-43 was steaming steadily making turns for 20 knots through the night toward their scheduled launch point. At 01:00 hours the weapons assembly crew was broken out to begin assembling weapons for a scheduled 04:00 hour strike launch. The Air Group operations schedule called for a mixed load of live 500 and 1000-pound general purpose bombs and 5" Zuni rockets. Concurrently, the flight deck crew was pulling back and spotting aircraft for load as assigned by the spotting board in flight deck control.

The mess deck assembly area was alive with men steadily installing tail vanes, bomb fuze's and arming wires as the ammunition came up the weapons elevators from the magazines. Once fully assembled the bomb skids were moved to the deck edge elevators and hoisted to the flight deck. Here they were picked up by ship and squadron loading crews and manhandled over the cross deck pennants to the appropriate aircraft.

The flight deck weapons safety Chief Petty Officer slowly moved through the tightly packed aircraft assuring that all safety procedures were being observed and that all ordnance had been fully loaded before he went forward to flight deck control to notify the Air Boss that we had a safe deck ready for launch. The pilots had already come up from their ready rooms and manned their aircraft while the loading was in progress. All operations were moving smoothly with just one last 500lb bomb to load.

Suddenly the night air was split with the sound of the flight deck speaker. It loudly announced, "The deck is clear, pilots start your engines!" The Chief was shocked! "What the hell happened? The "Clear Deck" word hadn't been passed to the Air Boss!" As the propellers began to spin and the engines started to fire up, he ordered, "Lets get the hell off this deck! Hurry, snake that bomb and skid into the starboard catwalk. Move it!" Once in the catwalk he counted noses. Damn, one man was missing. He had to be still on deck under the aircraft!

Quickly the Chief crawled back out between the main gear and tail wheels of the aircraft toward the center of the deck. He finally located the man frozen in a crouched fetal position afraid to move. He had to physically knock the man over and began to drag him toward the catwalk. Once nearing the edge his crew helped get the man off the deck into the catwalk.

Badly shaken, this Chief was really a lot more than just angry. With blood in his eye he raced through the compartments below the flight deck to the port side and up into Flight Deck Control. He flipped on the primary fly switch to the Air Boss and without thought of reprisal, he shouted, "What the hell is going on up there? I never passed a "Clear Deck" signal to start engines! We still had a loading crew and a live bomb on deck! Plus, that was topped off with the fact we came damn close to having a man killed out there. I had to crawl back out and drag that scared kid off the deck!" The Air Boss responded, "Calm down Chief, get up here immediately."

When the Chief arrived at the Commander's station they discussed the situation in detail. The Air Boss then advised him that the Captain wanted to see him because he had heard his angry outburst over the speaker system. Still shaken, but not with fear, the Chief proceeded to the Captain's bridge. On arrival he saluted with a "Reporting as ordered sir."

Now this particular Captain was also noted for his ability to occasionally fly off the handle. He had the Chief follow him out on the open wing of the bridge. His comment was, "I definitely understand your problem but, I can't have you chewing out the Air Boss in public like that, do you understand me?" The Chief responded with a quick "Aye, Aye Sir. The Air Boss and I normally work well together. He had no idea where the all clear signal came from." As the Captain dismissed the Chief, he quietly stated, "Chief, I hope that man of yours realizes and remembers that you probably saved his life."

THE SPLENDER OF ROME & THE VATICAN

Having always been interested in history and historical items the 1952 USS Coral Sea, CV-43 Mediterranean summer cruise provided a excellent opportunity to view, and investigate, the ancient historical sites of Europe. Our large Aircraft Carrier had just dropped anchor off the city of Naples, the sin city of Italy. All hands, who had money, were excitingly preparing for their up and coming liberty ashore. As a collateral duty as a member of the ships Recreation Department I had become friends with the Catholic Chaplain, who was also a member. While making arrangements for various shore visits, he questioned if it was my intention to make the tour to Rome.

Disappointed, the answer to him was no. It was explained that desire had been out voted by forwarding funding home. This had made me a little short of cash. He suggested that the problem might be easily solved. If I had no objection, he would request my assignment as tour Shore Patrol Chief. Traveling in duty status with the Chaplains tour group would cover all basic trip expenses. I really was unable to thank him enough for the opportunity.

Because of the priest's request, my Shore Patrol badge, pistol belt and night-stick was making this Rome trip possible. Over 40 ship's company personnel boarded the train for Italy's ancient capital. The train trip, Naples to Rome, was less than interesting as well as uneventful. On arrival, tour buses motored our sailors to the resident hotel located at the top of the Spanish Stairs. Daily, the Shore Patrol Chief, "supervised" the loading of the buses that carried the group to the various scheduled ancient attractions of the city. There were excellent on site views of the Roman forum, the Coliseum, Victor Emmanuel's Monument, Mussolini's former HQ and many others sights to see.

However, the most interesting was the visit to the Vatican City and the Basilica of St. Peter. It's really complicated to define the splendor of this fantastic edifice. As a part of the visit, the ships Chaplain had been able to obtain permission for a Ships Company audience with Pope Pius XII. To my knowledge your scribe was the only non-Catholic in the group. However, being married to a Catholic girl and having two sons enrolled in Catholic school, I had purchased several religious articles to be blessed.

When Pope Pius XII entered the room, he spoke briefly to the group and blessed everyone's religious articles. He then went to each man individually and put out his hand. Everyone sort of kneeled down and kissed his ring. I immediately tried to visualize what I would do when he got to me. When he extended his hand, I just sort of gripped his hand and said, "Good Morning Pope." He smiled at me and questioned, "I take it you're a protestant?" Responding nervously, I said, "Yes Sir, however I'm married to a good Catholic girl." He smiled again, reached into his pocket, took out a small medal and handed it to me. "Give this to your wife when you get home." He then moved on to the next group of men. I was astonished. I stood there looking at the medal then put it in my pocket. When we left the room and were again back outside, I caught "Holy" hell from most of the guys. The subject was, only one protestant in the crowd and who do you think the Pope gave a medal to?

This happened over fifty-eight years ago. To this day the wife still carries this medal in her purse wherever she goes.

1952 Rome The Basilica of St Peter
Construction began 1450 and took 176 years to complete

MARSHAL JOSIP BROZ TITO
Former President of Yugoslavia

Tito was a strong brave man, who had defied the Germans during World War II as well as becoming the first communist to also defy Stalin and the Soviets. He and his followers had solidified the provisional government of the Democratic Federal Yugoslavia. Following the 1945 elections he became Prime Minister as well as Minister of Foreign Affairs. Tito's rule of the combined provinces definitely had the flavor of a dictatorship.

During World War II his subversive operations against Germany and their Allies actually aided the war efforts of United States, England and the other Allied Nations. As a result British and American staff officers had been assigned to Tito's headquarters. Because of their help, the partisans continually received military support by way of needed Allied airdrops.

After the war his friendship with Stalin definitely cooled which angered Stalin. The Soviets on occasion made several attempts to physically solve the problem. Tito's response message to Stalin stated, "Stop sending people to kill me. If you don't stop sending killers, I'll send one to Moscow and I won't have to send a second." By the early 50's the U. S. had a fully established Ambassador in place and it had been agreed we would send a special visiting vessel to entertain, and be entertained by Marshal Tito.

The USS Coral Sea CVB 43 was selected to conduct that visit. To my knowledge we would be the first vessels to ever visit Yugoslavia. Our course was reset and we proceeded north through the Straits of Otranto into the Adriatic Sea. The approximate distance from the heel of the Italian boot to Split, Croatia was about 275 miles to where we would meet with the famous Tito.

It was a short run up the river from the sea to the city of Split. Vice Admiral Cassidy, Commander Sixth Fleet had arrived earlier to aid Captain Pirie in welcoming Marshal Tito aboard. When the Marshal arrived accompanied by United States Ambassador Allen, our band played the Yugoslavian National Anthem as the celebrities were piped aboard. The guests were given a special tour of the most interesting compartments of the vessel. Tito's comments indicated the most interesting area was the enlisted men's mess. However, he was fed and entertained in the Admiral's quarters. Shore liberty the first day began at 13:00 hours but I guess that Tito was familiar with the desires of young American sailors. All the ladies age 6 to 60 were not to be found anywhere in town!

Early the next morning Marshal Tito and his entourage returned aboard. We immediately put to sea and began to prepare for the big air and ordnance display. The weapons assembly crew had risen early to make ready for loading rockets, bombs, napalm, you name it we loaded it on Air Group Four's planes. As we made ready for launch, the dignitaries watched with interest from the wing of the Admirals bridge. Once CAG 4's planes were airborne the towed target sled was streamed. Wardroom chairs were rigged aft on the flight deck for Tito and the rest of the viewing party to witness the show.

Captain Pirie positioned his flight deck ordnance Chief behind Tito's interpreter to respond to the Marshal's questions concerning the ordnance being expended. He had several questions, but was really impressed with the Tiny Tim 11.75 rockets. The air show was really impressive and was concluded with the Air Group planes spelling out the Marshal name TITO with a flyover. As the party returned to the Admirals bridge to witness the Air Groups flight deck recovery, the Marshal shook hands with the Chief and thanked him for his responses.

On the return to Split, Tito and his party was ceremonially piped ashore again. However, he never returned the favor by permitting his hidden ladies back in town!

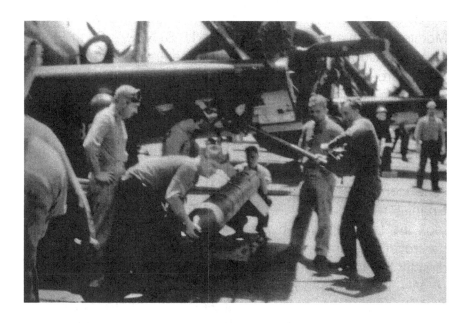

Loading Tiny Tim 11.75 Rockets for Marshal Tito,
off split Yugoslavia 1952, Keneman behind
sailor bending over rocket nose.
"I'm supervising the load"

"OLAY, OLAY, OLAY!"

Once upon a time long ago, ('52-'53), we sailed the Mediterranean as an element of the U. S. Navy's Sixth Fleet. The USS Coral Sea CVB 43 was the central part of a Carrier Battle Group lead by the Command Ship, the USS Salem CA 139. For quite some time, President, or Dictator, (your choice), Franco of Spain was trying every trick in the book to entice the U.S. to have their vessels begin visiting Spanish Ports. Well, it seemed he had finally used the right bait.

It had been agreed our Battle Group would be the first American vessels to visit Spain since the beginning of the Spanish revolution. As we departed Taranto, Italy, The Salem took the lead followed by the Coral Sea and flanked by our destroyer entourage. We steered an easterly heading aimed directly toward the City of Barcelona, Spain.

We had been advised that Senor Franco was doing everything possible to insure our welcome upon our arrival in Barcelona. For example, the bullfight season was over but they had scheduled a special showing for the American's pleasure. Hey, it was even rumored that he would be paying a special bonus to any young lady that gave birth to an American child! How happy could a bunch of young sailors get?

At the bull-fighting arena they had reserved a whole section for our visiting sea fairing men. Everyone was in a happy joyful mood. I doubt if there was an empty seat anywhere in the arena. The opening ceremony was spectacular. As the band played, the toreadors entered dressed in their colorful outfits and capes, followed by the picadors on horseback marched in, they turned and faced the Navy attendees. The band shifted to the Star Spangled Banner while our white uniformed men stood up cheering and saluting, it was a colorful sight!

It was now time for the first Bullfight. In charged the first snorting bull shaking his head. The Toreador approached cautiously manipulating his red cape. The bull watched him closely pawing with his right front foot. Charge! The red cape was flipped sideways. The startled bull looked around wondering what happened to that damn red rag! The Spaniards screamed Olay! So the Sailors followed with their Olay. The bull got madder and madder making numerous attempts but that two legged guy in the fancy pants kept jerking that flashing red rag out of the way! Suddenly the Toreador bravely turned his back on the bull, threw his cape over his shoulder and walked behind a barrier. A mighty "Olay" went up from the Spanish audience with some help from our Bluejackets. The bull just stood in the middle of the arena wondering what the heck all the shouting was about.

The bull then turned to watch two guys with long lances charging him on horseback. Sticking him in the back of the neck with those blunt sharp lances. A muttering sound began to rumble in the crowd of sailors. As for the bull, he must have thought that was his punishment for missing that damned red rag so many times. The sailors didn't particularly cotton up to the brutal bloody action by those fancy dressed guys on horseback. The Toreador returned with his cape over his shoulder and a shiny sword in his right hand. He began teasing the bull with his sword cocked at the ready. The low sound of boo's started to resonate out of the sailors in white. Following up, the Toreador stepped forward with the sword raised shining in the sun as he plunged it to the hilt behind the bull's head. The Spanish audience roared in appreciation as the section of sailors sat in dead silence while the slain bull was dragged out of the arena. Some of the sailors immediately departed but the majority remained.

As the second fight began the Spanish attendees cheered Olay on the first couple of passes. The sailors remained silent. Suddenly on the third pass the bull knocked the Toreador down. Instantly, many of the sailors jumped to their feet screaming Olay, Olay! The Spanish attendees, just as suddenly shifted to a dead silence! The downed Toreador immediately jumped up and recovered his cape but the bull knocked him down again. Instantly, the entire sailor audience leaped to their feet screaming Olay, Olay at their top of their lungs as the Toreador raced out of the arena. The Shore Patrol worked like crazy trying their best to get the American sailors to shut up with little success.

Many of the Spanish were in an angry mood and were beginning to depart the stadium. Some of the more levelheaded people began to wonder about getting out of the stadium without one heck of a fight. Our departure was finally reduced to total silence as our personnel left the stadium. It took quite a bit of negotiation for the Spaniards to understand the American reaction as it was finally explained to their final satisfaction. However, I fail to recall ever being invited to another bullfight! One sailors comment was, "It was kind of a lousy bloody show. I doubt it could ever replace football or baseball!

"LISBON COMEDY SHORE PATROL"

After World War II the United States established the Navy's Sixth Fleet. The specific purpose for positioning a Carrier Battle Group in the Mediterranean Sea was to insure the protection of U.S. interests in the bordering nations. This force was kept fresh through the establishment of a deployment rotation system of 6 to 7 months in length. Shore liberty in the various countries was excellent because it accomplished several benefits. First it produced a certain amount of revenue for the nations visited and secondly it made available to our personnel the ability to visit many interesting European historical places.

For example, The home of the French Foreign Legion at Sedi Bel Abbey outside Oran, Algeria, the French Riviera, Columbus's birth place, Genoa, the wonders of Naples and Rome, Italy as well as the Isle of Rhodes and the majestic ancient city of Athens, Greece.

However, married sailors, particular those who allotted a major portion of their income to their families at home, had to develop an outside source of shore leave funds. Some became outstanding poker players but many were not. An alternative for senior Petty Officers was to volunteer for Shore Patrol duty as a means of financing a shore leave break from shipboard routines. Working the patrol night shift gave you free time during the day to admire the wonders of Europe!

Now as a senior CPO with SP experience you could make the effort more interesting by working Riot Squad from 16:00 hours to midnight. You would be stationed at the main Police station with a Jeep, a Petty Officer driver and a cop that spoke English. No actual work was involved unless you received a phone call reporting a disturbance. It also provided you with some of the juiciest or most humorist events.

On Patrol one evening in Lisbon, this CPO experienced one of the most comical events he ever experienced on Shore Patrol. It seems this very large Boatswain Mate 2nd had a small misunderstanding in a bar where a table and some glass wear had been damaged. The proprietor called the cops. The sailor knew he was at fault and waited peacefully for the police. The cops spoke no English and the P.O. no Portuguese. Because of their failure to communicate, made the cheese get more binding on the trip back to the police sub-station.

As they progressed on foot the cops, as they usually did, began poking the sailor with their nightsticks. The sailor not understanding, nor liked being poked, stopped and complained. This action caused the cops to poke him even harder which angered this 6'5" 250 lb sailor. He immediately wrestled the nightsticks away from the cops and began poking them as they all ran toward the sub-station. Shortly thereafter the Riot Squad phone began ringing off the hook. The local cop listened to the call and the Jeep and Riot squad was on their way hell bent, for the police sub-station.

On arrival the Chief and his squad walked through the door. On our entry, there was no doubt in anybody's mind who was in charge of that Police Station. The big Boatswain mate stated in English, "Boy, Chief am I glad to see You!" When we arrived he had two cops penned up in a cell, one cop hiding under a desk and one behind the file cabinets. Now that communications was finally introduced, it appeared like the four local cops tried to overpower the sailor and put him in the cell. However, they were no match for this big kid. He man handled 2 into the cell and keep the other 2 at bay with a nightstick in each hand. He did permit one cop to make the call. As a result everyone was laughing as we took the big sailor into custody. We apologized to the Portuguese Police and advised them to post any financial claims with the U.S. embassy. However, no claim was ever filed. We figured they were too embarrassed to do so.

"LIFE OF RILEY"

Many years have slipped away from the great wars of the twentieth century. To most of our citizens they are just a distant memory. However to many of our remaining elderly they will always remain a bright memory despite their frailness of body. Broad steps have been taken as we passed into the 21 Century. However, as the brightness of prosperity begins to dim when the economy started to decline, it suddenly becomes possible that much of this shift might prove to be the fault of the elderly. After all, when times are good many may lose sight of the possibility of financial change and suddenly wake up to the fact they had over extended themselves. They are amazed to realize they have lost some, or all, their ability to cope with their debts.

Historically, this country has been an industrial nation that used our manufacturing capability to make us a world leader, a winner of wars, and provided the backbone to pull ourselves up by our own bootstraps! But we have since sold that capability to foreign nations. How long has it been since you have seen "Made in the USA" in a piece of our clothing? Why? Because most people wanted bigger profits while others wanted more for less. Viewing the national debt sort of tells me it is actually costing us a hell of a lot more for less!!

Now when trouble arrives we have a lot of patriotic people in Congress, some good, some not as good, who do a lot of work trying to keep the people back home happy. But anybody in his right mind has to know that those 635 people are only human and are unable to keep track of everything going on themselves. That's the reason for an intelligent staff, a hundred, more or less, specialists trying to keep those people informed. Sometimes for a minor problem, the simplest and quickest process is to throw some money at it and hope the problem goes away. However, this is not a satisfactory method for conquering the mounting Health care situation, or taking over major industrial production. Nor, should age suddenly become a factor in determining if you deserve help or not.

Some members of Congress have reflected the feeling that some of us elderly, or "the greatest generation," should learn to sacrifice like some of the younger generation has learned. Well, I guess our little secret is out. Seems like up till now we have been living the Life of Riley and it is now time that we pay the piper. Based thereon, I would like to pass on some of my personal thoughts as to what maybe some of our learned representatives seemed to have forgotten.

During the so-called depression of the 30's we really lived it up dancing to the tune of "Brother can you spare a dime". In those days many of us had to choose to dine at one of those fabulous Soup Kitchens with other members of our family. In the early 40's others had the opportunity to travel to the tropical Pacific to view the great pre-Christmas Fireworks Display provided by the Japanese on 7 December '41.

Then our cup really runneth over. Quite a few of us were invited to participate in the exhilarating stroll from Bataan to a luxury oriental resort. While others cruised the balmy Pacific on special luxury cruises with the U.S. Navy occasionally enjoying both day and night fireworks displays. Even luckier, were those who won prize cruises to fun filled spots like Midway, the Solomon's and Murmansk.

We even basked on the sunny beaches of Guadalcanal, Iwo Jima, and Okinawa where we observed the wonders of the "Divine Wind". Better known to us as Kamikaze! Or, even fritter away our youth wandering through the lush jungles of Burma and New Guinea. Also, those of us visiting Europe's vacation spots had good times, boating and swimming on a Normandy beach on a pleasant day in June '44. With side visits to such scenic locations like Bastogne, Malmady and Monte Cassino. And please, don't forget the lush winter mountain snow resorts of Korea! And the lust jungles of Vietnam. Plus it won't be long before all these newer Middle East fiascos can be added to this list.

Yes, I guess we were pampered and spoiled rotten. In the opinion of some we never learned what the word sacrifice really meant. For example, we didn't even rate a government WW II memorial approved by the government. Top that off with the fact we could only get it, if we the people were willing to pay for it ourselves! Our generation is getting old. Most of us probably won't live long enough to ever view this monument. However, if you run across any of those that felt we need lessons in sacrifice, just suggest they take a moment, stop and think, they will discover we were the ones that REALLY knew the true meaning of the term sacrifice.

Duty, Honor, and Country!

THE NAVY CHIEF

In the 1700's when the first group of naval sailing vessels set out to sea the title "Chief" or Chief Petty Officer did not exist. Your writer had to assume that in those days the senior boatswain probably fit the bill. As the years passed the Navy, like our nation, definitely grew in size. As a result the requirement for some form of senior enlisted service rating existed.

As a young Seaman 2nd class back in the mid 1930's an old Chief Boatswain Mate with hash marks up to his elbow, tried to sell me the story that God himself had called the senior Admirals together and told them that they had to invent the Chiefs to make sure all those 2nd Class Seaman become good sailors, as well as to insure that those nice young Canoe College Division Officers make Lt. (jg) in four, or 5 years. After all it was embarrassing, most of the sailors in their Divisions were older and had been to sea longer than those nice young Ensigns!

The rating of Chief Petty Officer, E 7 became official on 1 April 1897. Under normal circumstances, it took the average Petty Office about 14 to 16 years to reach that position level. In the intervening years, this person became a true man of the sea. His brain absorbed a monumental amount of information concerning the workings of his designated rating, but also the Navy's personnel requirements as well as a work management philosophy. By then he has developed a quality of leadership necessary for application in the workplace. When one of these senior personnel were directly questioned in relation to just who is running the Navy, his reply with a slight smile would be, "We Chiefs Do".

On promotion to Chief they actually entered an elite organization. They were immediately elevated to private living and messing quarters. In earlier days once promoted to Chief he was required to serve one year as Acting Appointment. At the successful completion of that trial year he was designated as Permanent Appointment. Which was accompanied by a slight pay increase. During the 1940 war years some of us advanced more rapidly and had to instantly prove we deserved those quick advancements.

In that time frame we also had our personal Uniforms. The blue and white uniforms were identical and reflected real authority. Each blouse was secured by 8 gold button's, count "em", two more than the officers. On his weather beaten head perched a uniform cover identical to the officers. But the only gold thereon were two brass buttons that anchored the black chinstrap. The gold plated fowled anchor marked USN was pinned to the center of the white cover. However, they eventually made uniform changes that removed the two jacket lower buttons. The snappy white uniform we liked so well was also cancelled and replaced with that officers style choke collar without any Gold Crow or 4 or 5 Gold service strips. The man in the uniform shop said, I guess you old guys can't make them nice young officers look bad!

When a Chief arrived on the weather deck, he might arrive with a pipe clinched in his teeth, and a cup of jo in one hand. His appearance thereon might make the bluejackets snap to and work even harder without his not even making a sound. This might depend on each individuals thoughts running from respect to a small element of fear. I guess in the personal opinion of some, it places the Chief some where between God and the flaming Devil.

When necessary these men ruled with a certain amount of fear and a little bit of intimidation. In my service period from the lowly Seaman 2nd up to the Lt. (jg), he may have been considered a little scary but well respected. Despite all their visual toughness most of them really had a heart of gold. His personnel feelings and love for the Navy, eventually filtered down to the youngest element in which he had direct contact.

He occasionally might assign extra duty or illegal restriction or even save a young tars naval career with an illegal "Chiefs

Mast." As to his positions with "young Officers" several of some of our best high ranking officers I have known can look back to a time when some Chief helped him through a tough or challenging situation by instilling confidence in a young officer's leadership.

As the years rolled by modification of regulations have outlawed some of the most effective management procedures and techniques invented by many sly old Chiefs. It might have resulted in the necessity for expanding the Chiefs Corp to include Senior and Master Chiefs. However, my recent reading of Naval Institutes Magazine, proceedings concerning the present state of the 3 Chiefs system should leave the old time Permanent-Appointment Chiefs with a happy, I told you so!!

AOC Harry L. Keneman USN (Ret.)

"HAIL TO THE CHIEF'S"

As our nation grew, the Naval sea services had to have someone responsible to insure everything was kept shipshape and operating properly. You must remember that many of those young Division Officers, I'm referring to those young graduates right out of the Canoe College, were really good kids but were still on a learning curve. Plus the fact, a majority of their division Bluejacket's were a bit older than their officers with longer sea going experiences.

I was once advised by a five hash mark Chief that the good Lord himself called the Admirals together and told them it was time to invent the rank of Chief Petty Officer. Now everyone knew Chiefs had to be important because they rated their own private quarters and mess where even the Commanding Officer of the vessel always requested permission to enter. Further, in the earlier stages they were the only single rank in the Naval service that rated their own special uniform!

Their original blue and white uniforms differed from all other Naval uniforms. For example, for years their dress blue and white blouses were adorned with eight, (count 'em) shiny double-breasted brass buttons. Which were two buttons more than that of the officers. Their whites uniforms were identical to their blues except for one difference. The blue uniform jacket for those with less than 12 years service, (there actually were a few), the sleeve rating badge identification and service stripes were bright red topped with a woven silver eagle. Those with 12 or more years of excellent service the red insignia's were replaced with gold topped by a silver woven eagle and slick silver occupational designator, plus their service stripes consisted of one bright Gold hash mark for each four years of service.

Now someone had to be jealous and submitted a complaint because they eventually made the Chiefs cut their gold buttons back to six the same as the officer's. Plus, they totally eliminated that fancy white uniform we had and made the Chief's wear that choke collar officers blouse with not a single stripe of any kind! I guess they didn't want the Chief's to make the young junior officers look bad.

Today its got to the point Navy expansion indicated we needed even more Chief's to take charge, so they invented Senior and Master Chiefs. Which is sort of modeled after the Warrant Officers. Now some of the old Chiefs wonder if these new fangled ones still form up their Divisions in the old fashion way. In the old days all he had to do was order, "Squat", and all hands responded accordingly. After all, some of those young canoe college boys hadn't been aboard long enough to understand "squat"!

Thinking back some of those old chiefs loved to listen to military music. They especially appreciated the sound of "Hail to the Chief". When that played, they would lean back, smile, and think, "They're playing our song". One day at a Washington, D. C. affair, when the President arrived the Band struck up "Hail to the Chief". There were two elderly Chiefs present. One whispered to the other, "Why are they playing it for him?" The old Chief next to him shrugged his shoulders and whispered back, "He must be an Ex-Chief." "Yea, Must be!"

THE AEROPLANE

For thousands of years man had studied the flying birds trying to figure out how man might achieve the same capability. Many gave it a good try but most of them spun in either breaking their necks or other various body parts. However, after many mistakes and errors and solving small bitts and pieces, they began learning about things called weight, lift and thrust.

Just after the turn in the century two bicycle mechanics had built a lightwood and fabric winged vehicle installed with a small internal combustion engine and a carved propeller. They felt like they had studied extensively and were ready to test it in an area where they could get assistance from the wind. So they packed up their invention and headed for North Carolina.

Little did they realize, once those two bicycle mechanics actually got that very first flying machine airborne in 1903 at Kitty Hawk, North Carolina, they just assumed that they had constructed another small extension of the internal combustion engine. I assume they felt they had just designed something comparable to the automobile. Now I'm not trying to say the auto wasn't a wonderful invention. After all, it is still the first choice of every kid who can reach the age of 16 all in one piece. Besides a good car in every garage, or driveway, is an absolute necessity while in fact an airplane was not.

The one thing that Orville and Wilber failed to realize at the time was that flimsy little biplane would eventually materialize into one of the most effective military fighting machine ever devised by man. Now this didn't happen over night. It took awhile. The airplane quickly became less flimsy and some smart guy put wheels on it in order to get it safely into the air and back on the ground without doing too much damage.

However, it took a special type of adventurous kind of individual that was willing to try and drive one. He had to be the type of guy, known to be either, dumb, crazy and/or stupid enough to try things the average sane individual wouldn't do. Those adventurous individuals brave enough to operate one of these flying machines, instantly became compared to race car drivers and deep sea divers. He suddenly became a Knight of the Sky who was making a few bucks around the country stunting in air shows and taking other adventurous people up for thrill rides.

Visionary people, most of them in military uniform concerned about the future, began watching closely to the rapid advancements being made in aircraft and wondered if it might eventually have some commercial or military possibilities. Even the Army and Navy were both dabbling with the idea. In fact, the Navy had converted their Pensacola, Florida Shipyard into their first Naval Air Station in 1911. Being active up in the air was definitely quite different than operating at ground level. That flying machine opened the sky to exploration of wide open spaces that contained fewer hazards other than high, tricky winds, driving rain, blinding snow, damned high mountain peaks, and crash landings.

As growth, progressed, the speed of the airplane was beginning to approach a speed category of a 100 miles per hour, or more. When war broke out in Europe in 1914, the airplane received its first taste of military warfare. At first, the big military wheels in command only considered the airplane valuable for conducting reconnaissance flights over enemy territory. Both sides flew observation flights back and forth over each other's lines; They sort of waved and smiled at each other as they went by. However, one day, one of the pilots while he was waving and smiling he was shocked to notice that dirty SOB in the other plane was shooting at him with his pistol! So he pulled out his own gun and starting firing back! Mid-air combat had finally come to the fore! On his flight the following days that angry guy's observer was armed with a light machine gun! Aerial combat was about to come into its own!

Aircraft designers, like old man Fokker tried hard to sell his aircraft designs to the British but they turned him down, so he then went to Germany. There he designed some of best new fighter aircraft ever flown during WW I. His D-7 model was recognized as one of the best combat designs of that war.

Probably the best aerial combat design feature was the invention of the synchronized machine gun. This mechanical device was mounted on the planes engine that timed the guns fire with the rotation of the propeller that permitted the gun to fire through the propeller without shooting the propeller up. This simplified the pilots aiming ability by adjusting the aircrafts line of flight to correct his aiming ability.

Fighter pilots were a new kind of war hero, true Knight of the sky. When they downed five or more victories they were given a new title, ACE. Pilots on both sides with exceptionally high victory scores made front-page news. For example, Germany's "Red Baron," Manfred Von Richthofen, was overall leader with a total of 80 victory's. These new combat hero's were celebrated and admired by their countryman as exceptional warriors of the sky!

Following the war things slowed down for a short period. Somebody, probably the government, invented the airmail system. The Post Office was happy the mail could get to its destination faster, if they didn't hit a storm or run out of gas and crash. But either way the Post Office made a few cents more selling Air Mail stamps.

Our Navy had been keeping track of all the aircraft advancements. They studied some of the British early experiments at converting lesser vessels to seaplane carriers during WW I. This eventually led to the conversion of a collier, the USS Jupiter AC-3 to the USS Langley CV 1. In the early 1920's it had been modified with a wooden landing surface 530 feet long. First official air operations began in 1923.

When the Naval Conference outlawed the construction of the Lexington class battle cruisers there were two vessels that had already been launched, The Lexington and Saratoga. However, the approved conference limits did not apply to aircraft carriers.

Therefore, in order to salvage the construction cost of these two proposed battle cruisers, it was immediately determined to convert them to aircraft carriers. This was the official beginning of our fast carrier Navy.

By the time of the Japanese attack on Pearl Harbor we had seven Carriers in operation and several Essex Class vessels were under construction or on the drawing board. Early in WW II, the value and power of the airplane was well demonstrated in Africa, Europe and the Pacific. It had been proven that victory on the ground in many cases depended strictly on the ability to maintain control of the air. The first major sea battle, where surface ships never fired a shot at each other, was won by air-to-air action. WW II proved conclusively that no matter how large the vessel; a sustained accurate air attack could eventually send it to the bottom!

As we progressed through the Korean Police action, the Vietnam War, Desert Storm and several other little fracases our military aircraft have become more important, more sophisticated as well as more expensive. It's nice to be able to compare the Wright Brothers motorized kite to our dual jet engine mach two sound busters. Now as we progress into a new century it's beginning to look like the computer and TV might even be replacing requirements for some of those crazy fly-boys we needed so badly when the aircraft first began.

BIRTH OF NAVAL AVIATION

Our military has always been able to develop visionary personnel who constantly searched for ways and means to provide our nation with the best national security methods and procedures. This is specifically true of individuals with exceptional engineering backgrounds. Like it, or not, this world has always been dominated by nations that participate in a continuous arms race for personal gain and military superiority. They are constantly conducting research for new methods and procedures to constantly provide the means to improve and expand the physical capability of their armed forces.

For over 200 years the United States had preferred to remain fairly neutral. However, in the interest of national security it had chosen to maintain a high performance sea service to protect our vast shorelines. Plus, we also continued to encourage the support of a national back-up industrial capability, which in reality, is the very backbone, strength and power of any armed force.

Those of us who have dedicated our lives as military professionals are more aware than anyone of the possible horrors and devastation of all out war. The living veterans are well aware that the best war deterrent is an outstanding secure defensive posture. Superior military power allows this nation to present, or even in certain cases dictate, if you prefer, a strong diplomatic position. However, several times in our history, the civilian powers that be, have taken a more peaceful approach, which in the long run, has usually cost us dearly in both funds and manpower.

Down through the century's, warfare and research technology continued to make our world seem like a smaller place. What formally took years to accomplish now take only months, weeks, or even days. Our vessels of war began with wooden hulls, sails, and muzzle loaded cannon, which over the years progressively upgraded to steel, coal, oil, and breach loaded guns. The last 80 years of the 20th Century progressively brought improved combat vessels, jet aircraft, super submarines, nuclear power, atomic energy and guided missiles.

Our Navy began studying the possibility of some form of airborne vehicles almost 15 years before the Wright brothers got their motorized kite airborne at Kitty Hawk in 1903. There was a small group of visionary Naval Officers that actually believed in the eventual possibility of airborne weaponry and that in the very near future man would finally construct a vehicle that would be airborne!

The internal combustion engine already existed. It was just a matter of time before man would figure out how to mount one in a vehicle with wings. For more than a hundred years there were all kinds of curious industrious people, who were considered crazy because they were breaking their bones and necks building different kinds of wings, so they could jump off buildings or out of balloons. Sooner or later somebody had to come up with the correct solution. Now there was a couple of bicycle mechanics named Wilber and Orville Wright. Little did they realize when they give birth to the first vehicle to lift off the ground, it would eventually develop into a future combat weapon that would move the mighty battleship and their monstrous guns into 2nd place.

Naval Aviation actually began 14 November 1910 when Eugene Ely flew Glen Curtiss's heavier than air biplane off the USS Birmingham. However, neither the aircraft, nor the pilot, were part of the military. Captain W. I. Chambers, Officer in Charge of Naval Aviation, (which was nothing more than a retirement position, with no staff or funding), persuaded Curtiss to provide an aircraft and pilot for the test. He had managed to talk the navy into building a wooden deck on a ship. It's assumed the navy said, Why not. All this stupid stunt was costing them was the price of the lumber.

Predicated on the favorable news reports of Ely's takeoff from the USS Birmingham, Captain Chambers was able to talk the navy into attempting a shipboard landing. The USS Pennsylvania was selected for the test. Mare Island Navy Yard constructed a wooden platform 120 x 32 ft. on the USS Pennsylvania's stern. In the originally plan they intended that the vessel be underway during the landing. However, the ships Captain insisted that the traffic in the bay made it too restrictive. He stated that it would be necessary for the landing be made underway, it would have to be accomplished in the open Pacific or while the ship was at anchor in the Bay. The pilot Ely chose the latter.

To prepare for the first ever, shipboard landing, Pilot Ely made an on shore duplicate layout of the identical dimensions of the Pennsylvania's stern landing platform. He even experimented with different types of arresting devices to stop the aircraft. He quickly discovered that the Arresting Gear weights on each arresting line had to be the exact same weight to keep the aircraft from yawing to one side. Once ready to give it a try, they were held up for several days because of California's rainy weather. By 18 January 1911 the weather was just misting so they decided it was a go. The engine was started and Pilot Ely took off for the twelve mile flight to San Francisco Bay and the USS Pennsylvania.

The visibility was poor but as Ely progressed toward the ship landing, he viewed a good number of small boats heading in the USS Pennsylvania direction that just about everyone was interested in viewing the event. From just a couple of miles away he picked out the USS Pennsylvania.

As he flew passed and around the ship he noted that he would have to compensate for a slight wind blowing from about 10 degrees from the right. Once he lined up with the deck, he began to throttle back. About 50 feet from the end of the deck he cut his engine to idle. The plane ballooned slightly as he passed through stack turbulence but he eased it back down. As his wheels touched the deck his arresting hook caught one of the arresting lines and the dragging weights brought the plane to a stop with almost fifty feet of deck still left.

There was a long moment of silence as he cut the engine and climbed out of the aircraft. His arrival was followed by an uproar of cheering. He had arrived aboard at 10:59 hours, one minute early! An hour later, Pilot Ely's plane had been repositioned for takeoff. He started his engine and safely departed the USS Pennsylvania returning to the Army base were the flight began.

Captain W. I. Chambers, while waiting his retirement, had been buried in a thankless job titled, Officer in Charge of Naval Aviation. He had no staff, no funding and no aircraft! The Captain, during his three years in the position did a darn good job, working alone, without direction or a funding allowance. Chambers did quite a bit to increase the navy's interest in continuing to research the probability of using this new invention in the navy's future inventory. His efforts during this particular period were surely remembered. For nearly a century Chambers Field, at NAS Pensacola had operated under his name in memory of his contributions to Naval Aviation.

With the aid of Glen Curtiss Naval Aviation officially began in January 1911. Curtiss had leased North Island in San Diego Bay in order to establish a flying school. He had formally written the Secretary of the Navy offering to give free flying lessons to a naval officer. After volunteering Lt. Theodore G. Ellyson, a qualified submariner received orders on 23 December 1910, to report to the Glenn Curtiss Aviation Camp at North Island to under go flight training. Ellyson arrived at North Island in January 1911 where his efforts began toward becoming Naval Aviator #1.

Knowing the navy was a deep-water service; Curtiss had also been experimenting with a floatplane concept. Captain Chambers also believed that an airplane that could take off and land on water would be beneficial to the navy because it would simplify the landing field problem. Curtiss successfully built a plane on floats. This vehicle which eventually was to become known as a seaplane, first operated off the waters of North Island on 26 January 1911. Six days later the twin floats were replaced by a single float, which also proved successful. That successful single float proved that the single float concept necessary for the catapulting of shipboard aircraft now existed.

In March 1911 Captain Chambers finally received his first funding. The Navy's Bureau of Navigation received $25,000 dollars for experiments in aeronautics. After numerous expenditure discussions, on 8 May Chambers prepared purchase requisitions for two Curtiss biplanes, one an amphibian equipped for take off on land or water, designed for a speed of at least 45 miles per hour, and with a passenger seat next to the pilot, plus a dual control setup for control by either passenger. This plane eventually became the Navy's first airplane, the A-1. The date 8 May has since been considered as the first purchase of an Airplane and was officially proclaimed as Naval Aviation's Birthday.

By now two additional Naval Officers had been cut orders to flight training. Lt. John Rogers to the Wright Brothers at Dayton, Ohio and Lt. (jg) J. H. Towers to join Lt. Ellyson at the Curtiss Hammondsport, New York Plant. On 3 July Ellyson made a night flight from Lake Keuka to Hammonds port and landed safely, on the water without lights.

Working together Curtiss and Ellyson had been attempting to design a system to use aircraft on a cruising vessel. On 7 September 1911 they made a miraculous experiment toward solving the problem of developing a shipboard aircraft launching devise. Lt. Ellyson made a successful take-off in a Curtiss airplane equipped with a slotted float using a cable type launching system. However the cable launching system was abandoned after only one successful launch.

A compressed air catapult launching system was designed and built by the Naval Gun Factory in Washington D.C. and was mounted on a dock at Annapolis. On 12 July 1912 Ellyson attempted the first catapult launch. The fact that the A-1 aircraft was not physically attached to the catapult it reared up in mid-stroke. When it left the catapult nose up, it was caught by a crosswind and crashed in the water. Luckily, Ellyson was unhurt and was able to swim ashore. It was pretty obvious a redesign was required to keep the aircraft on the catapult until the end of the stroke. It was back to the drawing board at the Washington Navy yard. By the fall of 1912 an improved catapult was mounted on a barge at the Navy Yard. On 19 November Lt. Ellison again attempted, and completed, the first successful aircraft catapult launch in a Curtiss AH-3. One month later he also made a successful launch with the navy's first flying boat the C-1.

By now it was becoming obvious these new fly-boys needed a home of their own. First, in the interest of background lets drop our thoughts back a few years. In 1825 President John Q. Adams and Secretary of the Navy Samuel Southard originally conceived the idea for the Pensacola Naval Station. Construction began in 1826 where it became one of best equipped Naval Yards in the United States. During the Civil war the Navy Yard was totally destroyed by the Confederates when the Yankees captured New Orleans. After the war, the ruins were cleared and reconstruction began. Many of the structures built during this period including the two and three story houses on North Avenue still exist to this day. However, many of the newly built structures were destroyed in 1906 by a terrific hurricane and a tidal wave.

Because the need for wooden vessels declined, the Naval aircraft research and development increased. It was agreed in 1911 that the Aviators required a base of their own. The Pensacola Navy Yard was available and the weather was perfect for the aviators and their equipment. Therefore, the navy yard was renamed the Naval Aeronautical Station. The first ship designed to carry an aircraft began construction in 1911. A few weeks later the first Navy seaplane made its appearance.

By 1913 a Board was established by Secretary of Navy Joseph Daniels to make a survey to determine the policy to guide the future of naval aviation. Their most important recommendation was to also establish a permanent aviation training station at Pensacola. As a result all future navy pilots would now receive their flight training at Pensacola. Shortly thereafter, the station began to be known as the "Cradle of Naval Aviation".

Naval Aviation had finally been recognized as an official element of the naval service. Those young men that worked so hard and given so much effort to make it all happen are now mostly a fading memory. However, they will never be forgotten. Their portraits in shiny bronze grace the Wall of Honor at the Pensacola Naval Aviation Museum.

FIRST NAVAL AIRCRAFT FLIGHT MANUAL

Resurrected from old Naval Air System Command files

Instructions issued with the 1911
Glen Curtiss "Pusher"

Rules governing the use of
Aeronautical Apparatus

1.) The aeronaut should seat himself in the apparatus, and secure himself firmly to the chair by means of the strap provided. On the attendant crying "Contact" the aeronaut should close the switch, which supplies electrical current to the motor, thus enabling the attendant to set the same in motion.

2.) Opening the control valve of the motor, the aeronaut should at the same time firmly grasp the vertical stick, or control pole, which is to be found directly before the chair. The power from the motor will cause the device to roll gently forward and the aeronaut should govern the direction of motion by use of the rudder bars.

3.) When the mechanism is facing into the wind, the aeronaut should open the control valve of the motor to the fullest extent, at the same time pulling the control pole gently toward his (the aeronaut's) middle anatomy.

4.) When sufficient speed has been attained the device will leave the ground and assume the position of aeronautical assent.

5.) Should the aeronaut decide to return to terra firma, he should close the control valve of the motor. This will cause the apparatus to assume what is known as the "gliding position", except in the case of those flying machines, which are inherently unstable. These latter will assume the position known as "involuntary spin" and will return to earth without further action on the part of the astronaut.

6.) On approaching closely to the chosen field or terrain, the aeronaut should move the control pole gently toward himself, thus causing the mechanism to alight more of less gently on terra firma.

"THOSE CRAZY BEGOGGLED VISIONARIES"

Since the beginning of time man has watched and wondered about the graceful flight of the birds. He also thought how wonderful it would be if man might some day attain the same capability. For hundreds of years they pondered about this subject and even risked their lives experimenting with various homemade wings and tail designs that eventually failed due to the lack of thrust.

Thrust in those days meant something you did with knives, swords or spears. As time progressed, the world's scientific efforts advanced as well. They finally concluded that wing design kept the bird in the air but it was the wing power that got him airborne and kept him there. Therefore, it was easy to recognize the need for wings. However, the problem was, devising a system of thrust to compensate for mans weight in order to provide him the ability to fly.

By the end of the nineteenth century, man had invented the internal combustion engine and the automobile was born. I would not have been surprised if someone didn't try to put wings on the auto, because one thing it did have was thrust! Those visionaries finally realized that it required a combination of both thrust and lift to become airborne and remain in the air. They also concluded wing designs had to be curved in order to pack air pressure under the wings to keep the vehicle airborne as it moved forward.

However, I doubt if all those deep thinkers realized that the maximum amount of lift depended on the proper curve design of the airfoil. The lighter curved air pressure created on the upper wing surface provided the most lift. The heavier pressure exerted on the lower wing surface caused the wing to be lifted upward. Once fully understood it only took a short while to learn to flatten out the lower side and curve the upper to obtain a better airfoil. As a result, the greater the forward thrust of the engine, the swifter the airflow under and over the wing the greater the lift necessary for a flying machine. Wilber and Orville Wright finally conquered the thrust and lift problem at Kitty Hawk in 1903. Forevermore, man would finally be able to fly just like the birds!

As always, when anything new is invented, every nation with an armed force, no matter how small or large, starts sniffing around to determine its possible military advantages. Naturally, anything that would be capable of moving from one place to another by air might definitely have military possibilities. Even the U. S., especially the navy visionaries were sitting up taking notice of these fragile flying kites. It's amazing, once it's proved to be successful, how unbelievable rapidly it can become less fragile and more sturdy in its construction.

When the U.S. Navy began showing a real interest in the new flying machine, many were curious about what possible use could a water bound navy make of these weird little aeroplanes's. What the navy had in their favor was a group of young officers who were real visionaries vitally interested in improving future naval operations. With the assistance of Glen Curtiss they conducted early tests with landings and take offs from temporary wood decking on real combat vessels. It didn't look like much, but stop and think, if it worked with simple jury rigged decks, there had to be a damn good possibility of working on a vessel specially constructed for support of aircraft operations.

At this stage of its activities, navy fleets participating in battle drills were practically conducting maneuvers in the blind. Lookouts high in the rigging with the best available spy glasses were restricted to a short range line of sight to the horizon capability, aided solely by high speed destroyer search and discover missions ahead of the fleet. Our visionaries believed the possible addition of an airborne reconnaissance vehicle, with a variable visible range dictated by time, speed and altitude would permit a whole new early search and warning capability.

Now Mr. Curtiss had a good thing going with these young naval officers. As a practical businessman he was strictly interested in getting the jump on everyone involved in new airplane development. However, there were many things that were forcing limitations. The major obstacle being the non-believers that controlled military funding, who in their opinion considered that goggled flyers, were all nuts, willing to waste government money on a fly by night idea that was considered impractical for over water use.

Based thereon, Curtiss had an idea. He made an offer to the Secretary of the Navy to teach a Naval Officer to fly for free. You and I know our government never turns anything down that you could get for nothing! Lt. Ted Ellyson, a submariner, because thereof who already had to be a little bit nuts, volunteered. He was issued orders to report to Curtiss at North Island, San Diego, California to learn to fly and become what was to be known as Naval Aviator # 1. Curtiss also knew that the word Navy rhymed with water so he modified his basic pusher design by the addition of a hull float and called it a flying boat. This was eventually sold to the navy. As a new purchase, there was no aircraft designator established for flying machines, so it was named A-1 meaning Aeroplane #1. Pretty clever wasn't it?

Lt. Ellyson worked well with Curtiss and performed most of the early tests using the A-1. One of which was to convert the aircraft to an amphibian by the addition of two manually retractable wheels to the float hull. In 1912 aeroplane A-1 also established a seaplane altitude record of 900 feet. Our visionaries went on undaunted because they were certain that the construction of a large flying boat had definite possibilities for successful long range overseas missions like the possibility of flying across the Atlantic or non-stop to Pearl.

A few months later aircraft A-2 was delivered in the land plane configuration. Approximately a year later it was converted to a seaplane by the addition of a pontoon structure. In 1912 while a seaplane it completed an endurance flight of six hours ten minutes. A bit later A-2 was again modified to add manually retractable wheels to the hull to permit both land and water operational capability.

Based on their many short trials and experiments, they began to visualize the possibility of Battleships and Cruisers at sea equipped with their own reconnaissance aircraft. Catapults were nothing new therefore, properly designed they might well be capable of applying the necessary initial thrust to get an aircraft airborne from a surface vessel. It was just a matter of time, and the right funding to design an aircraft strong enough to withstand the thrust of the launch pressure as well as to develop the ability to land close to the vessel in the open sea for underway recovery by the mother vessel.

There were those with the mental visibility that could close their eyes and envision wheel mounted combat airframes returning to the mother ship, landing on aboard, then rearming and refueling for the next mission. It's just that things moved rather slowly when you were fighting the big gun money shufflers over nickels and dimes!

With the threat of war rumbling in Europe our Naval Aviation personnel were already working with Curtiss for the construction of a series of special long range, three to four engine flying boats capable of an attempt to fly the Atlantic Ocean or, fly neutrality patrols in the event of war. The proposed aircraft were simply identified as NC-1 through NC-4. (NC, could that mean Navy Curtiss?)

When World War I erupted in Europe in 1914 the proposed transatlantic flight plan had to be shelved and held in abeyance. The United States remained neutral and gave little to no thought of early preparation based on the possibility of being drawn into the conflict at a later date.

When the day finally arrived forcing them to declare war, they were far from ready to train and arm a military force for deployment to France. For example, despite designing the most accurate bolt-action rifle in modern history, Springfield Armory was only capable of arming companies not divisions. Luckily,

Remington and Winchester were contracted to manufacture British Enfield's. By converting them to be capable to fire U.S. .30-06 caliber rifle ammunition, the U.S. was lucky to be able to buy into those contracts. The majority of our troops in France were armed with the M 17 Enfield conversions. Only a small number of troops were armed with the 1903 Springfield. In relation to aircraft we were in even worse shape. Not one aircraft manufactured in the United States ever fought in World War I. We had to unlock some of those tightly squeezed military funds to buy aircraft from the British and French in order for our aviators to have something to fly. However, we did have the four NC flying boats under construction but the war ended and the Neutrality Patrols never materialized.

Once the war was over the British Daily Mail's 1913 prize money of 10,000 pound sterling for the first non-stop flight across the Atlantic was still on the table. Commander Towers, Officer in Charge of the NC-1 through NC-4 flying boats felt the time was ripe to make the long planned attempt to fly across the Atlantic. Cdr. Towers wasn't interested in the prize money. His only interest was his desire for the U.S. Navy being the first military activity to perform such a feat.

The NC-4 was one of four, almost, identical flying boats under Navy construction during the war. The original plan for the Atlantic crossing called for the four plane formation to depart from Far Rockaway NY, with stops at Halifax, NS. Then proceed to Trepassey, Newfoundland. From there to fly across the Atlantic to Horta, in the Azores, then continue on to Lisbon, Portugal thus completing the transatlantic passage.

On 10 May 1919, NC-1, NC-3, and NC-4 departed from Far Rockaway. It was necessary to strike NC-2 from the formation due to a damaged wing. Enroute to Halifax NC-4 developed engine trouble and landed off Cape Cod and sought repair at Chatham, Mass. The others arrived at Halifax safely.

NC-1 & -3 continued the flight to Trepassey with NC-4 returning to the formation on the 15th of May. On the evening of the 16th all three aircraft departed Newfoundland headed east for the Azores with an arrival for early morning the following day. Twenty-one destroyers had been positioned at fifty mile intervals along the route as a navigational aid due to the fact that in 1919 flight instruments and aerial navigation was in its infancy.

During the night the planes broke formation in the interest of safety. The night passed without any problems. However, dawn and sunrise was followed by dense fog. To take a navigational sighting Cdr. Towers NC-3 decided to make an open sea landing. Unfortunately, the sea was running high and the landing was so rough it damaged some of the engine mounting struts. Thus the Flying Boat NC-3 was now just that, a boat. For the remainder of the trip to the Azores they became a surface craft. NC-1 also landed without any problems but the seas were so rough they were unable to take off again. They were able to stay afloat until a Greek freighter broke through the fog and rescued the crew. The NC-1 sank later.

After over 15 hours in the air, dead reckoning and radio reports lead the crew to feel the NC-4 was close to their objective in the Azores. There was a break in the fog and they spotted greenery on one of the Azores Islands. At noon on 17 May 1919 the NC-4 landed at Horta in the Azores. The badly damaged NC-3 sailed bravely into Horta as a non-flying boat the following day.

Bad weather and engine trouble kept the NC-4 at Horta until the 17 of May when its crew took off for Lisbon. Thus, the U.S. Navy finally completed the first transatlantic flight in history. The Navy got the credit but they accomplished the feat with a rarely mentioned fact. The NC-4's Copilot was, Lt. E. F. Stone, U.S. Coast Guard's' Aviator #1.

The NC-4 is still available for viewing today. It was originally placed on display at the Smithsonian Institute but later transferred to the Naval Air Museum at Pensacola, FL where it is currently on display.

The leather helmet and goggled aviators were still determined to seek the availability of a vessel designed for the launch and recovery of wheeled aircraft capable of air to air combat as well as the delivery of new aerial weaponry, against enemy vessels. World War I had led the Army to believe this was the sole purview of the Army Air Force, but the Navy disagreed. With the right type vessel designed as a mobile landing field, the matching attack capability could be applied against enemy fleets and shipping. Finally, the navy had a break through.

With the receipt of basic funding, the Collier Jupiter on 19 July 1919 was ordered to the Navy Yard Norfolk, Va. for conversion to an aircraft Carrier. The purpose, to conduct experiments on the idea of using combat aircraft on war maneuvers at sea. The vessels name was changed to Langley in April 1920 and received the designation CV-1. It was officially commissioned in March 1922. The vessel now sported a wooden landing deck 530 feet long. On 17 October 1922 the first pilot to take off from her decks was Lt. Virgil Griffin. While underway 9 days later Lt Cdr Chavalier was the first man to land on a Carrier deck. Comdr Kenneth Whiting, the Langley's Commanding Officer was first to be catapulted from a carrier. In its hey-day, this vessel developed most of the basic ground rules covering Carrier operations.

The two available battle cruiser hulls left over from the 1922 treaty construction restrictions were saved for conversion and shortly followed the Langley to became the new large carriers USS Lexington CV-2 and USS Saratoga CV-3.

This is basically where my planned story ends. However, as an after thought, aerial combat and bombing during World War II was proof positive that those crazy pioneer airdale's were really true visionaries. For over 200 years the monster gun ships ruled the waves. But those crazy aviators and their flying machines became both the rulers of the air as well as the seas. The big guns of the battle wagons have been silenced forever.

Today science still continues to advance. We now fly Mach two aircraft off nuclear powered Carriers, and have shed the old leather helmet and goggles for a space suit so we can now learn to fly to and explore distant worlds.

THE UNITED STATES NAVAL AIR FORCE

It might be of interest to know that in 2010 our Navy Air Force is really getting old! Believe it or not, in exactly one hundred years the whistles of this massive force, will blow loudly on every aircraft carrier and aviation support vessel to honor one hundred years of faithful aviation service to the United States of America!

Like anything historical it started out slowly and small with a bunch of smart alec young crack-pots who were smart enough to believe that Navy men should fly. Off a combat vessel no less!! No way, some thought. Just one shot out of a 6 to 16 inch gun, or maybe even a .30 caliber rifle and that flimsy flying machine might fall apart!

But the joke was on those 16 inch gun lovers. Those crazy young Fly-boys were right. They might of started out small potato's but I just saw on TV, (another dumb invention}, an F/A—18E/F Super Hornet make a neat landing on the USS Ninitz-CVN 68. Oh, and by the way have you read about the new F-35 Lightning II tearing up the sky in their new test performances. Well it's good to know that the might of our Naval Air services are stretched out over this mean old earth protecting our interests in far away places.

It's hard to believe that it all began in 1911 when, believe it or not, a qualified submarine Officer volunteered to accept Glen Curtiss's free offer to teach a naval officer how to fly and become Naval Aviator #1. All those big Gun sailors laughed with glee at the sub nut wanting to fly, because anyone with any brains at all realized that those flimsy motorized kites had nothing to offer the navy. People in their right minds all realized the power of the navy rested in the great distance we could toss a large heavy explosive projectile through the air!

In January 1911, Lt. Theodore G. Ellyson, reported to Glen Curtis at North Island, San Diego for the purpose of training to become the Navy's first Naval Aviator. Now stop and think, in those days what possible military mission could those flimsy stick and paper type aircraft perform for a military service that operated principally on deep sea vessels? There was a small visionary group that followed Ellyson that realized that a combat ships sight capability was limited to the power of their lookouts telescope and the speed and ability of their destroyer escort. Their crazy early visions rested mainly on gaining the possibility of aerial long range scouting and reconnaissance.

These adventurous young men were the basic floor plan upon which today's mighty Naval Air Fleet was built. It took them awhile to get their visions in motion because of money shortages and the U.S. Army's leg up with the Congress. Their first concerns was getting aircraft built strongly enough to withstand catapulting off combat vessels like cruisers and battleships. Plus the design of seaplanes for long range overseas flights and anti-submarine and rescue missions. Curtiss was a big help in the design and placement of aircraft on large combat vessels.

Despite their successes, the major design in the back of their minds was the possibility of operating land based combat aircraft from a vessel at sea. There were numerous problems to consider but it was finally agreed that studies be conducted to determine the feasibility of designing a vessel that could launch and recover aircraft underway at sea. A former collier the USS Jupiter was selected to enter the Navy Yard, Norfolk, Va. for an experiential conversion to support a compliment of aircraft. Her name was changed to USS Langley CV-1. On 20 March 1922 she was commissioned as the Navy's first Aircraft Carrier containing a flat wooden flight deck 530 ft long. Commander Whiting was assigned as its first Skipper.

When the first aircraft was launched from her decks shortly there after, the era of the Navy aircraft Carrier began. Much was learned about the launching and recovery of aircraft at sea and the initial shipboard flight doctrine was developed on that experimental vessel. Concurrently, we had installed catapults on the battleships and cruisers. Single engine floatplanes designed and built by Curtiss manned these cats. The flyers of these small aircraft became the eyes and ears of the fleet until finally replaced by the installation of the radar system during World War II.

In 1922 international conference resulted in the signing of an international treaty limiting the size of Military vessels. These limits resulted in the cancellation of the two proposed battle cruisers the USS Lexington and the USS Saratoga. The Aviation personnel immediately laid claim to the two hulls stating the treaty never outlawed Aircraft Carriers. It was a great break for the airdales because they were able to put two hulls back on the ways for redesign and modification into good size aircraft carriers. It was a major event in Naval Aviation History when both were launched again in 1925 as aircraft Carriers CV-2 and CV-3. Upon their commissioning in 1927 carrier aviation got underway for real. It was finally obvious that aircraft at sea was coming into its own as both an offensive as well as a defensive weapon.

From that point on ships, aircraft, and weaponry began to come off the production line specifically designed for aerial combat at sea. A new element of warfare had come into being. As a result all the major world nations all established offense and defensive aircraft programs to include this new element of warfare. The U. S Navy surface personnel of the big ship navy suddenly found itself in a funding struggle with the upstart "Airdales."

Secretly the Japanese Admiral, Yamamoto, who was also a sharp cookie and a firm believer in the value of aerial combat capability had defied the 1922 treaty limitations and had secretly constructed a massive Imperial Fleet with special emphasis on aircraft carriers, fighter and attack aircraft and the specially trained combat aviator. The Admirals 7 December 1941 attack on Pearl Harbor and the destruction they caused in slightly over an hour with a little over 200 plus aircraft was proof positive of the value of military air. Another example was the battle of the Coral Sea were opposing air forces were able to do considerable damage without a singe shot being fired by vessels on either side.

In reality the modern aircraft with its outstanding selection of special armament was beginning to silence forever the big guns of the mighty battleships. These historical vessels are now manned by happy youths and curious visitors trying to get the feel of a time long past when those vessels were the rulers of the seas. It may seem hard to believe that more than sixty years have passed and the nuclear fueled carrier and the Mach two aircraft are still supreme.

THE NAVAL AVIATOR

It takes a special type of individual to train to become a military Aviator. But, in the personal opinion of your writer, it takes an extra special type of individual to fly for the Navy. Having spent a major portion of my life committed to Naval aviation, both in uniform and as a civilian, I hope it's obvious that I might be considered qualified to make such a statement. After all, just think about it, when you are out there it's obvious there is little out there but water! Now the average individual might wonder how does the pilot know where he is going and how long is it going to take him to get there, accurately?

Battleship Cruiser Aviators:—Beginning in the middle 1930's I spent a good part of my life working and flying with these Navy fly boys. In that time period I rarely ever gave much thought about the pilot with his hand on the throttle, failing to bring us safely back to the vessel of departure.

Actually there was a real good reason to think differently when it comes to mind. In the early days when they catapulted you off a ship making twenty five, or more, knots in order to fly a four hour search mission, how could you be sure the ship was going to be in the right place where you returned? Even with everything working perfectly how would you find your way back? After all like it was said before, there was absolutely nothing out there except water!

Unlike Air Force flyers there was no roads or railroad tracks like those Army guys had to follow! There weren't any maps to follow because they wouldn't look any different than looking out of the cockpit at all that damn water! Here we are at 5000 ft altitude, which provided us with good visibility but what did we have to look at but one hell of a lot water!

Now we were not exactly helpless we had instruments. The altimeter told us how high up we were, the compass kept us aware of our flight direction while the fuel gage kept us advised at how long we can remain airborne. We also knew the speed of the departed vessel and the course it would be sailing during our scheduled time of flight. Plus, at altitude our line of visibility was one heck of a long way. That was unless if a cloud got in the way. Now you know why they paid us brave Navy aircrews the big bucks of an extra thirty dollars each month for sticking our necks out for a total of about a hundred hours of airtime per month!

Now the reason our Navy pilots were so good they were excellent at figuring. Their proposed flight schedule was worked out on a plotting board. Once airborne, the search was plotted on a preplanned triangular course. When reaching the determined flight altitude, a compass course was planned to fly away from the ship while still remaining parallel with the course of the vessel. At the end of your search time it was really just a matter of turning toward the ships expected position with both you and the ship arriving at the predetermined spot at the completion of the prescribed four hours of flight time.

Besides if there might be a slight error in plotting, at altitude you can see one heck of a long ways! Plus the fact you could be in constant contact with the ship by radio, that is except when operating at radio silence. Just a couple of years later our vessels were equipped with an electronic locator signal.

Now the flight wasn't really over until you were safely back on board securely locked on the catapult car. Aircraft recovery was in reality, the most dangerous part of the flight. Upon arrival the ship would make a wide turn toward the prevailing wind to make a nice smooth slick for us to land on. Once safely on the water the ship would launch a special sled with an attached net for us to taxi up on. Our centerline float had a hook that would engage in the net and tow the aircraft. As the pilot cut the engine back to idle, the man in the rear cockpit could then straddle the pilot and remove the hoisting sling from the upper wing center section and prepare to engage the hoisting cranes hook as the tow lines brought the aircraft in closer to the vessel for pick up. This is actually the most dangerous part of the flight operation because the ship is still progressing underway through the entire operation. Once the hook and sling was engaged and the aircraft replaced and locked on the Catapult Car the flight was over. We then washed the plane to remove the salt spray and prepared for the Next flight.

The Aircraft Carrier:—These were the Aviators that in just a few days completely changed Naval warfare. For over 200 years the mighty battleships had ruled the waves of navy's throughout the world. In just a few engagements the Carrier Aviators not only moved the battleships into second place they eventually transferred them into historical monuments.

All Navy pilots are trained at Pensacola, Florida and all are eligible for various assignments. However, the carrier combat pilots are the ones we hear the most about. It all began when early visionary aviators got the idea that a sea going landing field would be a revolutionary idea. The big gun sailors thought they were all nuts looking for a short cut to Arlington Cemetery.

They finally succeeded in talking their way into getting funds to convert an old collier with a little over 500 foot flat wooden deck to handle those motorized kites they were building in those days. I don't know if it was true or not, but some of the big gun club members were hoping they would all break their necks and the problem would go away.

However, it was the beginning of a new era for Naval history. The new ship AV 1 the USS Langley began the development of sea borne landing field doctrine some of which is still in use today. Actually, landing an aircraft on a moving carrier in a heavy sea, especially in the early days and on the short decked jeep carrier's was tricky but they learned how. In fact, we are getting to the point where today's pilots just point his jet at the stern and the ship system lands the aircraft all by itself!

It is amazing, almost unbelievable the changes the aircraft made to our Navy's combat capability. It was proved early in World War II how extremely important that control of the air over the operating fleet was to the safety and protection of the surface combat vessels. Plus, it also proved that aerial operation and delivery of weapons against enemy vessels was far more effective than long range gunnery. The manned aircraft had proved conclusively that it had importance as a defensive weapon as well as an offensive weapon!

THE BLUE ANGELS

The U. S. Navy Flight Demonstration Squadron

After the Japanese signing of the papers of unconditional surrender in September 1945 aboard the USS Missouri Chief of Naval Operations Chester W. Nimitz, ordered the formation of an aerial demonstration team. Its mission was to enhance Navy and Marine Corps recruiting efforts as well as keep the public interested in Naval Aviation. Its purpose also included impressing the political elected leadership of both the United States and the foreign nations of the world.

The leading expert naval aviators were selected to be trained for this special duty under the Officer in Charge, LCdr Roy Voris, a WW II Fighter Ace. The team perfected its first maneuvers in secret over the Florida Everglades. LCdr Voris personal statement was, "*If anything happens just the Alligators will know.*" The team's first demo before Navy Officials conducted 10 May 1946 was met with surprised admiration and approval to proceed officially.

On 15 June 1946, at Craig Field, Florida, LCdr Voris conducted their first public demonstration flying four Grumman famous WW II F6F Hellcat fighters through a 15 minute aerobatic program. The spectators were thrilled by their fancy low flying maneuvers in tight formation. This public team demonstration was honored by its receipt of its first trophy, which is proudly displayed at its current home. Surprisingly, the teams name was finely derived from a New York Nightclub called the "Blue Angel". LCdr Voris liked the name and made it official on 19 July 1947.

On 25 August 1946 their display aircraft was upgraded to the Grumman F8F Bearcat. In the same year their famous tight "Diamond Formation" was introduced to the viewers at the World Air Carnival in Birmingham, Alabama. LCdr Voris departed the team 30 May 1947 returning to active duty. LCdr Bob Clark replaced him as Officer in Charge.

The "Blues" introduced their first Jet aircraft, the Grumman F9F-2 Panthers in late 1949. However, that tour was short lived. The outbreak of the Korean War put their demo flight activities on hold. The team was returned to combat duty with Fighter Squadron VF-191, the "Satan's Kittens" aboard the USS Princeton in 1950.

The team was officially recommissioned on 25 October 1951 and reported to NAS (Naval Air Station) Corpus Christi, Texas where, LCdr Voris returned as Officer in Charge (he was the first of two officers to lead the Blue's twice). They began operations with the much improved Grumman Panther F9F-5. The Blue's continued to operate out of Corpus until the winter of 1954. They were then moved to what proved to be their permanent home for over fifty years, NAS Pensacola, Florida. They were now flying the Grumman swept wing F9F-8 Cougar.

In the next 20 years that followed, the team transitioned to two more aircraft. In 1957 they began to perform with the Grumman F11F-1 Tiger aircraft, which continued for a period of twelve years. The Tiger was best known as the demonstration aircraft. Mainly because it survived longer as a demo aircraft then it did in active service. In 1969 they received "Big Ugly," the famous McDonnell Douglas F4J Phantom II. (The twin engine F4J was the jet fighter yours truly cut his Navy civilian teeth on as Bureau of Aeronautics Ordnance Logistics Manager.) The F4J Phantom II was the only aircraft ever used by both the Navy and the Air Force Flight Demonstration teams.

In December 1974 the Navy Flight Demonstration team was, out of necessity, downsized to the more economical subsonic McDonnell Douglas A4F Skyhawk II aircraft. Concurrently it was reorganized into the Navy as the Flight Demonstration

Squadron. This revision finely permitted the establishment of a Commanding Officer vice an Officer in Charge. Cdr Tony Less became the Squadrons first official Commanding Officer.

On 8 November 1986 the Blue Angles celebrated their 40th anniversary. During the celebration they introduced their present aircraft. They unveiled the new McDonnell Douglas F/A-18 Hornet which was the first twin role fighter/attack aircraft assigned the responsibility of serving the nation as the Navy's front line of defense. The F/A-18's power and aerodynamics allowed the Blues to perform a slow high angle attack, "tail sitting maneuver" and also gave them the ability to perform a formation loop with the landing gear extended.

Aiding the Blues with their demonstration travels they also operated a Marine Corp C-130T Hercules aircraft. This plane has been nicknamed "Fat Albert" due to its unusual shape. Plus it also participates in the Blues demonstrations. It performs a jet assisted (JATO) take off prior to the beginning of the blues fighter/attack demo. The "Fat Albert Airlines" is operated by a eight man Marine Corps crew of three officers and five enlisted personnel.

The Blues perform seventy or more shows each year at thirty-four or more different locations in the U. S. They still fly many of the basic formations displayed at previous locations as far back as 1946. Since their 1946 beginning they have performed for almost 500 million spectators. Their flying has always been spectacular. Take it from your scribe who has followed their performances ever since his first viewing them in 1947.

During the show season, the Squadron is stationed at NAS Pensacola. During the off season, January through March, they operate out of the Naval Air Facility El Centro, California. Here they train and practice with newly assigned pilots. An item of special interest, during normal flight of high performance aircraft the pilots always wear G Suits to prevent blackout caused by blood rushing from their head.

During their training, due to the stress experienced in sharp demonstration maneuvers the Blue Angel pilots must learn to control the aircraft without a G suit because the air bladders in the suits would be constantly inflating and deflating at each sharp change in direction. This could be dangerous and interfere with the pilots operation of the control stick. To compensate the pilots tense their stomach muscles and legs to prevent blood flow from leaving the head and rendering them unconscious.

During the current year 2007, the Blues have been scheduled to perform 55 air show at 35 different sites. Concurrently they have also been celebrating the 20th year of operation with the F/A-18 Hornet. If you ever have an opportunity to witness a Blue Angels demonstration, I strongly recommend you not miss this show. You will not only enjoy their performance, it's proof positive of how good our Naval Aviators really are! May our "Blue Angels" continue to fly on into eternity!

WATER, WATER, EVERYWHERE!!

The earth is a small planet, the third from the sun, which is the center of our universe. In theory the earth just happened to be the only planet correctly positioned to sustained life. In the early days, man was a rather simple satisfied creature. There was no work, no construction, why bother just so long as there were caves to live in. Ownership was a simple matter, just walk in and take over. He also carried a simple tool, a club. This he carried mainly to satisfy his hunger. It was a simple life style. When hungry just bash what ever was available on the head, and eat it before it had a chance to eat you.

However, there was one thing that really bothered him. Two thirds of the earth's surface was covered with water, salt water. The remaining third consists of irregular ground areas which were later called continents, and islands. They appeared to him to be nothing more than tops of hills or mountains that stuck out of the water and have become living surfaces.

For this short trip down prehistoric lane, the main item of discussion between cave people had be water. It didn't take our first human beings long to learn that water was an absolute necessity. But for some damn fool reason the largest quantity available was useless and undrinkable. Only the clear sparkling water that seeped out of the ground and flowed in the in-land creeks and streams was tasty.

The early thought process dwelt on the fact that salty water had to be good for something otherwise there wouldn't be so damn much of it. It did provide a larger, tastier supply of fish, which may have been possibly because it was pre salted! Just a prehistoric joke!

Once man suddenly discovered that wood floated, the boating business was born. Man's natural curiosity finally led to the desire to find out what hell was on the other side of all that damn water. This persistence down through the ages finally resulted in the expensive Cruise Ship industry and huge Navy's to protect their side from the other sides.

The winds and waters of the world on normal occasions can be an item of infinite beauty. To a sailor there is nothing more beautiful than the reflection of a setting sun on a smooth slow rolling sea of blue water. However, on other occasions, with the aid of a stiff wind, it could raise up causing terror and destruction. During these moments they discovered that for some reason the safest course of action was heading directly into the direction of the wind. A hurricane, or typhoon, at sea is a special unnerving experience. The shifting high winds turns that beautiful smooth blue water into a roaring green chop with waves that sometimes exceed eighty to a hundred feet high. Small vessels have totally disappeared in weather of this magnitude. I'll bet our little caveman wished he never found the value of a piece of wood when he experienced his first storm at sea.

Personal knowledge had been experienced on an aircraft carrier almost 1000 feet long that displacing over 55,000 tons. We were taking solid green water over that 80 ft bow that stripped the flight deck of every wired down item that couldn't be stored below on the hanger deck. Considerable additional damage was sustained to the hanger decks roller curtains and other top side items. On returning to port it was necessary our large vessel to enter the yard for minor repairs.

If you can visualize what happened to that carrier, you might be able to imagine what similar conditions might have been on a smaller vessel. But compared to the size of our fleets, only a few vessels have ever been lost because of storms. Experienced Navy crews can normally conquer a raging sea. Therefore, the true sailorman worries only slightly about the sea of darkness and thinks only of the sun kissed waters that carry him to far away places to view the many wonders of the world.

THE SUBMARINE

Being an aviation type, discussing the submarine service is not generally my forte. However, down through the ages military personnel have always been interested in unique methods for sneaking up on enemy vessels and surprising them. Now for the Navy approaching an enemy vessel unidentifiable has always been difficult for a fully armed attack group because of the inability to keep their powder dry plus the distinct possibility of drowning.

Everyone was fully aware the solution rested in some of underwater vessel. However, at the same time the mere suggestion of such a vehicle brought laughter and a possible measurement for a straight jacket! But man was intelligent and progressive in nature and continually moved toward some sort of solution. It didn't take much of a brain to figure out that the availability of air or oxygen was the major problem. Many early attempts were made by the British, but there was little success until the Civil War and a man named Huntley.

In 1863 and 64 Mr. H.L. Huntley had been experimenting with the construction of a under sea vessel and finally built one for the Confederates. It required an eight man crew that propelled the boat manually. I have searched to find out how he resolved the air/oxygen but failed to locate an answer. On their first, and also their final mission, they were armed with a Spar Torpedo loaded with 90lbs of gunpowder. They approached their target the USS Housatomi at night with the Spar Torpedo mounted on their bow. They rammed the spear of the spar into the side of the Union vessel and exploded it as they backed away from the holed vessel, which immediately began to sink.   Historically they were the first submersible to successfully sink an enemy vessel. However, the mission was not a total success. The Huntley sank with all her crew on board during the return trip to their own base. There they rested as a casket for her volunteer crew until August 2000. She was finally raised by efforts of the National Park Service and the Smithsonian. The crew's remains were identified and finally buried with full military honors.

The first official U. S. Navy submarine was the USS Holland SS 1. It was accepted after demonstration trials on the Potomac River. However, it was not a sea going boat and could not operate in open waters. But it was a formal start. As of the current year, the Navy's Submarine Service celebrated 102 years of service as well as the advancement of undersea technology.

The first Navy to successfully deploy submarines in combat service was the Germans during WW I. They constructed a complete fleet of these vessels that were serviced at sea by disguised sea going supply vessels. The U.S. was finally brought into this conflict because a German sub sank the Lusitanian with American citizens on board.

During the period between WW I and WW II, The United States designed and progressively improved our own submarine fleet and trained our sub-surface personnel into a formidable force. It was in this period your writer had his first, personnel contact with our sub service. It was aboard an old S boat acting as a torpedo firing observer. It was amazing to witness the ability of the crew to work and operate in such a limited space. One of their torpedomen noted my aviation insignia an asked if aviation wasn't dangerous. The reply was, "It can't be as dangerous as subs. What goes up always comes down. But what goes down doesn't necessarily have to come back up."

Prior to WW II the Navy spent considerable time and money developing an efficient and effective submarine force. We soon found out the Germans had done the same. From 1939 and the following war years German submarines and their wolf packs used the Atlantic ocean as their own happy hunting ground. Many U.S. and Allies cargo vessels now line the Atlantics bottom.

In the Pacific, following Japan's attack on Pearl Harbor, for several months, the American submarine was the nations primary defense force in the central Pacific. During, the four plus years of that war, our submarines destroyed almost 90% of the Japanese supply vessels, well over 1,100 ships amounting to hundreds of thousands of tonnage. But again success wasn't free. Fifty-two of our vessels and over 4,000 brave seamen are considered still on station.

Today, since the demise of the Soviet Union, The United States now deploys the largest Nuclear submarine force in the world. Since the launching of the first nuclear powdered boat we have sailed million of undersea miles without an accident. For over a 100 years it took thousands of brave submarine sailors to volunteer a portion of their life to establish a record of that magnitude.

MILITARY INTELLIGENCE

A Brief Analysis

The collecting of Military intelligence began a long time ago when man began to expand his horizons with the use of force of arms. As the world grew, man became increasingly more intelligent. Concurrently, the collection and analysis of said intelligence progressively became more sophisticated. Today the government and its military continue to collect foreign intelligence. Said information is fed to our trained intelligence analysis for the specific purpose for determining the proper methods and procedures for updating national security requirements, for combat applications and when necessary the specific movement and positioning of troop strength.

Despite its increased scientific methodology and importance, intelligence gathering, still cannot be considered a perfect science. Because it's a two or more sided science working against each other it will probably continue to remain as a best guess! It consists of analyzing a massive collection of facts and assembling them in an orderly fashion that makes sense. When completed and analyzed the human element may consider it lucky if the results fall into a 50 to 90 percent accuracy range. Basically, it is hoped the quality of the material being analyzed is fairly accurate to begin with. For example, direct copies of original documents as compared to verbal statements or notes. It must be understood that possible unrecognizable errors can reduce the quality of the effort.

Until a few years ago little of this intelligence information reached out to the general public. However, in today's environment, it has become difficult to keep a lid on intelligence keeping. In many cases the military and our intelligence services regrets the necessity to make reports to the government or media activities. There may be many individuals within this chain that seem to believe they can make brownie points by releasing fresh information to the public through the media's eagerness to be the first to release any and all sorts of information, true or not. We now find the ordinary citizenry discussing, commenting and complaining, about the mishandling of intelligence. It's surprising, how many people in this land of free speech, are often talking and making a big deal about subjects they really don't know a damn thing about!

Another stumbling block is the fact the oppositions counter intelligence personnel are concurrently working against us and may be deliberately releasing tainted information specifically designed to lead our military or politicians astray. In the good old days intelligence was gathered by courageous human elements. Many of who were specially trained spies operating in enemy territory, direct, on the spot, gathering of information was more effective, but at the same time might be misleading. Even then there were possible flaws because when the information arrived at the desk of the analyst, it was the under-cover agents interpretation of what he thought he saw or heard.

As electronic technology became more advanced we began to drift away from the human element to electronic surveillance. But even this has its limitations. Orbiting satellites can be programmed, tracked and timed. One can assure the opposition is aware of the approximate time the satellite will make its pass and therefore be able to hide or arrange what he wants the analyst to see.

For 250 years this nation has been involved in 12 or more shooting conflicts of one size or another. I'm positive that in each and every conflict, smart capable high-ranking military commanders have been subjected to the use of flawed information. Even before our own revolution, during the French and Indian wars, the British Commander received information that his planned attack against the French would be a walk in the park. It turned out to be a shoot out in the woods, with the "cowardly" French and Indians, shooting from behind trees.

The British force was nearly cut to pieces. Luckily, one of the Commanders officers, named Washington, who was familiar with the frontier style warfare, saved the command by ordering a hasty withdrawal.

Our Revolutionary War battles were pock marked with bad intelligence. Plus we lost our first heroic American spy. Patriot Nathan Hale who, just before his hanging in 1776, stated, "I regret that I have only one life to give for my Country". We finely won that war due mainly to bad British Intelligence. Lord Cornwallis would never have allowed himself to be trapped in Yorktown if he had known the French Admiral de Grasse's Fleet would block his withdrawal by sea.

In the war of 1812 the British overrun Washington D.C., burned the White House, (that's why it's still painted white) and were advised, that everything to the south was theirs for the taking. They were surprised when Andy Jackson, supported by his frontiersmen and pirate sailors, volley firing from behind hasty built barricades, broke the British line by shooting the British officers thus leaving the troops leaderless. The British never fought us again. They claimed we failed to fight in accordance with the European rules of engagement as well as having the audacity to shoot officers. I guess they finally figured out we made better friends than enemies.

More recently in 1941, the successful Japanese attack on Pearl was due to the superior intelligence and the lack of an urgent secret Op-Immediate warning message transmission from Washington. Just the reverse situation assured us the victory at the battle of Midway, prior to the Battle of Leyte Gulf, a deliberate Japanese feint to the Northeast caused Adm. Halsey's hasty decision to sail north to chase a shadow fleet. Leaving a few destroyers and jeep carriers to fight an over welling Japanese force. However, with the battle almost won, bad Japanese intelligence caused their Admiral to beat a hasty retreat.

During the Korean police action, imagine General McArthur's embarrassment after he declared that the Chinese regulars would not cross the river into Korea. Approximately, two weeks later they charged across the river in superior strength driving the United Nation forces into the southern end of the peninsula.

In time of war Military Intelligence regardless of its accuracy is extremely important in determining troop movements and combat decisions. However, I doubt if any could ever consider it a major controlling factor for a declaration of war. It's an after thought mainly used to aid in the constructive planning of a course of action. But be warned, if you haven't seen it personally, use with caution. Error's, and mistakes in judgment are common in the heat of battle but if you gain your objective with the minimum of casualties, you must have done something right.

Now a word of caution, to those who, in time of war, wish to publicly complain or criticize your military and government officials about what should, or should not, be done. Not only are you skating close to treason, remember the enemy is always listening, but when you have troops in the field, you are doing your country, as well as your troops, a disservice. Politically, or treason wise, it can be classified as lending aid and comfort to the enemy.

SHIPMATES STAND TOGETHER

Military personnel, for the most part, are aware that service friends can be here today and gone tomorrow. In the navy, ship and squadron friendships usually last for the period of the tour. Once transfer orders come through, those friendships often quietly pass into history. However, occasionally there are exceptions to this rule.

For reasons unknown, certain individual friendships click. On these instances, names and memories remain fresh in mind despite long periods of separation. When I first started this short story I picked up the phone and called an old shipmate, AOC Jesse L. Batson, USN (retired). I first met Jesse over 50 years ago when he reported for duty with Patrol Squadron VP-44 at NAS, Norfolk.

At the time I was Chief in Charge of VP 44's Ordnance Department. The Ordnance Officer had also assigned me the task of briefing his recently assigned (Lt.jg) assistant, his administrative duties. I really appreciated Jesse's arrival. It gave me someone knowledgeable to share the squadron's ordnance workload.

We both had considerable weapons experience, but also had other outside interests in common. We had a mutual interest in small arms and their associated use and maintenance. I had purchased two surplus military firearms from Uncle Sam and had converted them to hunting rifles. Jesse was also a gun nut with a neat gun bluing operation set up in his garage. Further, he owned a duck blind in Back Bay, VA, and I later took over a deploying buddies blind on the Virginia inland waterway. Many a delightful hour was spent in building decoys and hunting ducks and geese. Plus, when the birds weren't flying, many a wild sea story was spun.

When a weapons position opened on the staff of the Commander Air Force's U.S. Atlantic Fleet, Jesse suggested I apply for the post. His claim with my Training Command and integrated Logistics background, I was already trained for the job. He convinced me to actually apply for the position. Despite my doubts, I was surprised on receiving orders to report to the Admiral's staff for duty in a position I held almost four years.

Jesse and I remained close during this period. In fact I had a lot to thank him for. My staff work resulted in being requested to retire and accept a position with the Navy Department, Bureau of Aeronautics, Washington D.C. There I spent 20 years in the Navy Department, retiring from the Naval Air Systems Command in December 1978.

Jesse also retired from active duty and accepted a job at The Naval Air Station Jacksonville. We never saw each other much during this period but kept in touch by telephone and correspondence. Most of what we talked about was past military experiences. Particularly things like shipboard and squadron life before WW II and what we enjoyed doing during our careers. People we told our stories to, found things we explained hard to believe. They were skeptical and seemed to feel like old Chief Petty Officers had a tendency to embellish things!

Old Jesse joined the Navy in 1935 two years before I did. We were both what was termed as "lifers." Our careers were tied to the naval service. Today, Jesse will be almost 96 years old. He has recently given up driving his own car and lives quietly close to his son in a Wilmington, NC. In an assisted living facility. Our usual "How the heck are you doin?" phone calls, a couple a times a year was great to hear his voice and again realize we were both still enjoying life. However, we are both fully aware that we will soon be eligible to receive that last set of transfer orders us old Chiefs are unable to change. One thing for sure old Jesse Batson was one of my oldest living friends and no man could ever have a better one.

When you have friends similar to this, hang on to them. It will mean a lot to you before you take that long trip into the setting sun.

OUR FRIENDS
"The Gun Show Guys"

It always gives me a special pleasure to talk about dedicated military veterans that for an unaccountable number of years have devoted a vast period volunteering their personal time and even their money to support the Legion and Fleet Reserve in its continuous battle to increase the membership to help support and maintain the pressure on government as it relates to veterans rights and benefits earned serving this nation in its times of need.

Out of all the people in a crowd you will usually find certain individuals that despite their stature, or physical features, these selective veterans tend to stand out above the crowd. He, or she, is not only a member, they are active individuals willing to freely give of their personal time and energy, to complete tasks that contributes to the success of their Post as well as the American Legion and Fleet Reserve as a whole.

Las Vegas Post 76 Past Commander Joe Fulsom and Adjutant Paul Jon Hemsley are such individuals. Over the years they has contributed much to the success and expansion of the Spirit of Freedom Post 76. My first personal contact with Joe was via the telephone. The wife and I had been living a satisfactory retiree life one block north of Clearwater, Florida when family requested we sell our house on the Gulf coast and move to the even sunnier state of Nevada.

In a period of over forty years this was the greatest distance yours truly had been a block or two away from salt water! It reminded me of the old sea story about how when old sailors retire they throw an anchor over their shoulder and start walking inland. The first person that questioned him as to what he was carrying, he was supposed to drop the anchor and build a chicken ranch. However, it appeared that Nevada already had several "chicken ranches" and didn't need any more. Once seeing this desert and its so-called soil, even the chickens would wonder about living here!

But, it really wasn't that bad. Being use to military moving about every three years and having partially owned about ten or more different houses, it didn't take us long to get settled in and began enjoying our stay. In those early days even the slot machines were friendlier! Then one day the telephone rang and for a change it wasn't somebody calling the animal hospital to find out how their pet was doing. When the guy on the other end began his machine gun spiel, I began to think this guy might be even worse!

Now this old sailor has a pretty good rep for being an ear bender, but old Joe was a real pro salesman. He could unload a ten-word sentence without taken a deep breath! I got the distinct impression he was a Legion membership recruiter. About all my contribution was admitting I was already a Legion member in a Florida Post. He assured me that retaining a membership in a Post a couple of thousand miles away wasn't doing me a damn bit of good.

After a few minutes it was easy to figure the only way I was ever going to get this man off the phone, before he wore it out, was to agree to the transfer. Surrender had to be my only choice. This old sailor had to admit when it came to a comparison with good old Joe, this old Legionnaire wasn't in the same League! After I finally got to know him better, being a ex-Army Man he must have developed all that stamina from diggin' all them there fox holes to have a place to sleep at night. When this sailor thinks of that it makes me shiver. I can assure you I'd preferred to sleep under clean sheet and a blanket at night. In our discussions about this Joe's argument is what do you do when a torpedo blows a hole in the tin under your bunk? That phone call did a lot for this sailor. It made me a lot closer and more interested in the Legion than I ever had before. Plus, it provided me with a friend with similar or like interests.

Now his Gun show helper was another one of those fox hole diggers by the name of Paul Jon Hemsley who wasn't one damn bit like Joe. Thank the good Lord. You would never figure them as a pair. Paul never had anything to say unless it was extremely important. Plus you had to listen closely because compared to Joe; Paul spoke about one octave above a whisper! Maybe he was tired from all the work he did when he was Sgt at Arms. I think he got the job because nobody ever taught Paul how to say NO! If anyone ever asks me who works hardest for this Post, Paul sure gets my vote!

Despite the fact that Joe still works in California, he still retains a home in Vegas and returns each week, if possible, plus to be the Legion and Post 76's face to the general public at the Gun Shows. His motorized pitch to the veterans is rather fantastic. Plus, I think he kind of stretches the facts a little if he thinks he's going to make a sale. It's obvious that if they don't always sign up immediately, they depart from his presence with one heck of a guilt trip. His big sign says Post 76 but I assure you he is pitching for every Post in the Valley. Take it from me. His pitch is hard to say no to.

For the 90 some years of the American Legion's history, it has been people like old Army Joe, and Paul, the former Foxhole diggers, that has made the Legion the strong, successful friend of our nations millions of former warriors.

WHAT'S HAPPENING TO OUR MILITARY HISTORY?

A few months ago the news media released a statement stating that certain College and University professors had decided to discontinue the study of 20th Century and earlier military warfare. Being a veteran of two major wars and a couple of minor shooting fracases and a Cold War, many Veterans, and intelligent citizens have taken this unbelievable decision as a grave error in judgment on the part of our professional educators.

The opinion expressed herein will attempt to define the fallacy of such an idiotic politically correct view which, in the immediate future, would definitely fail to prepare current citizens and the coming generations the means to cope with the possibility of all out war.

Never forget that Man, or as scientifically defined as the human animal that has been certified, at least in theory, as the most intelligent animal on the face of this earth. However, at the same time, when angered, they may become an unstable, extremely dangerous individual. Therefore, he might be mentally capable of designing and building the most dangerous combat devises ever imagined. Stop and think. In just a few century's he had mentally progressed from the stone hammer to the atomic bomb.

Up until the final quarter of the twentieth century the historical study of American warfare had been handled in a rather heroic, patriotic manner. In recent years it seems that this same history of warfare has drifted toward a political correct interpretation of warfare as being considered too violent for today's classroom. Many of our current history books treat past war events like something ugly that should be swept under the rug and forgotten.

Eliminating these teachings is a major mistake. People must know and understand a problem in order to be able to intelligently deal with it. No one in his right mind should favor war, however, in the event war should occur, the average adult should have sufficient knowledge to properly prepare for, and be able to more knowledgably cope with the events that might be happening around them.

Many of today's historians preparing study books for use in our classrooms seem to prefer placing their historical emphasize on the wonderful things that may have become marketable items because of a war instead of discussing the negative devastation and horrors and how the people best coped with the problem. Despite some of the outstanding technological advancements, little good results from the horrors of war.

However, never forget that down through the ages, our livelihood and the safety of the nation has been seriously challenged. The citizens of this country must always be prepared to cope when necessary to take up arms in defense of our rights and freedoms. In the final analysis, despite the negatives we must be nationally prepared to prevail. Further, never forget that a well-trained, fully equipped, military service ready for either internal action or deployment can actually be a protective force safety net. There is an excellent possibility it could be a perfect war deterrent as well. The so called former "Cold War" proved conclusively that military strength and the determination to use it can very well keep an "enemy" from firing the first shot.

Burying the details of what happened during the 20th century wars can be a catastrophic mistake that might lead to the possibility of repeating the so called mistakes of the past. If you view what transpired in Vietnam and what is currently happening in the middle east, add to that, negative miss directed media coverage, might cause elected government personnel to jockey for political advantage. This seems to have developed an anti-military, anti-war attitude within our miss-informed general public. This definitely leaves us with the conclusion that current historical presentations has not prepared the citizens of this nation on how to cope with war time conditions or requirements!

The little fracas in the Middle East is a damned expensive tea party compared to WW II. Using today's advanced scientific knowledge in conducting future world wars might make what went on before during WW II look like a walk in the park. For example, take a long look at the devastation and the cost of what is currently happening in the Middle East. This event is just an expensive minor scuffle compared to what might happen in a future all out conflict.

If you consider yourself a model citizen and against war, your not even in the ball park with today's veteran that has seen combat. Veterans are really anti-war for a heck of a lot better reasons than the average citizen. They have been to see the elephant and have felt the fear and pain of his might.

In reality, fighting our current mid-eastern enemy's, in a way, resembles the American Indian wars of the old west. Like the Indians, the militant Muslims are not a trained army interested in establishing a defined battlefront. They prefer to fight battles based on instant windows of opportunity, based on the hit and run style. They are an angry people primed from childhood to saver vicious hatred and dispense instant destruction and fear. They believe that war against the infidel is Holy, that dieing in battle is preferable to defeat, and that ever infidel killed is a battle won.

How do you fight an enemy with destructible thoughts and intentions? You use the same basic approach as the enemy! Face it; the true definition of war is overwhelming the enemy by destroying his fighting spirit and ability. You must apply Gen. Patton's philosophy. In the interest of self-preservation, you must instinctively be willing to kill your enemy before he has a chance to kill you. This nation must believe we want as few combatants dying for our country as possible! I'm hoping this form of discussion does not appall anti-war citizens. I'm certain that despite their anti-war feelings, they would prefer that any war be fought in the enemy's back yard rather than their own! We also hope that certain Congress members would stop referring to our military efforts as a losing proposition and stick to supporting our military in the field so they can properly bring our combat efforts to a successful conclusion! SUPPORT OUR TROOPS!

As a final statement never forget one fact. Down through the years we have been able to defend ourselves for two main reasons. When attacked the young patriots of this nation have rushed forward to become our first line of defense. These brave men were able to be victorious for the second reason. Up till now it has been the force and ability of our powerful industrial capability to design and build the materials necessary to preserve this nation, its freedoms and way of life.

WARNING! In the interest of quantity at reduced cost we are rapidly selling our industrial capability overseas. Especially to nations that in reality have always envied us and would like to put us in 2nd place! That move might be slowly approaching. When was the last time you saw a tag that said "Made in the USA"?

AN OUTSIDE DEDICATION TO "MOM"

As a retired Navy Chief Petty Officer, with only a high school education, my interest in educational perfection for children has never subsided. Further, as a retired military, my special thanks goes out to those retired military personnel that continue to serve this nation in the field of Education as part of an organization known as the Junior Reserve Officers Training Corps (JROTC). These are very unusual personnel who have chosen to dedicate the later part of their lives to the special instruction of our nations youth.

From my personal observations in the numerous states in which I have lived since my retirement from the Department of the Navy I have discovered that JROTC students receive more learning about our nation and its government through the JROTC than that taught in any other school classroom.

Having lived in Nevada for 11 years I have been able to visit several schools JROTC's. However, being retired Navy I've sort of settled in with Captain Hardeman's JNROTC at Centennial High School. He is well supported by Senior Chief Petty Officer Borders and Petty Officer 1st Class Gail Johnson. Now these three individuals each year have the outstanding ability to successfully control and instruct over 100 students that operate not only in true military fashion but the majority of their unit also excel academically.

Now I feel the Captain and the Senior Chief through their apparent military bearing strongly influence the units military stature. However, Petty Officer Johnson uses an even stronger semi-silent weapon better understood as the feminine touch, better known as the "Mom" approach which has for century's made even strong men walk a straight line! How do I know? Because I could wrap my Dad around my little finger but I was sure as hell scared of my mother!

The right female, such as the one I speak, using the "Mom" complex has the uncanny ability to draw individuals together. She provides the drive to get people to work together as a single unit such as a silent drill team, a championship color guard and any other effort that requires individuals to work together as a solid unit.

For two years the Centennial High School JNROTC and their trained teams have visited the Naval Air Station, Pensacola, FL, Home of the Navy Blue Angles, and famous Naval Aviation Museum to participate in the Navy JNROTC competition and have returned victorious. They have captured the National Championship for two years running. If they capture any more trophies they will have to construct an extension on the building!

OUR WORLD AT WAR!

This short piece has been prepared for the specific purpose of honoring those military personnel, both volunteers and inductees, who in the event of an unfortunate conflict, they became the conflicting fodder that is sacrificed to determine who winds or looser said conflict.

Why is said honor being extended? It's the fact that in most cases they heroically perform because of love of country, the protection of our national freedoms, as well as our superior life styles. In most cases, they never forgot their formal teaching as they grew from laughing toddlers, where even then, a good many of their early toys already reflected what they were supposed to do in the even of war. Remember that little tank whose little gun fired lollypop sticks?

Let's give a little thought as to whether going to war was really necessary. It seems like it all starts with some sort of election. In the very beginning it was determined by the fact of just who had the biggest club. So for safety sake everybody wanted to be his friend. At least that was until someone came along with a bigger club. The ancient war of the world was resolved when the winner took over all the local caves!

As man grew smarter and more intelligent, those who happened to end up in charge were possibly obsessed with both greed and physical power. This same failing has followed man down through the centuries. Wars were usually fought for the same basic reasons Greed and Power. Almost every war resulted because one side had something the other side wanted while the other side refused to give it up.

The short term solution was a totally unnecessary war. Most early wars were really individual people combatants. Each faction fought each other face to face using hand held weapons and spears. The major "reach" weapons in those days was the invention of the long bow and the arrow and the rock throwing catapult. Further, it really wasn't surprising to discover the individuals that actually started the fighting, sat on the side lines and observed but never participated in the conflict unless they were being overrun.

As battles increased in the depth of devastation it became even more obvious to everyone that the powers who were providing direction never seemed to actually participate in any of the conflicts. They made damn sure their observations were from a safe distance.

But by the end of WW I, the mobilization of heavy movable armament, like the invention of the tank and the almost unheard of item the first introduction of the combat airplane resulted in major changes to the mechanics of warfare. The intelligence of man, through the use of science had finally given the common man the capability to kill millions of human beings rather than just a few hundreds or thousands.

By now we had advanced to the late 1930's. The world was just recovering from a vast depression. So it was absolutely necessary that something be done to insure that all the people have steady employment. The Germans and Russians were beginning to specialize in activities that seemed to always to end up in conflicts directed by Power and Greed.

Therefore, in order to put some of their desires in motion German troops rushed across the borders of Poland with a surprise attack. A viscous, sneaky totally unnecessary war! But it seemed good way to get even for their first World War defeat and concurrently begin their unbelievable deliberate extermination of a human race.

Actually, this piece doesn't wish to discuss the basic battles fought during World War II. We would prefer to discuss some of the various approaches and results. For example, the airplane quickly became a major weapon of war. It suddenly provided all combatants a long-range capability to fly thousands of miles into the enemy's homeland, where it could drop bombs in the enemy's families back yards. This was able to make the people at home as miserable as the combat soldier at the front.

Plus they discovered that a properly armed aircraft could sink more ships faster than 16-inch guns on a battleship. Improved mobility trench warfare had been replaced by fast massive armor attacks designed specifically to overrun and eliminate the common foot soldier.

For a short period the U.S. had been able to stay out of the war. However, our President had initiated an embargo that stopped the sale of Oil to Japan. Without oil Japan would have been unable to conduct naval operations. That sort of Pee-Ode Adm. Yamamoto, Commander of the imperial Japanese Fleet. He happened to be one of the worlds sharpest Naval Officer. Like many of our own Naval Officers, he also believed the command of the Air would eventually increase the speed of naval warfare and put slow costly battleships out of business.

He also realized from his duties in the U.S. that Japan would eventually have to do battle with the United States in order to control the Pacific. However, he was also well aware that our industrial capability was far greater than that of Japan. Therefore, he felt our Pacific fleet had to be destroyed in a single monumental battle.

Welcome to an early Sunday morning visitor observation flight over Pearl Harbor. Unfortunate for the Japanese and exceptionally lucky for the United States, a couple Japanese errors and a little American luck, the fleet was badly damaged but not destroyed. Blood had been spilled and like it or not we were now committed to a major war in the Pacific as well as providing aid to the English and the defeated French in Europe.

Time for us to get down to business, but would you believe our military were unable to negotiate a unified command procedure? Despite their urgent need for cooperative recovery planning a lack of inter-service trust existed between the Army and the Navy. It was sort of expected because of Gen. MacArthur and Adm. King's hatred of each other's guts. What a wonderful way to begin a war against a powerful enemy who in fact had landed a terrific blow in the first round of the fight!

The problem was only partially solved when Adm. Nimitz was assigned Commander Central Pacific and Gen. MacArthur was announced as Commander of Western Pacific. What MacArthur had really wanted was a new Title of Supreme Commander of all hands on both sides.

What I had stated previously was zeroing in on the unbelievable materials and loss of human life. During this war we had an excess of 16 million individuals under arms. Between 1941 and 1945 over a half million American servicemen lost their lives. The nation's personnel losses exceeded 400,000 combat deaths and 100,000 non-combatant deaths. In France, we have three major military cemeteries where 15,000 young men rest that failed to return home. This was the body count for just the Normandy operation. This number doesn't count the thousands that were wounded or crippled. The totals lost during the various European battles ran into the millions.

In the Pacific the battle count was also tremendous. For example, in the first sea battle at Savo Island in 32 minutes we lost 4 large battle cruiser's and a total of 1,270 dead and 706 wounded. In addition nothing could be more death defying than an amphibious landing. On Tarawa, a piece of land of about one square mile, U.S. casualty count was 7,991 while on the island of Peleliu the casualties were 9,804 of which 1,794 were killed. On Iwo Jima we lost 6,821 killed and 19,179 wounded, with our total causality count at 26,310. I doubt if I have to go any further. I'm sure that you would understand that many additional might have passed away before the atomic missions wiped out two Japanese cities and finally brought WW II to a swift conclusion.

When you listen to today's unbelievable discussion about present losses in the middle-east, I feel it's time to remember what another major war might do to this crusty old world of ours.

WAR OR TERROR IN THE 21ST CENTURY

On 11 September 2001 the United States of America was attacked by one of the most disastrous act of Terrorism in our nations history. The targets selected for destruction were the trade towers in New York City, the Pentagon in Arlington, Virginia just outside the nations Capital and the White House in Washington, D.C, which through the courage and bravery of the passengers who chose to die for their country fighting the terrorist in the fourth aircraft which was headed for a crash attempt on the Presidential residence. I'm certain no reason exists for me to recreate the terrible acts of destruction and devastation that you may have already witnessed several times on your television.

These cowardly despicable acts of terrorism failed to bring us to the brink of war, however, I'm certain our government tried to figure out an international method for getting even. One activity definitely capable of providing any help was the United Nations. In the opinion of the writer, there were several member nations that definitely enjoyed seeing us get clobbered.

Since 1830 the U.S. had some form of on and off friendly relations with the nation of Afghanistan. After the 09/11 attacks with their permission, the U. S. launched an air attack on the Taliban and al Qaeda for the specific purpose of closing in on Osama bin Laden but the old boy disappeared into thin air, or should I say holed up in some cave like a scared rat. Thousands of U.S. troops were stationed in country to support the new Afgan government, and, began to hunt down insurgents. In 2005 we signed a long-term policy relationship with the Afgans. Actually, no declaration of war was ever made against the

Taliban or Al Quadia but quite a few rounds were exchanged regardless.

At that point in time almost everyone in America was waving the flag and demanding that we immediately do something to get even. The powers that seemed to be felt were, it was time to act and so did the general public. In fact, our government assumed we could solve two problems in the middle east with a single action. All hands were well aware we stopped too soon when we kicked Iraq's Sadden Hussein out of Kuwait. At that point in time we should have pushed on to Baghdad. No matter what the reason, it was concluded the time was ripe to hit the Taliban, Al Quadia and ole Sadden all at the same time.

It was easier than expected, on entering Iraq we motored all the way to Baghdad, almost by invitation. There we finally found Sadden hiding in a hole in the ground like a scared rabbit. Everybody was happy, even the Congress. However, there was a problem. Even though the Iraqi people were very happy that we got rid of Sadden for them, their population included three or more separate sects that jointly hated Sadden, but it soon became obvious they didn't like, or trust, each other.

Now it's obvious that most of these people are firm believers in their chosen religion but they have failed to conform with or make any allowances for many of life's personal advancements developed over the years, unfortunately. In a manner of speaking, they had left themselves a couple of thousand years behind the times. The men are still wearing the same style hats, pants and shoes as they did back in the year 0001 plus there wasn't a ladies beauty salon or fashion boutique within flying distance!

Some factions believe it is both honorable and heroic to become a suicide bomber to destroy an "enemy," whether they might be an infidel or a Moslem of a different sect. It seems when you do this your supposed to get a whole bunch of virgins when you go to heaven. That I don't quite understand, if you blew yourself up, who puts you back together to enjoy their company? In addition, they were now convincing young women to blow themselves up. What would they do with all those virgins?

During WW I both sides introduce aerial combat and the British introduced the first armored tank, almost all nations noted the advantages and began to develop and train for conducting mechanized warfare. WW II frontal attacks with fast armored vehicles rapidly overran objectives, quickly followed by the infantry to hold and control the gained territory. By the end of WW II, major land warfare was conducted with the use of heavy armor followed by motorized infantry to clean up and occupy conquered territory.

Our current war in Iraq may have started in that manner, but it soon reversed itself. What happens today has reverted back mostly to human endeavors. It's actually reminiscent of old western Indian warfare. Armed personnel, without uniforms, suddenly, without warning, attack targets of opportunity, and then quickly withdraw to reform later to attack a different site. Sporadic surprise attacks and rapid changes to fighting locations are difficult to combat. It is complicated for the untrained citizenry and elected politicians with minimal, or complete lack of military experiences, to understand or cope with. Therefore, it is recommended that they withhold judgment, refuse to publicly condemn military efforts for political gain that might also tend to lend aid and comfort to the enemy. In fact printed comments of any kind should be processed through military authority prior to release.

It is also recommended that modifications be made to existing Rules of Engagement. Someone has forgotten the definition of War. Wars means more than just kill or just destroy your enemy before he has a chance to kill you. A split second does not permit you time to ask an opponent for his military ID card before you shoot him. It may not be that bad but my newspaper indicates that many of our troops are being jailed for killing enemy's. Isn't that what we sent them over there to do?

PEARL HARBOR DAY
7 December 2008

Sixty-seven years now seems to have rushed away. However, for those of us that were alive that day and serving with the military, the memory of what happened that morning is still fresh in our minds. The day dawned a bright, sunny December Sunday morning. On our moored vessels, members of their ships company bands had arrived on deck prepared to welcome the new day by honoring our colors as they rose to the masthead. Suddenly, the stillness of a quiet Sunday morning was broken by the roar of hundreds of aircraft engines, followed by the explosive bursts and flames from incoming bombs, the blast of torpedoes blowing holes in helpless vessels and the metallic rattle of intensive machine gun fire. The Imperial Japanese Navy had just rudely invited the sleeping United States Navy into the combat of World War II!

Luckily, your scribe had personally missed that engagement. My four year enlistment had expired in November 1941 and I was happily on my way to the Receiving Ship, New York, Pier 92 for discharge. Unfortunately, only two days out of New York we listened to the attack reports on the ships radio. What passed through my mind was the fact that the attack on Pearl was never going to let my discharge happen.

On arrival at the Navy Receiving Ship, at Pier 92, the officer on duty advised that there was only two options available. Choice No. 1 was to reenlist for four years and receive a double reenlisted bonus of $400 or, choice No. 2 meant the Navy was going to withhold my release for the duration of war! Not having ever seen that much long green in one pile, a four year cruise suddenly turned into a life time career.

There were several people I would know in my lifetime who were Pearl Harbor survivors. One of who happens to be the only Pearl Harbor Medal of Honor recipient Former Chief Aviation Ordnanceman John Finn, who was later promoted to Lieutenant, was sleeping in on Sunday morning. Please note, I did not say Lt. Finn won the medal. It does not happen to be an award you can win. It's the highest possible honor that our nation can bestow for outstanding bravery under fire above and beyond the call of duty. At the time John was a Chief Aviation Ordnanceman stationed at the Naval Air Station, Kaneohe Bay. That fateful morning he and his wife, happened to be sleeping in on a quiet Sunday morning when they were awaken by the roar of many aircraft engines. He wondered what was happening. No flights were scheduled that morning. The sudden additional sound of machine gun fire and the explosion of incoming ordnance quickly spelled attack. Half dressed, he jumped into his car and headed for his hanger space. Japanese aircraft in mass formations were making bombing and strafing runs on the airdrome.

In the hanger he had a Browning .50 caliber machine gun used in training sessions. He yelled for ammo as he dragged the .50 Caliber out onto the tarmac. Once loaded he began making sustained fire at the incoming aircraft. The Japanese pilots instantly noted his return fire so some pilots began making direct runs that included fire on his ground position. Bullets and shrapnel began hitting all around him. He himself began taking hits but his adrenal rush was so great he barely noticed.

When the attack subsided they rushed him to the sick bay. John had sustained in excess of 20 shrapnel and bullet wounds. Despite his many wounds, he returned to his workstation to direct battle damage cleanup and prepared for a possible follow up attack. For his exceptional bravery he was recommended for the Navy Medal of Honor.

Another friend at Pearl that day was a 1st Class Petty Officer NAP (Naval Aviation Pilot) named, "Chubby" Lyons. He had just reported for work at the hanger that morning when one of the first bombs blew out a part of the hanger. His statement was, "Then all Hell broke loose!" After the attack subsided they located Chubby wounded with a badly damaged lower left leg. At the hospital they found it necessary to remove that part of his leg below the knee because it was found to be beyond repair. Once back on his foot, it was determined that he appeared before a survey review board for discharged from the service. Chubby fought his discharge all the way to Washington where Admiral King finally authorized his retention and even later returned him to flight status. He became what I believe was the Navy's first carrier qualified one-legged Naval Aviator. He was then Commissioned and years later he retired as a Navy Captain. Unfortunately, he has now become a small part of Naval Aviation history.

Machinist Mate Chief Petty Officer Frank Adamson, another friend, was also a Pearl Survivor. Prior to the war he had twice been declared a world class Navy wrestling champion. However, he was more often remembered for having served aboard the Battleship USS Tennessee for over fourteen years straight. During that period of WW II he earned two Purple Hearts and other awards. He was a true Navy "lifer" retiring after 30 years total service to his home in west central Florida. At age 88 he passed on to an even greater reward.

Greater detail on all three of the fine sailors may be found elsewhere in this volume.

The attack on Pearl added 15 new names to the list of naval hero's who were recipients of the Medal of Honor. Just 5 of these survived to be personally knowledgeable of receiving this prestigious award. Plus, one other was killed in action almost a year later. Nine other awards where made posthumously to next of kin. Only one went unclaimed. No living relative could be found for the presentation of the Medal for Chief Watertender Peter Tomich. For a while the medal remained aboard the small destroyer that bore his name. However, at the decommissioning of the USS Tomich I believe it was presented to the Smithsonian for safekeeping. After 65 years a relative was finely located in Europe, a copy had finally found a home.

I just hope the readers enjoyed this short rendition. It has been an honor for this 89 year old Navy veteran, who first went to sea in 1937, to have the opportunity to honor the memory of those living and dead that were serving this nation on that historic day, 7 December 1941. The people of this nation must never forget what the men in uniform, living or dead, may have personally sacrificed for the American citizen.

IT'S JUST UNDERSTOOD?

When your invited to an activity as a conference speaker, or dealing with highly trained subordinates it some times becomes necessary to use special terminology to cut off foolish or argumentative questioning. Or it could be used to stop a discussion of possible classified information, or as a visiting speaker it might even be used to avoid the embarrassment of not knowing an answer to a question, or in some cases just to be able to shift the subject material completely. Over the years many short stopper phrases have been originated to serve this purpose. After all, you can't let the audience know there is something you don't know, or to be hit with a question like where is it printed or defined?

I wish to talk about one of these simple phrases, specifically like, "It's just understood." For some unknown reason, it seems like the only sensible response to this statement would be, "What the hell does that mean?" Now no intelligent person in his right mind wants to be the one to mouth a question like that out loud.

For example, The American Legion constitutes an association of veterans. In reality, the Legion is a vast business corporation similar to any other commercial activities. It exists for the specific purpose of service to the special defined rights and desires of individuals that have served this nation in times of national emergency or armed conflict. Like any corporation the Legion is managed and controlled at various levels, National, State, District and Post by elected Commanders and Vice Commanders, that maintain membership and the various programs designed to best serve veterans and their families.

My interest in researching this phenomenon started with a question to a high-ranking Officer of the Legion concerning the definition of a certain regulation. The answer received sent me to the Officers Guide for further clarification. The search was fruitless, no such explanation could be found. When reporting back to the Officer to explain my failure to locate a written explanation the response was, "It must have been removed from the book as superfluous, because "it's just understood." Oh, Oh, you were just hit with one of those offbeat quotes. Damn, are you going to show your stupidity with a follow up like, "What the hell does that mean?" It's a matter of how stupid you want to look!

Ploys like this have been used for centuries to stop questions in their tracks. In 1776 The N.Y. representative entered Jefferson's office and asked, "Tom, I've been going over your draft of the Constitution and I just can't follow some of the phraseology." Jefferson at the moment couldn't think of a good reason for having written it that way either, so he stated. "John, it had to be that way, "it's just understood." As a result, for over 200 years not a single word of that Constitution has been changed or questioned. It's probably the reason it takes so long to prepare an amendment and get it passed. Changes must be prepared separately, approved by a Congressional majority and 32 states must ratify it within 10 years. As you well know that the proper procedure, "It's just understood."

A newly elected Congressman reporting in January for his first Congressional session was reviewing a draft of a Ways and Means resolution, where he hit a snag, and called in his "new" Chief of Staff. This character was probably a holdover from the former office resident. When the new Congressman questioned the resolution processing and routing procedure, he was advised, "Don't worry about it. We have at least 100 political science grads in the outer office to analyze and set up your work schedule. All Congressional procedures are "just understood," "Right now it's more important for you to hit the phone circuits and start collecting funds for your reelection. Besides the Majority Whip will be here shortly to advise you on what and who to vote for. Plus I'll be standing behind him shaking my head Yes or No while he's briefing you. You see "it's just understood" how things work around here!"

Now if you the reader are scratching your head trying to figure out what the devil I've been talking about. Just relax, think about it, "It's just understood".

"LIFE IS WHAT YOU MAKE OF IT"

In October 1929 the financial structure of this nation was destroyed by the collapse of the stock market. It was the beginning of "The Great Depression." There was instant panic as we hit a low point in our country's history. Many people lost their so-called fortunes. Former millionaires jumped out of windows and those lucky enough to still have jobs took heavy cutbacks. Even the military was reduced to enlisting only high school graduates. Moreover, Navy crews on our combat vessels were unfortunately undermanned.

For example, you are reading about a hopeful young hero, me, who had a position in both a Port and Starboard 6" 53 gun crew. However, those that were willing to choose employment with the military were in a sense rather lucky. The military didn't pay much but it did have certain special advantages. It was all-inclusive. It covered food, clothing, housing and even extensive world travel.

It sometimes took a new recruit a little while to figure it out, but in the military, the young soldier or sailor was the master of his own destiny. If you wished to advance as soon as possible, it was entirely up to you. No one pushed, or attempted to force you. It was a perfect example of being completely in charge of your own success and exactly how you planned to handle it.

When a sailor began to recognize the advantages that were available to him, it was time to close in and choose a specific profession. Now in peacetime the military defined specific periods in which one could be eligible for scheduled advancement. There were specific study courses as well as elementary and advanced service trade schools that could be applied for to aid you in your climb up your personal ladder of success.

It is also true that in time of war you would be expected to operate in harms way. However, the more you learn, and the higher you advance in rank, the better your knowledge and chance of survival. By expanding your ability to think faster, survey situations and make decisive decisions, your performance under stress during war time conditions could very well contribute to your ability to advance more rapidly. Once you have chosen a specific skill field, for example electronics or ordnance, you must constantly expand your knowledge on your occupation of choice.

Down through the year's only intelligence, technology, training skills and capabilities have changed. The ability to succeed still rests in an individual's personal desire to achieve. Never forget, the officers over you in many situations are totally dependant on your technical knowledge and specific skill. It's especially important for your future that your capability be recognized by your seniors at various levels. Being a stand out performer can establish a successful military career. Your career, no matter how long you may have served can be a direct aid to your future endeavors all the way to final retirement.

Take it from one who applied this philosophy. Properly executed the government will assure you a comfortable, worry free life style during your so-called golden years. Take it from one who followed this course. Because everything this old ex-sailor owns belongs to him free and clear.

A 41 PLUS YEARS NAVAL CAREER
Reduced to a Few Hundred Words

We have here today an old worn out Chief Petty Officer who has now pushing to the age 92. He is still recognized by those familiar with the early 20th Century military as one of those thick headed old retired Chief's who refuses to let the whole damn world forget how he and all them there tough "old navy" bluejacket's survived hard labor and low pay defending the eastern and western water fronts back in the old days of the mid 1930's and the years shortly there after.

In 1937 with an $18.00 a week job, I was too young and stupid to see very far into the future. This kid loved salt water and that there sign that read, "Join the Navy and see the World" sounded great, so he signed up as a $21.00 a month Apprentice Seaman Recruit. Financially, this was a big step backward, however at age 18 he really didn't worry about it!

Shortly thereafter I was freezing my fanny off hoping for an old Chief Boatswain Mate at the Newport, R.I. Naval Training Station, a fieldstone penal institute look-a-like. While there I applied for Aerial Photo School however the Navy selected me for Ordnance School. What the Hell, he liked Ordnance especially them there fancy aircraft machine guns and the other kinds of weapons they mounted on them there slick fancy fabric covered winged fighting biplanes.

When school was over, what the devil was I doin" swabbing decks on that old Cruiser USS Memphis CL-13? After all didn't I get top marks on that ordnance stuff I was studying? It actually took him over a year to finally talk his way into aviation. Was it because I had great marks at the Ordnance school? Heck no, it was due to the fact I held a small boat coxswain qualification!

I could care less about the Navy's reason because I was now attached to Patrol Squadron 11, later changed to #54, which flew them there fancy PBY-2 flyin boats. With good luck and help from Chief Pop Sammons and Strawberry Varner I was finally promoted to AOM3rd where I could now work full time on them 50 Caliber machine guns and bomb racks, having a pay increase to 60 bucks a month was a big improvement also!

Then, be damned if I wasn't transferred a year later, (1940), back to that old USS Memphis just because I got married. On there we Cruiser airdales flew South Atlantic Neutrality Patrols in those old SOC-2 biplane catapult aircraft. It also must have been a good luck move for a change because I passed the test to make AOM2nd Class prior to the end of my first 4-year cruise. Plus it made me eligible for that outstanding 36 bucks a month family allowance. That sure was a heck of a lot better than the normal processing time of not receiving an E-5 upgrade until your 2nd or 3rd cruise!

Having finished my first cruise they shipped me back to the Receiving Ship NY for discharge. The wife and I figured we would take a 90 day vacation to get to know each other again, then maybe ship over. On yea, that would be the day! Two days out of NY those dang Japanese deliberately bombed Pearl for no other purpose than beat him out of that long vacation with the wife. On shipping over he got $400.00 double shipping over money and only 10 days leave instead of 90!

Once again he applied for a couple of squadrons or a carrier. On returning to the Receiving Ship to pick up his new orders they read NAS Argentia. Never heard of it. Where in the hell was that? The Answer, they didn't know either till we called the Navy Dept. and asked. We were told it was some place in Newfoundland. What in Gods name was he supposed to do in Newfoundland besides freeze his butt off? He was also advised to be lucky enough to be in charge of a draft of about 40 kids right out of Newport's boot Camp! For transportation they boarded on one of them Navy special cruise ships named the USS Pyro. It was actually an ammunition ship loaded with explosives. I wanted to make these new kids comfortable, so

I told them that they would be issued parachutes rather than life jackets. I explained to the kids, it was a joke, because if the ship was hit on their way north the chute would be more appropriate!

On arrival in Argentia it was oh so obvious this was going to be a lousy duty. It was more than just a new Air Station; the place wasn't half way constructed yet. Our arrival more than doubled the size of Ships Company. Lucky me, I was now the only Ordnanceman on board the station. I immediately became the entire Ordnance Supply Department. Wasn't it great to find out you were the boss and at the same time be the only man on the totem poll close to being qualified for the job? At least I thought I was! Duty here was unbelievable and I won't bore you with the details. One thing we all found out about was you don't have to fall in battle in order to die for your country!

After more of a year of backbreaking work the Navy Department recognized my efforts and automatically promoted me to AOM1st Class for special services rendered, plus they issued a set of new orders to NAS Pensacola, Fla. Halleluiah. Back to warm sunshine and married life! The wife and I really appreciated the change. With the exception of the short tour with VP-11-54 I hadn't spent more than a few weeks at a time on U.S. soil in almost six years!

In Pensacola as a qualified Combat Aircrewman I was assigned as a gunnery instructor. During this tour I qualified for promotion to ACOM and at age 25 became one of youngest Chief Petty Officers in the Navy. On my first trip to the CPO Club they laughingly ran me out and told me I could back once I grew up! After an excellent tour and the arrival of our first son he received orders to report to the Naval Air Training Command.

As Chief in Charge of a mobile training detachment, which spent temporary duty on several Air Station's this was the beginning version of an operating station Integrated Logistic Support system, which eventually became permanent units.

Due to having spent considerable time on temporary duty, orders were issued for transfer to Shore Duty at O&R Norfolk.

There he served in several capacities, none of which had anything to do with ordnance except for the flight test part of my duties of Leading Chief of Multi-Engine Flight Test. However, I must admit this did add much to my total aviation education.

From there I returned to sea duty aboard the USS Coral Sea CVB-43. It was an excellent two years and a butt as the Air Department Leading Chief of the V3-0 Ordnance Division of 180 men. Except for time away from family, it was the excellent carrier duty he had been looking for since the beginning of his Naval career. It included two summer tours with the Sixth Fleet in the Mediterranean Sea, and the southern Nations of Europe. Said tour was a real education on shipboard air operations.

At tour completion his new orders read report to Patrol Squadron 44, Naval Air Station, Norfolk, VA for duty involving flying. My duties again involved Leading Chief of the Ordnance Department. This duty was short lived due to the fact I had been recommended and interviewed for a position in the Weapons Department on the staff of the Commander, Naval Air Forces U.S. Atlantic Fleet. Here I worked for nearly four years. This duty actually led to determining my career for the remainder of my working life.

When relieved from the staff I was assigned temporary duty with Fighter Squadron 61. This short duty tour lasted until my retirement transfer to Fleet Reserve, which took place 28 January 1959. Three Days later I entered civil service with the U. S. Navy, Bureau if Aeronautics. Wash, DC. February 1 1959 I started as an in-training Equipment Specialist, Ordnance GS-9 attached to the Electronics Department. After approximately 4 to 5 weeks of introductory service, I found himself at McDonnell Douglas Corp. St. Louis, MO serving as the Maintenance Inspection Review Board as Chairman of the Ordnance Team for the new F-4 (F4H) Aircraft. Note:—I figured the Navy's Idea was if your new on the job, put him in Charge of something. It was one heck of a good system for him to learn and get up to speed in a big hurry!

I also figured I was now in a position to finally influence the Naval Air Technical Service Facility to get field Maintenance

Manual Specifications updated to insure that contractors prepared manuals that were compatible with field maintenance conditions. Opening a manual that spoke about how smart the engineer was to have designed it that way didn't help the poor sailor in the field to fix it. For my troubles I did obtained some success. They made me Program Manager for Aviation Technical Maintenance Manuals. When the Bureau of Aeronautics and Ordnance combined into the Bureau of Naval Weapons and then eventually became the Naval Air Systems Command, I eventually found myself promoted to a top management position and became NavAir's documentation representative to the Naval Materials Command and the U.S. Air Force.

After over 20 years with the Navy Department my life's partner decided that after 41 plus years with the Navy it was time I stayed at home for a while. On 7 December 1978 I closed out a successful Navy career with the Naval Air Systems Command as Head, Naval Air Documentation Policy and Programs Office. The pay I received for that job was a heck of a lot better than the 21 bucks a month I started out with! It's granted I only started with just a High School Education however, with desire and dedication visible success and comfort can eventually become your reward.

Harry L. Keneman, USN (Ret.)

A VOICE FROM THE
GREAT BEYOND

Despite the title of this piece and being well aware that the title capability does not really exist, I would like to imagine I could. Therefore, I decided to put these words on paper before I loose my ability to do so. My question is, do I still have the proper mental capability to properly word everything I actually wanted to say? So, please remember me for what I'm really trying to accomplish. That was to leave behind an honest mental description, as well as a personal opinion, of a variety of experiences and sights I've witnessed during my military career. In this volume your scribe has tried to capture, true items some good, some bad, some in conjunction with various individuals whom I had personal contact while serving my country. After all, I started my navy career at the paltry sum of six cents an hour and eventually retired as a top salaried civilian, Head of one of the working aviation sections of the Department of the Navy. Therefore, I must assume along the way I must have done something right.

Please forgive me for the simple quality of my writing efforts. After all, I'm an amateur, not an established professional writer. Plus during my many years of service I had never given much thought or had the time available for keeping a journal to record the names of people with whom I had contact or the interesting events that happened along the way. But I'm certain my hard head contained a fairly normal brain, (At least I thought so), that seemed to remember things fairly well with only a few flaws of forgetfulness.

As I grew older, I began to realize that many people around me, particularly the young people, have either forgotten, or, had never been taught a complete study of the political and military history of this nation. I am proud to say I think we live in a great and powerful nation that had successfully progressed for over 200 plus years old. A major portion of our citizens enjoy the greatest personal freedoms, plus enjoy an outstanding family life style mostly unknown in many other parts of the world.

It appears that almost all our citizens take our life style for granted, without really knowing, or even understanding, the national power that permit him or her to do so. From many of our various oral history studies that have been collected in recent years, it's obvious that someone beside this old duffer has also been worrying about this historical knowledge problem. However, it appears that a lot of the results of this great effort has been stored in memorials and archives which leaves me wondering as to how available this information will be to the general public.

As I relax here at my computer and think back over my life, I believe this old guy experienced most of the normal ups and downs of trying to raise a fine family in conjunction with a military career. It actually involves what the ladies who are left behind termed as deployment separation. The average civilian family hardly ever experiences this type situation. It definitely requires a lady with exceptional determination, and will power to succeed at single parent management while her man is deployed anywhere from 6 months to a year! However, I understand in today's military where you will now find ladies going to sea or serving overseas, that the shoe can be squeezed onto another foot. When I think about it, I'm happy to say I never ever had that reversal experience.

In addition our educational system requires some revision. We must return to the proper study of government beginning with simple civics and an understandable version of the operation of our three branches of federal government. Today it's easy to conclude that, government, for the people and, by the people, as stipulated by our Constitution no longer really exists. It has been turned over to the political parties and politicians who constantly beg for and collect vast amounts of money, and set up fancy campaigns, in order to grab up even more voters money while making fancy, glass thin, breakable promises declaring they will take care of you just so long as you fund and vote for them.

The current generation appears to have already lost the political battle. There were hopes the new younger generation would break the current mold. However, we think they have already lost it. When the party cheerleaders jump up and yell "Cheer for the candidate," the new 18 to 25 year old voters jump up, scream, wave their hand-out name support cards at the TV cameras then bellow their heads off because the only words they can remember is, "we will take care of you". A disappointed witness sorrowfully whispered. "Yea, just as soon as you pay your new tax bill."

Please, please, someone take the time to teach the 10 to 18 year olds on the way up, to better understand the true workings of a democratic government. A system protected for over 200 years by a strong joint military force that will continue to do so for many decades to come.